STANDING UP TO HITLER

The Story of Norfolk's Home Guard and "Secret Army" 1940-1944

Adrian Hoare

*"We shall defend our island whatever the cost may be...
We shall never surrender"*   Winston Churchill, June 1940

*"Men of fearless disposition will be stationed near the Village
Strong Post to throw Molotov bombs at the enemy"*
     From 'Actions Stations' Drill at Salle, Norfolk, July 1940

COUNTRYSIDE BOOKS
NEWBURY, BERKSHIRE

First published 1997
by Geo. R. Reeve Ltd, Wymondham

This new edition published 2002

COUNTRYSIDE BOOKS
3 Catherine Road
Newbury, Berkshire

To view our complete range of books,
please visit us at
www.countrysidebooks.co.uk

ISBN 1 85306 722 9

Note to Second Edition

Since this book was first published, the author
has been fortunate in meeting more former
members of the "Secret Army" and their families.
Their personal memories have been included in
this edition. The map showing locations of OBs
(operational bases) has also been updated.

Produced through MRM Associates Ltd., Reading
Printed by Woolnough Bookbinding Ltd., Irthlingborough

STANDING UP TO HITLER

This book is dedicated to all who served in the Norfolk Home Guard or Resistance Units.

The British Resistance Organisation Museum is now open at Parham, Suffolk.

Opening times: March to October on
Sundays and Bank Holidays,
11 am to 6 pm; July to September
also Wednesdays 11 am to 4 pm.
Tel. 01206 844041 for further details.

CONTENTS

ACKNOWLEDGEMENTS

My grateful thanks are due to all those Norfolk Home Guard and Resistance Unit veterans or their families who have supplied information, lent documents and photographs and given so much of their time by talking or writing to me.

I also acknowledge the help of the Norfolk Record Office, the Norfolk Regimental Museum, the Imperial War Museum, Ben Stimpson, David Cleveland and the UEA Film Archive, Janet Smith and the Wymondham Archive, Tim Holt-Wilson, Curator of the Diss Museum and Valerie Woodrow, Wymondham College Librarian.

I am indebted to the Eastern Daily Press, the Eastern Evening News, the Diss Express and the Norfolk Chronicle (NRO), who have given permission for me to use information and quote from their newspapers for 1940-1944.

Dr. D.J.J. Harris has kindly permitted me to use and quote from his father's papers in the Imperial War Museum (ref: 84/54/1). Sub Lt. L.S. Harris, RNVR., served in the Norfolk Resistance from 1940-43.

All the illustrations given, loaned or copied, are acknowledged on the page they appear. Mr. C.W. Scott has kindly allowed me to take prints from a wartime film of King's Lynn Home Guard made by his father.

I acknowledge permission to quote from original documents held in the Norfolk Record Office, whose reference numbers are:- PD 238/113-118, WD 97 385X5, MC 158/1, 626X8, MC 158/2, 626-8, N/C1/154, MS 10605, DC11/1/1 and MC 419/1 696X5 by permission of Mrs. C.G. Lowden.

Every effort has been made to contact all copyright holders. Any omission from the list above is unintentional and my apologies are offered.

At Geo. R. Reeve Ltd., Brian Seager's help and advice has been much appreciated together with Tim Smith's cheerful tolerance and attention to detail. I am also very grateful to Ian Lavender, "Private Pike" in "Dad's Army" who has written a foreword to the book.

Last but not least I owe my wife an enormous debt for the countless tasks she has performed for me while researching and writing this book. She has also done all the line drawings and the map. Without her help, the book would not have been completed so quickly.

FOREWORD BY IAN LAVENDER

Thetford, Norfolk, the Summer of 1968; in a side bedroom of the Bell Hotel all the paraphernalia of a TV film unit starts to rumble into life and attempts to get a motley group of actors into make up and costume for the first day of filming of a new comedy series. As far as we were concerned it was going to be a pleasant way of spending the next ten weeks. None of us, no matter what our hopes were for continuing employment, ever thought that "Dad's Army" was going to become part of the fabric of the British way of life.

If there were any misgivings at all amongst us, they were that the people who were part of the L.D.V. and subsequently the Home Guard might be offended by the very fact that it was the subject of a comedy, and a pretty broad one at that.

I remember I went to audition for Dame Cicely Courtneidge after having recorded the first series but before it had been transmitted. "Now tell me what you have been doing", she said. I told her. A pause before, "Oh, no, no, no. You must be wrong. They wouldn't dream of making a comedy series about the Home Guard, far too serious". I assured her it was so. I didn't get the job.

To the best of my knowledge, there were no complaints from any Home Guard veterans. On the contrary, David Croft and Jimmy Perry were the recipients of letter after letter from them suggesting stories for future episodes, most of them too outrageous to use. It was as if at last somebody had remembered them.

Intentionally "Dad's Army" gave a lot of laughs to a lot of people all around the world. Accidentally and fortuitously it made us aware that there were thousands of men all over the country who really were prepared to give everything if the dreadful shadow of invasion became a reality. Like the platoon from Walmington on Sea, they had a lot of fun, experienced true friendship and camaraderie, spent far too many hours awake when they should have slept like everybody else, but most of all were deadly serious in their commitment, knowing that it might require the ultimate sacrifice.

For me, Norfolk is inextricably linked with the Home Guard. We did 98% of our filming in the county of Norfolk in and around the Battle Training Area near Thetford, and Adrian Hoare has chosen the Norfolk Home Guard as his subject. (Many of them were re-enrolled as extras in several of the episodes.) Norfolk is his adopted county, and where he spent 20 years teaching before retirement. Earlier, in Birmingham, he once attempted to teach me. His research has been local, intimate and personal, as well as archival. The result, a rich mixture of official and private memories and divulgencies.

I'm not that much of a "Stupid Boy"; I know you will enjoy it. You will meet characters with the same backgrounds as Pte. Godfrey, Pte. Fraser and Jack Jones the Butcher; people recognisable as Capt. Mainwaring, Sgt. Wilson, and – dare I say it? – Pte. Pike. The difference is Adrian Hoare's people are real.

Ian Lavender
Formerly of No.1 Platoon, Walmington on Sea Home Guard

A NOTE ON SOURCES

The evidence for Norfolk Home Guard battalions is fragmentary and scattered. References to particular units occur where documentary evidence has survived or when it has been possible to speak to Home Guard veterans or their families. Ben Stimpson has been especially helpful in providing his Home Guard papers for the Salle and Reepham areas. With regard to the Norfolk Resistance, I have been greatly helped by the personal memories of veterans of the "secret army" and the papers of Sub. Lt. L.S. Harris in the Imperial War Museum.

PREFACE

Most people's view of the Home Guard is probably coloured by the hilarious adventures of "Dad's Army". Of course there were many amusing moments, as the personal memories in this book show. However, serving in the Home Guard, and even more, running it, was a very serious business which was both demanding and time consuming. Although the men of the Norfolk Home Guard could laugh at things and themselves, they became justifiably proud of their achievements.

One of my earliest memories as a very young boy during the war, was watching my uncle getting ready to go out on Home Guard patrol or duty. Even at such a tender age, I realised that he was doing something important and was very proud of it.

The Norfolk Home Guard started off, as it did in other parts of the country as a very amateur force. It was a new type of citizen's army, the like of which had not been seen before. In time it became a very professional and proficient military organisation, albeit on a part-time basis. Men from all walks of life joined the Norfolk Home Guard, ranging from complete amateurs with no military experience whatsoever, to the likes of Sergeant Harry Cator, VC, MM, Croix de Guerre, one of Norfolk's most distinguished veterans of World War I. The force included both the young and middle-aged, as well as the retired and elderly. All offered to serve their country at a time of great national danger in the struggle against tyranny. They paraded, patrolled, went on guard duty and trained in all weathers, while continuing with their normal day jobs. Many would have had little sleep some nights, but they just got on with things.

It is impossible to say how the Home Guard would have coped in the event of an invasion. However, its presence and resistance would have caused an occupying force greater problems than it had ever experienced on the continent. If Norfolk had been attacked by the Nazis, we can be sure that its Home Guard would have fought fiercely. Later in the war, when more and more of our regular troops were fighting abroad, they had every confidence that their families and homes were in safe hands. No higher compliment could be paid to the Home Guard.

My interest in the Norfolk Resistance Units or "Secret Army" began some 10 years ago when my wife heard a talk given by Mr. Jack Gamble, who lived in the Wymondham area during the war, and who had served in the Norfolk Resistance. It is a remarkable story and because of its highly secret nature, has been a great challenge to research.

I am most grateful to all those men and their families who have offered so much enthusiastic help and information about their time in the Home Guard or the Resistance. The memories they have shared about that special period in their lives are included in two special sections of personal memories. To those countless people in Norfolk who missed my various appeals for help in the local press, I send my apologies. However, I would still be very happy to hear from them about their experiences and to see any documents and photographs they may have.

This account of the Norfolk Home Guard and Resistance Units, is tentative rather than definitive. There will still be sources of further information in the county which I have been unable to discover. However, I have tried not only to tell the story but also capture the spirit of the two organisations, together with the various problems and challenges they faced and largely overcame.

In one of his speeches, Churchill had spoken of, "the vast number who will render faithful service to their country, whose names will never be known and whose deeds never recorded". In this book I have portrayed some of the deeds and named some of the men and women, as representatives of the 32,000 or so, who served in the Norfolk Home Guard or Resistance Units. They were proud to belong to these organisations and were prepared to make the ultimate sacrifice in standing up to Hitler. We too can be proud to be citizens of a country which created them.

Adrian Hoare

Dialogue following a lecture to a Norfolk Home Guard Platoon!

Home Guardsman:	*"Do you think this Hitler be a coming?"*
Officer:	*"Quite possibly".*
Home Guardsman:	*"Well, du if he don't. I shall be wholly put out after all the trouble I've taken".*

(This anecdote by kind permission of The Norfolk Regimental Museum)

PART ONE

The Story of The Norfolk Home Guard

CHAPTER ONE

How it all began

WORLD WAR TWO BEGINS – EARLY SUCCESSES FOR GERMANY

When Germany invaded Poland on 1 September, 1939, few could have anticipated the speed and ferocity with which the Nazi Blitzkrieg broke Poland's resistance. By the end of September, Warsaw had fallen and Poland was defeated.

After the lull of the "phoney war", there was nothing phoney about the Spring of 1940, when the German onslaught was renewed with a massive attack on north western Europe. In April, Denmark and Norway were occupied in a few days and an allied

The Author's uncle being inspected by King George VI.
Photo kindly donated by Arthur Teasell

1

force was forced to withdraw three weeks later. On 10 May, Holland, Belgium and Luxembourg were invaded and by 20 May, France's north eastern defences had been penetrated and Nazi troops were in control of the Channel ports of Calais and Boulogne. The threat to Britain's security was obvious.

THE MIRACLE OF DUNKIRK

British troops who had fought in the Low Countries and France against the might of the German army, retreated to Dunkirk. Between 28 May and 3 June, over 335,000 British soldiers escaped across the Channel, in a remarkable operation involving the Navy, Merchant Marine and an "armada" of little ships of every kind, including tugboats, pleasure steamers and river launches. Churchill described the episode as a "miracle of deliverance".

However, although the men had escaped, most of their equipment was lost, left on French soil, including, 1,000 field guns, 475 tanks, 38,000 military vehicles, 8,000 Bren guns, 90,000 rifles and 7,000 tons of ammunition. Such losses were a huge setback, especially at a time when Britain faced the prospect of an invasion by the most efficient military force the world had seen.

Nevertheless, the heroism displayed at Dunkirk showed the willingness of many people to do their bit in the face of national danger, for with the Germans in possession of the Channel ports, the threat of invasion loomed large. After Dunkirk, there was no army to oppose an invasion, except the defeated, demoralised and temporarily disorganised troops who had escaped from France without their heavy guns and equipment.

FRANCE FALLS – IS BRITAIN NEXT?

Meanwhile, the situation on the continent steadily worsened. On 14 June, Paris was occupied by the Nazis, and France surrendered a week later. Thus the whole of northern France and the coastal areas of western Europe were in German hands.

Less than a month later, on 16 July, Hitler ordered preparations to be made for the invasion of Britain. Already, Dutch airfields, within easy reach of Britain, were in Nazi hands. Only the Channel stood between Hitler and the conquest of this island. Now much would depend on the Navy and Air Force to prevent this – but if they failed?

ENTER THE HOME GUARD

It was against this critical background, when Churchill had said, "blood, tears and sweat" were all that he could offer, and when the nation's defences were perilously fragile, that the birth of the civilian force, initially called the Local Defence Volunteers (LDV), later to be known as the Home Guard, was born. "Dad's Army", as the Home Guard has affectionately been nicknamed, was to become a symbol of the spirit of national resistance against a foreign tyrant. It was a spontaneous response to the threat to British homes and families, which would be defended vigorously.

CHAPTER TWO

1940 "The Broomstick Army"
From Local Defence Volunteers
to Home Guard

THE GOVERNMENT APPEALS FOR HELP

On 14 May, 1940, Anthony Eden, Secretary of State for War, made a radio broadcast to the nation. He referred to the part played by German paratroopers in the defeat of Holland and Belgium, gave details of their methods and aims and stressed the need for a speedy response and information, in the event of a similar attack on Britain. He told his listeners that he was offering an opportunity for those men not in military service, to do something for their country. They were told that by enrolling in the LDV they would be making doubly sure that invasion would be repelled.

All men between the ages of 17 and 65 would be eligible for the new force, provided they were "capable of free movement". Reasonable fitness and a knowledge of firearms was desirable. The LDV would be a part-time civilian army. It would not be paid, but men would get uniforms and weapons and they would have vital duties to perform. However, it should be remembered, that in the aftermath of Dunkirk, the main priority was to arm and equip the regular soldiers. The LDV would for a time be left to their own resources and initiative, a challenge that many of the commanders of the hastily improvised units relished!

NORFOLK RESPONDS TO THE CALL

Men were told in the broadcast to report to their local police station. Stations throughout Norfolk were inundated with men wanting to join the LDV. Indeed, the voice of the first telephone applicant to Norwich police station could be heard against the background of Eden's appeal still coming over the radio! Most police stations had run out of enrolment forms within the first 24 hours!

People from all classes, ages and occupations wanted to enrol in the new force – professional men, artisans, factory, office, shop and farm workers, vets, doctors, jewellers, lorry drivers, vicars, etc. It was a real citizen's army, comprising the employed, the retired, those too young to join the forces, those who were too old and of course those in "reserved" occupations who could not be recruited by the Regular Forces because of the vital nature of their work. To all these, the LDV provided an opportunity to serve their country in time of national danger.

THOUSANDS JOIN THE LDV

Within 48 hours of Eden's broadcast, thousands of men from every corner of Norfolk, had enrolled in the new force. Newspapers of the time give figures for many Norfolk towns during these hectic early days, for example:

Norwich	1800	Diss	50
Yarmouth	700	Wells	70
King's Lynn	431	Harleston	500
Cromer	130	Sandringham	396
Sheringham	174	Downham Market &	
Dereham	150	local villages	150

Among these early recruits were men who were over 70 and also some who were under 17 years of age. Many of those who enrolled had World War One experience and therefore military competence, including one man who had also served in the Boer War (1899-1902) – Norfolk's "Corporal Jones" perhaps! Others with some proficiency with guns of course, were those recruits from the farming communities throughout the county. However, a woman from North Walsham who was an expert rifle shot, was disappointed to be rejected.

What had begun as a trickle of interest in the first hours of the life of the LDV, became a torrent of enthusiasm within the next few days. By 17 May, there were up to a quarter of a million who had volunteered throughout the country. In Norfolk the total at this stage was between 5-6,000 men. By the end of May, less than three weeks since the Government had appealed for help, the Norfolk LDV numbered in excess of 30,000, a powerful indication of the intense patriotic feeling at the time and the realization of imminent danger.

Getting kitted out in King's Lynn. L.D.V.s get their armbands.
Photo with kind permission of Mr. C.W. Scott

GETTING ORGANISED

The difficult task of getting the enthusiastic volunteers organised in a positive way, was delegated to the Lord Lieutenants in each county, where they would be expected to consult with the senior military commander in the area. In Norfolk, Mr. Russell Colman held a meeting of his Deputy Lieutenants, on 17 May, to give effect to the government's appeal. It was decided that the men should be organised into battalions corresponding with the eleven police districts in the county as soon as that was practical. In the meantime, Mr. Colman hoped that those in authority in every parish would nominate one resident as their local representative, who may become the eventual officer to command the parish force, a reminder of the fact that the parish was the basic unit of rural society. The response was swift in Wymondham, where on the same day, Lt. Col. Prior was nominated as the CO of the

Anti-Parachutists Volunteers (a name coined by the press). Furthermore, Lt. Col. Prior was offered an old surveyor's hut on Town Green as his HQ!

It would be some time before an organised structure could be set up of course and in the early weeks, much would depend on local initiative and improvization. Rather than wait for officers to be appointed some areas elected or acclaimed their own natural leaders to positions of command.

The LDVs were told that the key needs were local knowledge, vigilance and speed. It was believed that every parish was capable of providing a sufficient company of such men so that it would be impossible for any German landing to be effected without detection or prompt action. The organization of LDV units then, was an important part of the general preparations for an expected enemy attack.

THE RESPONSE OF THE LOCAL PRESS

Once the War Office had underlined the importance attached to an attack by air, and that the greatest need for action was in the small towns, villages, and less densely populated areas, the press was quick to report on the role of the LDV and to praise its contribution to national safety and morale. It was the press that had referred to the LDVs as "Parashots", and in doing so recognised that the LDVs were in the front line if a German air attack did materialise.

The Diss Express referred to "the spare time army of volunteers enrolling to combat sky raiders". The same newspaper published a detailed article on 24 May, 1940, entitled "PARACHUTE TROOPS – Their Methods and Detection". The information and advice was based on the experience of German paratroop attacks on Norway, Holland and Belgium. It advised readers of the weapons, tactics and methods such invaders would use. In concluding, the writer said that anyone who detected the approach of aircraft should immediately inform our "well-armed and determined groups of defence volunteers", (i.e. the LDVs) who would be "essential to the capture or extermination of troops before they became effective". The LDV were certainly determined but "well-armed" they were not!

The Eastern Evening News welcomed the LDV and was convinced of its value from the outset. It argued that joining the

LDV was a chance to serve and it would provide younger members with some military training which would be useful when they were called up for regular service later. Furthermore, the creation of the LDV would release regular units for more urgent duties. The paper was convinced that the LDV units *would* be able to deal with paratroops. Such optimism is to be expected from the press which played a big part in boosting national confidence. However, the Eastern Evening News was nearer the mark in its view that the LDV would be a great outlet for the patriotic desire to serve, which was so widespread at this time.

The Norfolk Chronicle was similarly confident in the part the LDV would play. It was convinced that no foot of Norfolk would go unwatched and no German who descended from the skies would go undetected. It told its readers that no one was safe from the kind of paratroop attacks that had occurred on the continent, and that because there would be many veterans of 1914-18 in the LDV units, readers could be confident, because, "The old soldiers are now young again" and "they know all about German tricks"! Was this perhaps a reference to the report that some Germans might land in ordinary clothing and not proper German uniform?!

THE ROLE OF THE LDV

On the 22nd May, Sir Edward Grigg, Secretary of State for War, set out three main purposes for the Local Defence Volunteers:

1: **Observation and Information** – The first duty was to stay alert for possible enemy attack and in the event of such an attack, to provide details swiftly to the local regular army authorities.

2: **Obstruction** – They were to prevent movement of enemy groups landed by air, by providing road blocks, so such groups would be hemmed in. They were also to ensure there would be no access for the enemy to motor vehicles, by removing spark plugs and distributors.

3: **Patrol and Protection** – They were to ensure that all vulnerable spots in their area – bridges, cross-roads, railway stations, telephone exchanges, etc. were guarded at all times.

This was seen as a largely passive defensive role but many LDV units, doubtless commanded by some local charismatic personality, wanted to take the initiative and act in a more aggressive and combative way. The fact that the weapons at their disposal were in extremely short supply did not seem to bother them. Many men had joined the LDV not, as in the contemporary jibe, to "**L**ook, **D**uck and **V**anish", but rather "to have a go" at the enemy which was threatening their homes and families. A more appropriate phrase for such spirited men, might be "**L**ook, **D**isrupt and **V**anquish"!!

This more positive and flexible role had been indicated in a letter to the Eastern Daily Press on 17 May, from Lt. Col. Barclay, who later became the CO of the 1st Home Guard Battalion, based at Dereham. Barclay argued that commando-type units of the "best men" from each village were needed. He also said that drill and bureaucracy should be minimal and that what was required in the current situation, was maximum flexibility and mobility. He assured readers that the character of Norfolk men would guarantee they would take particular delight in destroying the "locusts"

One of the LDV functions was checking civilian identity cards.
Photo with kind permission of Mr. C.W. Scott

(Nazis). He also suggested that boys on bikes could act as messengers. His final suggestion was that Boer tactics of doing thorough preliminary scouting, should be adopted before the Nazis arrived.

Barclay's belief in flexibility and local initiative was in part echoed in an Army Council Memorandum of 20 May, where stress was placed on simplicity, elasticity and decentralised control. The LDV it said, should have the minimum of regulations and formalities, no officers or NCOs and no pay! However, discipline would be subject to military law and each local regular army commander would be responsible for the issue of arms, ammunition and uniform to the LDV units in its area.

Although differences existed about the exact nature of the LDV's role, it was now clear that they did have a recognised part to play in the scheme of national defence. Of course, they had very few weapons with which to fight and that was one of the many problems which faced the LDV at this point.

EARLY PROBLEMS AND DIFFICULTIES OF THE LDV

The overnight creation of a citizen army without arms, uniform, equipment or an effective organization, inevitably led to many problems in the early stages. Initially, many of the police stations in Norfolk ran out of enrolment forms. Then they were not sure what to do with the forms!

Weapons – There was an acute shortage of weapons of all kinds for the regulars after the retreat from Dunkirk, let alone the LDV. A national appeal for firearms resulted in over 20,000 weapons of various types being handed in. Among those received in Norfolk were several guns from the royal gun room at Sandringham and some Crimean War (1854-56) muskets from Norwich Castle Museum! An 1850 sentry box was also made available by the museum. In a rural county like Norfolk where farms were plentiful, there were no doubt many men who had shotguns. However, the shortage of weapons was the main weakness in an organization which existed to resist an invasion.

But members of the LDV were not dismayed and set about arming themselves with a variety of improvised weapons such as, broomsticks, pitch forks, golf clubs or home-made cudgels! Some may have thought this was a joke, but such was the spirit of the men, they believed it was better to have some kind of weapon than nothing at all. Of course they expected to be supplied with weapons soon and Churchill's slogan, "Let every one, kill a Hun", which reflected his belief that every member of the LDV should have a weapon of some kind, helped to reinforce their demands for rifles for everyone. However, despite the arrival of thousands of rifles from the USA and Canada in early July, most LDV units continued to be desperately short of weapons, as well as ammunition during the summer of 1940. Certainly, the German propaganda machine had made fun of the so-called "arms" the LDV possessed, – broomsticks, pots of beer and darts, etc!!

Uniform – The Nazi government warned British civilians who took up arms against German soldiers that they would be treated with the utmost severity. It would take months before the LDV could be supplied with uniforms. Meanwhile, the Government announced that the LDV would wear civilian clothes with khaki arm-bands stitched to the sleeve, with the letters "LDV" stencilled on in white. Thus the original "uniform" was an arm-band, or in army terms, a brassard. This device would be the only faint hope the LDV had of being treated as soldiers if captured by the Germans.

On 22 May, it was announced that a quarter of a million arm-bands were being issued to LDV units. These were to be followed by denims, coarse jacket and trousers used by the Army for dirty jobs about camp and notorious for coming in odd sizes! Towards the end of 1940, these denims were gradually superseded by battledress. Additional items of uniform and equipment such as greatcoats, boots, helmets and army style respirators, would arrive later still as they became available.

Training – Many of the early volunteers were elderly men, past retirement age. Most of the rest were involved in work of national importance and tired after a long day's work. Few had cars and fewer still had petrol. Buses had been cut to a minimum to save on fuel. Yet despite these difficulties, many members of the LDV walked long distances to reach their post for duty or to attend evening drills and instruction. Although most had cycles, tyres and batteries for lights were very hard to come by. In the early stages there were few instructors and the officers and NCOs, when they were built into the structure, had to be trained to teach! Despite such difficulties however, the spirit and determination of the men remained high.

The force which had been created so quickly at a time of national danger and which now faced the best equipped army in the world, may have lacked proper weapons, ammunition and equipment. However, its spirit was unquenchable and its *attitude* very combative!

LDV ORGANIZATION DEVELOPS

The Lord Lieutenant of Norfolk, Mr. Russell Colman, liaised with senior military commanders in the area. As a result, retired officers were selected as area, zone and group organisers, who in turn chose commanders for the different locations throughout Norfolk. However, some parishes refused to have anyone imposed on them as they had already elected or acclaimed their own leaders!

On 24 May Colonel Cubitt, who had been appointed by Russell Colman to organise the Norfolk LDV, reported that there was satisfactory progress being made in the formation of an organised corps and that rifles were being distributed. He wisely did not say how many rifles were available!

By 29 May the press was reporting that morale was high in the LDV and that its organization was complete! In fact it had been decided that in due course the LDV would be formed into battalions with areas corresponding to the eleven police divisions of the county. Meanwhile, it seems that each LDV unit was as ready for action as it could be in the circumstances. Duties were allotted, patrols mounted and duty rotas posted. Indeed, according to one report the first LDV patrols were operating with effect from 18 May. Surviving documentary evidence of the unit in the Salle and Reepham areas confirms this. Such a rapid organizational response must surely compare favourably with any other part of the country.

Of course the response to the appeal to join the LDV had greatly exceeded expectations. The authorities were overwhelmed and many volunteers had been told to be patient in the face of a lack of instructions as to their precise duties. It was an immense challenge to transform a military force created overnight, into an effective organization under the control of the military authorities responsible for national defence. However, in Norfolk, by the end of May, morale was high and the press reported that the LDV was confident that they could give a good account of themselves if challenged. Some men were impatient because they had no rifles. On the other hand there would have been men who wouldn't know what to do with a rifle at this stage! Some concern was expressed that misplaced enthusiasm with a gun could do harm to the wrong people! To supplement whatever amateurish weapon they possessed, many LDVs made "Molotov Cocktails". These were home made grenades which consisted of a bottle filled with petrol and equipped with a fuse or wick. The "Molotov Cocktail" was typical of the improvised methods of the LDV in the early months of its history.

CENTRAL GOVERNMENT STARTS TO ACT OVER THE LDV

On 30 May, less than three weeks since the birth of the LDV, the War Office appointed a Director-General and a small staff to oversee this part-time force which had surprised so many with its enthusiasm and rapid progress. This was the first small step by the central government in the transfer of LDV administration from local to national control.

One of the first signs of the new situation in Norfolk, came ten days later on 9 June, when orders were received that 85 road blocks were to be constructed with the utmost speed and then manned in an appropriate way. On 18 June a Ministry of Information statement announced that either the military *or* the LDV were empowered to give orders when a road was to be blocked "if an invader comes".

On 18 June Lt. General Sir Henry Pownall was appointed Inspector General to the LDV. He immediately began to try and impose some order over a force whose spontaneous origins and essentially local and varied character, no doubt offended a traditional military mind!

In Churchill's "finest hour" speech, he referred to the half a million LDVs, for even though he knew they were still short of weapons, he recognized their vital importance to national morale. He continued to be a stout champion of the force and was central in the movement to change its name to the Home Guard. It was Churchill too who played a key role in expediting the supply of weapons to the LDV, because he wanted them to have the means of "killing a Hun". But even Churchill could not perform miracles and it was some time yet before all units had rifles in Norfolk as elsewhere in the country.

THE LDV AT WORK – SNAPSHOTS OF LDV ACTIVITY

Because the first duty of the LDV was Observation, an OP or Observation Post was established in every village and was manned day and night. In the larger towns in the county there would be several such OPs:

Wymondham – On 4 June Wymondham UDC received an application from the local LDV for the loan of some camp beds and mattresses for use at various OPs around the town. The council supplied 12 beds and 17 mattresses but told the LDV that they could only borrow these items for a short time because they may be needed for some expected evacuees!

Cromer – Here the first duty of the LDV was a nightly guard of the beach to watch for invaders. They used various places for their duty, such as an old brick kiln, a platelayer's hut by the railway line and a beach hut. The waiting room at High Station was found to be a good vantage point to watch for parachutists, though initially the watch was done from the top of the church tower. A beach hut on the promenade was used to house two searchlights with a 300 yard range, enough to illuminate the end of the pier! The Post Office had its own LDV unit to defend this key building.
There was also in this town an elementary plan to prevent Cromer being used as a base by the enemy for further inland advance. On the alarm being given, all troops and LDV would immediately turn out armed, "but not necessarily fully clothed or equipped".
On one occasion when an inspecting officer asked the Cromer Coastguard, "What steps would you take my man, if the Germans invaded?" The reply was, "Bloody long 'uns Sir!" The sense of humour does not disguise a shrewd appraisal of the likely military realities in the event of a German invasion in the summer of 1940.

King's Lynn – On 19 June, some girls were reported accidentally injured at one of the local LDV posts by gunshot! Clearly *this* unit had some weapons at this early stage.

West Norfolk – A rumour spread among the community that the local sugar beet factory had been raided by the police who had arrested 19 spies. It was alleged that they had found a barn full of rifles and ammunition and that a Fifth Column centre had thus been destroyed. Clearly local imagination had run riot. In fact, the British Sugar Beet Company had loaned the barn to the local LDV for their headquarters and this is where they stored their rifles and ammunition!

MORE RECRUITS TO THE LDV STILL NEEDED

Despite the great wave of enthusiasm for enrolling in the LDV in the first weeks, there was clearly room for more recruits. The Wymondham UDC received a letter in mid June asking it not to discourage its employees from joining the local LDV. A few days later the Diss Express reported that there was an urgent need for more people to become members of either the ARP or the LDV. It went on to inform its readers that there were many people available who could plug the gaps.

On 28 June there was a reference in an Eastern Daily Press leading article, to a letter in the Times. The writer stressed the difficulties facing LDV units in rural areas like Norfolk, by pointing out that some conventional officers failed to recognize the special problems for LDV recruits who were not simply soldiers, but men who were expected to combine defence of the homeland with long farming duties. However, it is clear that despite the long hours and onerous nature of their work, the farming community played a significant role in the formation of the early LDV units. Their detailed knowledge of the local countryside, made them an invaluable asset to the units to which they belonged.

"THIS IS WHAT WE'LL DO AND WE SHALL DO IT TO THE LAST MAN"

Although the LDV had experienced many difficulties and frustrations in the early summer of 1940, its impact on the local community and the county in general was remarkable. The Eastern Evening News captured the spirit of the force in an article in late June. It reported on the high state of alertness of the LDV and said that they had a clear idea of their role if an invasion came,

– "There we shall be, this is what we'll do and we shall do it to the last man". It then referred to the network of positions all over England and stated confidently, "Whatever happens, we do not budge".

The fiercely patriotic sentiments of the article then claimed that, "if we cannot mop up the invaders, then the Huns have begotten much better children than we ever thought possible in the last war". The paper expressed its complete confidence in the competence of the "fearsome LDV commanders" whose vigilance and determination will ensure that no invader will get through a parish unscathed. Having sung the praises of the LDV the article concluded with a cautionary note to the effect that there was a need for more help from the military, and that the standard of the best units should be reached by all.

THE DEBATE OVER THE LDV ROLE – SHOULD THEY "HAVE A GO" OR STAY PUT?

On 4 July, during a debate in the House of Lords, Lord Croft, the Under Secretary for War, stated that, to effectively combat an invasion, every possible landing place must be covered by gun and rifle fire. In this context he argued that it was vital that the LDV recruit to the full in the coastal towns and villages. It was equally important that the LDV units should be well organised so that they may move speedily to their positions. Doubtless he had in mind an "Action Stations" drill such as that drawn up by the LDV unit at Salle near Reepham (see page 21). Croft echoed Churchill's belief that every member of the LDV should have an effective weapon to "slay any German who sought to enslave him or his women and destroy the freedom of this fair land".

Such sentiments must have been well received by many members of the Norfolk LDV, who had, in the words of one of them, "not joined the LDV to become a glorified policeman". Still less it should be added, did they want to 'Look, Duck and Vanish'! They wanted to use their initiative and take positive action against the invader.

Unfortunately for such adventurous spirits, Anthony Eden defined the role of the LDV rather differently on 5 July. He stated that their job was to "observe, collect information and give it to the military authorities as soon as possible". Of course they were also to guard whatever points had been assigned to them. Eden's view was that the LDV were in a "static defence" role. He discouraged the "have a go" brigade and certainly disapproved of any attempted guerrilla activities. After all, plans were already advanced towards the creation of Resistance Units, whose job *was* to carry out acts of sabotage against the Nazis, should they actually land.

However, the Norfolk Chronicle was claiming in mid July that many men had discovered in LDV activity a return to physical fitness. It also mentioned that the advice of the King of Holland, whose country had suffered a German invasion, was that the LDV should carry arms at all times and arrest anyone they were suspicious of until his identity could be verified. This merely reinforced the opinion that the LDV should be active and aggressive, Churchill's view too!

MAKING IT DIFFICULT FOR JERRY IN NORFOLK

On a lighter note, the Eastern Evening News published an amusing article at the end of June in which the writer pointed out that the German view of a simple-minded yokel was inaccurate. The yokel was on his guard and countrymen were not going to give anything away to the enemy. Indeed, a fortnight later, the same newspaper was giving advice to its readers on Norfolk dialect and slang. The idea was that you would chat to a German paratrooper in "broad Norfolk".

The assumption was that the paratrooper might want to know the way to Norwich! By engaging him in a lengthy discussion in Norfolk dialect, a devious local would be giving the LDV time to arrive and deal with the enemy!

CHURCHILL'S RHETORIC STIFFENS LDV RESOLVE IN NORFOLK

On 15 July Churchill made a morale-boosting speech in which he said that behind our main army, now much improved in organization and weapons to destroy paratroopers or traitors, there existed, the Local Defence Volunteers or Home Guard as he now preferred to call them. He told the nation that these men had the strongest desire to grapple with the enemy, and he warned that there would be no placid lying down in submission (as in other countries!). On the contrary, "we shall defend village, town and city."

A Norfolk Village Ready for The Nazis

On 23 July an anonymous LDV commander in a Norfolk village proudly conveyed the spirit of his unit in the columns of the Eastern Daily Press. He said that his men ranged from 15 to 63 years of age. They had fortified the village green, were pleased with their "uniform", and were now looking forward to becoming real soldiers. He informed his readers that "there would be difficulty in restraining our 63 year old from tackling the Nazis with his fists!"

He then said that his unit had held a practice raid and "woe betide the real enemy!" His enthusiasm had also led him to challenge a neighbouring village to "mortal combat", although unfortunately he does not indicate whether his challenge was met! He concluded with a reference to the fact that his unit had received help and advice from the local regulars and felt sure that the lessons they had learned would not be in vain!

Such a fearless spirit in the face of the greatest army in the world was as much a feature of LDV attitudes as was the more natural response of, "what chance have we got?"

LDVs To Be Organized Into Battalions

Towards the end of July, the "broomstick army" was now caught up with the rush of recruits and it was felt that a detailed framework of organization was necessary, with a geographical basis of control. The basic unit would be the SECTION (about 25-30 men), usually based on a parish. Four Sections would form a PLATOON, four Platoons would form a COMPANY and four Companies would be organised into a BATTALION. The size of a battalion could vary considerably depending on the local population and number of recruits. Battalions would be formed into GROUPS with a Group Commander and the groups in turn would be organized into a ZONE.

To ensure that LDV organization fitted in with the proper military structure, the GOCs (General Officers Commanding) were responsible for command, organization, training, equipment, etc. for all the LDVs in their area. This was a turning point in the organization of the Norfolk Local Defence Volunteers. It would take some time to fully establish the battalion system but plans were now laid. Churchill's wish that a combative spirit should be displayed by all units appears to have been well received in Norfolk.

It was at this time that the German government issued instructions to the troops planning "Operation Sea Lion", (the code name for the invasion of Britain). They were told that "the British will resist with every means – bitter fighting is expected". Such a view is well borne out by the determined spirit of the Norfolk LDV at this stage! The fact that they were still desperately short of weapons made no difference. Their senior commanders had been told in June, by the Commander-in-Chief, that they should not misjudge the shotgun, because he had arranged for a million rounds of ammunition to be delivered from the USA "which will kill a leopard at 200 yards". Unfortunately, he added that there would be only enough for 3 or 4 cartridges for each LDV member. We don't know how many of these cartridges reached the hands of the Norfolk LDV! Also, when a quarter of a million rifles, together with 77 million rounds of ammunition did arrive from the USA, most went to the Regular Army.

THE LOCAL DEFENCE VOLUNTEERS ARE RENAMED THE "HOME GUARD"

It was at this point that another change came to the force that had been in existence for a little over two months. Churchill had been a keen supporter of the *idea* of the LDV which he felt was a powerful symbol of the British spirit, so important at this critical moment in our history. However, he did not like the *name,* "Local Defence Volunteer". "Local", he felt was uninspiring and imprecise, "Defence", was too negative, and he had always empathised with the desire of the force for an aggressive role, while "Volunteer", sounded amateurish. He had been too busy in May and June to give much thought to the subject, but came up with the idea of the new name of "Home Guard", which he said sounded much better and was precise, positive and professional. Though some in high places resisted the change, Churchill was determined and on 24 July, the "Home Guard" was officially adopted as the new name.

One of the first changes was to the LDV armlets, which were adapted accordingly. It was about this time that the government announced that the total number in the Home Guard had risen to 1,300,000. It was stated that there would be a temporary suspension of recruitment, except in areas where there was a shortfall, so that there would be time for the provision of equipment for all the Home Guard. There are no records of a lack of numbers for the ranks of the Norfolk Home Guard at this point.

The village pub was a popular haunt for the Home Guard. World War One veterans in khaki once more, relax with youth too young for the Regular Army and those in "Reserved Occupations".

IWM D4852   *Photo with kind permission of The Imperial War Museum*

EXAMPLES OF SOME NORFOLK HOME GUARD UNITS IN LATE SUMMER 1940

Documentary evidence for this early period is scarce. There was a need for hasty improvisation to deal with a dangerous, unpredictable and changing situation. In such circumstances, there was much scope for local initiative, and under imaginative and resolute leadership, local commanders could engender a confident and combative spirit among the men they organised into these first units. Doubtless, many rehearsed their own role on a local stage in the event of an attack such as manning motor launches, guarding bridges, post offices, important road junctions, country houses or railway stations, while others simply trudged windy fields. See Chapter 7 for some details of these activities.

Fragmentary though the evidence is of the LDV/Home Guard units in Norfolk during the Summer of 1940, fortunately, enough has survived to illuminate the problems, nature and spirit of the men who formed these units. What follows is a survey of a few of them!

SALLE (NEAR REEPHAM)

This has proved to be the most well-documented unit of the Home Guard during these months and quite a detailed picture of the realities of Home Guard life emerge from this source.

Perhaps the most interesting document in the collection is an "ACTION STATIONS" Drill for July/August 1940, which sets out the detailed procedure for men in the Home Guard, in the event of an imminent enemy attack. Extracts are quoted below:-

"ACTION STATIONS" FOR SALLE HOME GUARD

"In the event of the above taking place, and the necessary rifles forthcoming, the following points should be arranged for by each Parish Commander.

Each Village has been or will be sited with a 'Village Strong Post'. Therefore it is necessary, besides having the main Armoury and Observation Post, to prepare Sub-Armouries near each village post. To these Posts men should be allotted who live nearest, and they should be made up in Sections, under a Section Leader who is in sole charge.

In the event of Action Stations continuing for some time, a Relief Section should be ready to take its place on duty, to enable the first Section to get some food and sleep.

It would also be advisable to arrange with the cottagers near the Post to provide, where possible, sleeping accommodation for the men who live a long way away, also light refreshment. At the same time, all men should provide for themselves and keep handy, a packet of chocolate, a packet of biscuits and a full Waterbottle.

We now come to the question of Spare men who will not be using a rifle. Their duties are many and varied, and each man must be told exactly what he has to do and where his station is viz:-

*1. One or two **Runners** to go to the Section Leader to warn him of enemy approach, etc.*

2. **Stretcher Bearers** *Two stretchers should at once be made for each Post (two sacks and two poles are all that is needed), and these men should know exactly where the nearest ARP Post is situated.*

3. **Traffic Control** *One man should be stationed in the centre of the Village to assist the Military in giving directions.*

4. **Guides** *To go with the Military and be able to direct them anywhere in the district.*

5. *A* **Mechanic** *ready to go round and be able to put all Cars completely out of action and destroy all Petrol.*

6. *Men of* **Fearless Disposition** *stationed near the Post to throw Molotov Cocktails at the enemy.*

   If 'Action Stations' is received when men are on guard the Section Leader will see that the Church Bell is rung and the Parish Commander is notified. If this should happen during the daytime, men will, on hearing the Church Bell sounded, repair at once to their Sub-Armoury or the Main Armoury, draw their rifles and go at once to their Village Post under their own Section Leader".

The attention to detail in preparing to combat an invasion, is a remarkable tribute to the morale and organization of the Home Guard at this critical period.

On 1 August, 1940, the Salle Home Guard was listed as No.4 Section, of No.1 Platoon, of No.4 Company, of No.1 Battalion of the Norfolk Home Guard! The battalion structure mentioned earlier, had clearly been imposed. At this point the Salle Section consisted of 31 men of whom 6 were ex-servicemen. The section possessed 20 rifles and 501 rounds of ammunition. Nine of the men were recorded as having tunics, trousers and caps, there were 8 brassards, 8 rifle pull throughs, 4 rifle slings and 5 oil bottles. With such resources would the Salle Home Guard resist the enemy!

However, every effort was made to meet the "Action Stations Drill" set out earlier. Two Defence Posts were guarded and manned, no doubt by men of "fearless disposition", Runners were in place and the roles of stretcher bearers, guides and traffic control had been allotted. It appears that every man in the Salle Section knew exactly what his job was in the defence of his village and all of them helped to fill 200 sandbags to fortify the defence posts. Guard duty rotas were published too, and in the critical months of August and September, 5 men were on duty at the same time. By October, however, two men mounted guard from 9 pm to 5 am the next morning.

Two resignations from the Salle Home Guard occurred at this time, apparently due to illness or old age. In each case, an urgent request was sent to the men to return what equipment had been issued, to their section leader. In a third case, there was some delay in returning equipment. As a result, the man in question who had resigned without any good reason, was sent the following note from the Platoon Commander:-

"Since you do not appear willing to attend drills and lectures in order to train yourself to defend your home, family and village, I shall be glad to know if you wish to continue service in the Home Guard or not, as the equipment issued to you, is urgently required for volunteers who *are* willing to be trained" (2 Dec 1940).

Training was done in the main hall at the Linton White Institute in Reepham. The equipment situation gradually improved and by December 1940 the inventory of the Salle Home Guard shows that all men had caps, tunics, trousers and eye shields. Most had boots, but there were only 12 blankets, 13 sets of anklets, 5 groundsheets and 3 great coats!

With regard to rifles, the Salle Home Guard had a weapon check on 23 October, during which 16 rounds of ammunition were missing! The unit still only had the 20 rifles listed earlier but was told at this time that it would be issued with new arms and ammunition. It is not clear when these weapons arrived! However, the platoon commander did have copies of "The Home Guard Fieldcraft Manual" by Langdon-Davies, a pamphlet on training men in the use of the Thompson Machine gun, and a copy of the Army Act 1881!

Salle Home Guard then, was hardly ready to take on the might of the German army. However, one can only admire the spirit and determination with which it went about the business of defending, "home, family and village".

SNETTERTON

There were 23 men in this unit at the beginning. All of them were agricultural workers and the list of occupations included, cowmen, warreners, gamekeepers, farm stewards, tractor drivers, farmers, etc. The youngest man was 18 years old and the oldest 59. Nine of them had served in World War One but probably most of this unit were familiar with guns given their agricultural background. The headquarters of this unit was in a thatched house near "The Hole in the Wall" in Snetterton. Although none of the men were prepared to serve in any area other than their village, understandable, given their farming commitments, they were ready to turn out and do their bit to defend Snetterton.

SYDERSTONE

There were 36 men in this unit at first, of whom the youngest was 16 years of age and the oldest 60. Ten had previous military experience, and another ten had transferred to the regular forces by the end of 1940. By 1942, there were 78 men in the Syderstone Guard which included 12 NCOs and a lieutenant, formerly a World War One captain, now a vicar.

The evidence shows that this unit, like many others no doubt, kept a careful record of kit and weapons, issued and handed in, essential when resources were so scarce in the early months. The CSM or Company Sergeant Major, was an ex-World War One machine gunner who had served in the Machine Gun Corps from 1915-1918. Later in the war when units did get machine guns, such expertise would have proved invaluable.

"RATTLING THE DICTATORS"

Despite the limitations of the Home Guard, its progress since May had been remarkable. Towards the end of July, the German and Italian governments tried to intimidate it with warnings that it infringed international law and that the "illegal activities" of a civilian force created by the "vilest criminals" would be punished severely! The Nazi press also described the Home Guard as a "corps of hedgehoppers".

But the Home Guard was undeterred, and on 29 July, some Norfolk commanders, along with many others from all over the country, were sent on courses at the newly created Home Guard School at Osterley Park. Here they would learn how to sabotage a tank and the art of guerrilla fighting, taught by Tom Winteringham, who had commanded the British Battalion of the International Brigade in the Spanish Civil War (1936-39).

Winteringham took the view that the Home Guard should have an offensive as well as defensive role. However, the War Office was soon to take over Osterley and Spanish Civil War methods of fighting ceased to be taught. Very few realised that there were already in being, highly trained "Resistance Units", who would act very offensively if the enemy did manage to set foot on these shores!

The local press continued to express great confidence in the Home Guard, with a reference to "the old Norfolk cry of "that's stopped him" (referring to a shot pheasant), which may soon apply to Nazi paratroopers!" The Home Guard were now in the habit of stopping anyone as they went about their duties. In early August there was a Ministry of Information appeal to the general public to be courteous and co-operative when stopped at road blocks and asked for their identity. People were told that such duties were essential to national security and they must not misunderstand the activities of the Home Guard.

A Home Guard Sub-Section Officer is challenged and asked to produce his pass.
IWM D12230   Photo with kind permission of the Imperial War Museum

THE HOME GUARD MOVES FURTHER TOWARDS A MILITARY STRUCTURE

On 3 August, the Home Guard was to be affiliated to County Regiments and would now be known as the Norfolk Home Guard. Three days later, it was confirmed that the Home Guard was part of the armed forces of the Crown. This was so that it could not develop as a few had hoped, into a "people's army" of freebooting irregulars. However, the new status was welcomed by most men as they correctly saw that it gave the Home Guard a greater importance in the military defence of the nation.

By now the Norfolk Home Guard was organised into 11 Battalions:-

		COMMANDING OFFICER
No.1	East Dereham	Lt. Col. J.F. Barclay TD
No.2	Downham Market	Lt. Col. E.R. Pratt MC
No.3	Harleston	Capt. Sir Robert Bignold
No.4	Holt	Lt. Col. Lord Hastings
No.5	North Walsham	Col. Lord William Percy CBE, DSO
No.6	Norwich	Major S.W. Trafford
No.7	Kings Lynn & Sandringham	Col. O. Birkbeck
No.8	Swaffham	Capt. R.G. Buxton
No.9	Wymondham	Col. Lord Bury MC
No.10	Norwich	Capt. B.F. Hornor DSO
No.11	Great Yarmouth	Major F.R.B. Haward

Shortly after the formation of these battalions, they were re-organised into three zones which conformed to military boundaries in Norfolk:-

East Zone consisted of parts of 3 and 4 Battalions and 5, 6, 10 and 11 Battalions, commanded by Col. Cubitt and under the operational control of the Commander of 76 Division of the Regular Army.

Mid-Norfolk Zone comprised 1 and 9 Battalions plus parts of 3 and 8 Battalions, commanded by Maj-Gen. E.M. Steward CB, and under the operational control of the mid-Norfolk Sub-Area.

West Zone consisted of 2 and 7 Battalions and part of 4 and 8 Battalions, commanded by Col. E.R. Pratt.

However, this organizational structure was in its early stages, and most men in the Norfolk Home Guard were aware only of their own unit commanders whom they knew personally. The imposition of a battalion system did nothing to dull their enthusiasm and excellent morale at local level.

"THE MOST DESPERATE ENTHUSIASTS THE WORLD HAS EVER SEEN"

In a speech during July, Churchill had informed the nation that every village and town would be defended with the utmost vigour. Some of the Norfolk Home Guard units may have been short of weapons, but their spirit and determination to resist an invader could not be faulted.

The Eastern Evening News reported in early August that the confidence of Home Guard commanders was "sky high" as they constantly trained to achieve things which Britain's defeated allies, Belgium, Holland and France could not achieve. Among the many activities of the Home Guard at this stage apparently, was the men practicing bomb throwing with turnips! They were also preparing ambushes, imagining raids and diving into ditches. It was suggested that the Nazis had been successful so far because they had been opposed by men whose methods were open and irresolute, but they would not know what was in Britain's mind!

While such chauvinism is to be expected from the press in time of war, and the optimism about the ability of the British to see off a Nazi threat might have been excessive, nevertheless, both the government and the military authorities were convinced that Britain would have resisted Germany more effectively than France where the Nazis were allowed to roam freely without hindrance. As the local press saw it, in the English parishes, if the Home Guard was given its chance against the invader, the Germans would be meeting "the most desperate enthusiasts the world has ever seen – Englishmen defending their homes". If a Nazi tank got behind our lines, it was argued, this would not confuse the defenders; it would merely have travelled out of one parish of determined men into another!

This view of the importance of the Home Guard in the national defences is confirmed by B. Collier, a leading authority on the defence of the UK at this period. He describes the Home Guard as "a valuable adjunct to the Home Forces".

Never turn you back on a pint, Jimmy.

Percy Armstrong

Oh Percy wheres you Lewis

Charlie Stubbs – Butcher

Choice of weapons – Gentlemen

Mr Sturman
The Odd "Spot"!

Tishy
Tanktrap!

Bertie Wyer

Shall I shunt you boss?

I must wear my gold-braid
The Station Master

Every little
Lionel Tell!
The Artist?

Cartoons of members of Attleborough Home Guard
showing their varied occupations.
Kindly donated by Victor Woods

29

The Norfolk Home Guard, like countless other units throughout the country, provided a network of defended villages, parishes and townships, which would hamper the consolidation of enemy troops landed from the air into inland districts. At the same time, they reinforced the nation's defences near the coast. Churchill had famously said in June 1940, "Hitler knows that he will have to break us in this island or lose the war" and, "We shall defend our island, whatever the cost ... we shall never surrender". In stiffening the national resolve, Churchill provided the Home Guard with a message which especially appealed to the spirit of the men who had spontaneously responded to the government earlier in the year.

It was this spirit that was seized upon by the Norfolk press in August 1940. Whilst it recognised that the Home Guard needed technical help and advice from the Regular Army, it was vital that the early spirit of the force continued to flourish. The Eastern Evening News concluded that "if it is the spirit of the troops that counts, there might be no better troops in Europe than the Home Guard".

The same newspaper reported on the "continuing keenness which still bubbles ... in many of the village companies". Readers were reminded that the most ardent champions of the Home Guard, had said from the outset, that, properly organised, it would make invasion impossible, while at the same time releasing regular troops for counter measures against Germany. Many Norfolk units were commanded by experienced officers from World War One, who were aware of the need to master the tactics of the Second World War. The defence of their homes was a priority but the Norfolk Home Guard was also aware of the need to build on this role by providing an enthusiastic support to the regulars in the area.

HIGH MORALE AND HIGH ALERT

A headline in the Eastern Daily Press in early September 1940, "Invasion is still on!", underlined the importance of the utmost vigilance. A Watton man was fined ten shillings (50 pence) by Wymondham magistrates for failing to immobilize an unattended motor car at Hingham.

However, perhaps the most illuminating example of Home Guard attitudes in this critical summer in our national history, is

Pillboxes were familiar sights,
regularly used by the Home Guard in the early part of the war.

1. Strong point at
   Bromholm Priory,
   Bacton

2. Mileham

3. Ashill

to be found in a Secret Memo sent by a senior officer of the 53rd Infantry Brigade, to Home Guard commanders on 19 August 1940. The Memo was headed "PARACHUTES" and its purpose was perhaps, to convey the alertness of the country at this time, but also to illustrate the dangers of excessive zeal! The contents of the Memo are quoted below.

PARACHUTES

During a recent air battle with the Germans, one of our machines was so seriously damaged that the pilot was forced to take to his parachute. The alertness of the country in watching for parachutists may be judged by his own account of his descent, which runs as follows:-

"I was being blown for miles over the English countryside and saw masses of men bobbing up from hedges and other cover, all watching me. I eventually landed near Canterbury in a cornfield, fortunately not having been shot at on the way down, and was winded. The corn was about waist high.

I then saw a lot of very angry armed gentlemen ... who had posted themselves along a hedge at varying intervals. One group of three was particularly interesting, being led by an old farmer. I first saw him 80 yards away taking careful aim at me with a shot gun; my hands were up at the time and I shouted to him not to shoot, but his only answer was to walk a further 20 yards to a more advantageous position by a tree. He again took aim at me, but a soldier gave me a ray of hope by coming towards me from the left.

I then suddenly got the impression that somebody was behind me and I turned round quickly to find a yokel of the fiercest type coming at me with a 6 foot piece of railing! I said: 'Hey, for God's sake put that down!' and with my hands still up told him where to find my identity card. Whilst he was looking for the identity card, the old farmer advanced another 20 yards taking aim again.

At this point several soldiers with a corporal ran across the field and I was able to identify myself. The farmer was then told by them to lower his gun; his only comment was: 'You nearly got it; I'd like to blow your brains out'. After further conversation, he was convinced that I was English; then he was very helpful and took me across to his house to have my leg dressed. On the way there I noticed that two women from the house had rushed out, one with a heavy frying pan, and the other, with what looked like a large knife".

This story illustrates the spirit and degree of alertness which was typical at this time. In early September, the Norfolk Chronicle was assuring its readers that "the invader will be hunted and attacked and allowed no quiet; from the moment of his appearance he will be assailed". We can be sure that the Norfolk Home Guard was watchful and ready to take action if the occasion demanded it. The same newspaper also paid tribute to women "the other Home Guard", whose cooking and other domestic duties protected the men from ill health!

Another illustration of the spirit of the times is the case of a tractor driver of Horsham St. Faiths. A Home Guardsman, he did not like using rope as a rifle sling, and had persuaded a soldier to sell him a proper sling for 2 shillings. In court he told the magistrate he wanted to "look decent" when he went on guard duty. With such an attitude there was no option but to dismiss the case against him.

WILL THE INVASION COME?

If invasion was to come in 1940, the military authorities thought that early September was the most likely time, because of favourable tides and before the winter weather set in. Certainly the Home Forces in Southern and Eastern Commands were on full alert at this point. The codeword for invasion was "CROMWELL", which was duly passed down the chain of command. However, it appears that not all the Home Guard units seemed to have been properly briefed, which led to confusion and false alarms in some parts of the country. What was clear though, was that church bells would be rung to signal an invasion was in progress. Once again there was some confusion about the exact roles of the Police, the Army and the Home Guard. However, the Commander in Chief of the Home Forces, General Sir Alan Brooke, authorised the actual ringing of church bells by a Home Guard commander, provided he had himself seen at least 25 parachutists!

Some bad feeling seems to have developed at this time between some Home Guard units and the central authorities. It should be remembered that many units in Norfolk, had been raised, patrols organised, and guard duties set up, on a local basis without, they thought, much help from the War Office. It was only natural then, that these units of patriotic volunteers would be reluctant to submit to orders from above at this time of apparent crisis.

The expected invasion did not materialise but at least one member of the Norfolk Home Guard seems to have known that an invasion would not take place. On that night in the Autumn of 1940, when the codeword "Cromwell" was signalled and all England stood to arms, he refused to leave his bed saying:- "I'll get up if he comes, but I know he baint a-coming"!

TIGHTER CONTROL OF THE HOME GUARD – OFFICERS AND NCOS

The War Office felt by the end of October that the time had come to exercise more control over the Home Guard. In early November the proposed changes were announced. It was believed that they would not only bring it under greater central control, but also make it a more professional fighting force, boosting its morale in the process. While there was some concern about the democratic

A section of a village Home Guard ready for action. Men from a broad range of occupations made up each unit.

IWM D9260   *Photo with kind permission of The Imperial War Museum*

spirit of the Home Guard, the Under Secretary for War, Sir Edward Grigg, clearly recognised the local and diverse character of the force, indicating that he did not want it to lose its "free and easy, homespun, village green character".

Because the Home Guard was part of the Armed Forces, it should be appropriately organised. Firstly, there would be army ranks, i.e. commissioned officers and NCOs. Self-appointed Home Guard commanders who might be too old or even incompetent, however patriotic, would have to go. Each battalion would have regulars put in as instructors and administrative officers to give more coherence to the units. Furthermore, the shortfall in weapons would be made up, systematic training would be introduced and each member of the Home Guard would be properly equipped. Plain denim, which was the usual uniform by this time, would be replaced by standard army battle dress. Soon, the War Office promised, every member of the Home Guard would possess a steel helmet!

The regularising of the position of Home Guard commanders by giving them the usual military titles and ranks, was not a decision which was well received by all members of the Norfolk Home Guard. There were those who preferred the Home Guard to remain a separate militia; they felt that it would now become subject to bureaucratic regimentation. This was inevitable, given the increased powers of the Home Guard Directorate at the War Office.

Another result of the reforms in November, concerned the relationship between the Army and the Home Guard. If the enemy landed, the Home Guard would now come under the control of the local Army commander. However, there was some concession to Home Guard pride, in that the local Home Guard commander would have responsibility for directing defence measures in his immediate locality.

THE PRESS RESPONSE TO THE WAR OFFICE REFORMS

The Eastern Daily Press welcomed the reforms and was pleased that the War Office had recognised the "local and friendly" character of the Home Guard, arguing that it was important to preserve its individual identity and diverse character. However, it also supported the view that officers lacking enthusiasm and competence should be discarded. At the same time it pointed out that the Home Guard was born out of spontaneity and enthusiasm in the face of a grave threat to the security of homes and the safety of our land. In general, it went on, this enthusiasm had not waned but "burned with a steady flame". The paper also made the crucial point that the Home Guard had proved its worth by its very permanence and the high quality of its morale. With the new War Office reforms it argued, the force had truly come into its own and been duly recognised as an integral part of the nation's defences. Its military status had now come of age.

However, it was the paper's final comment which captured the national mood in 1940 so well. The Home Guard was specially symbolic in that it expressed the determination, should the need arise, "to fight in the fields, to fight in the streets, to defend the last ditch".

TRIBUTES TO THE HOME GUARD AT THE END OF 1940

Throughout the Summer and Autumn of 1940, the local press had paid enthusiastic tribute to the Norfolk Home Guard, assuring the county that no one could ask for a more determined force to do everything in its power to defend homes and families.

In December, the Inspector-General of the Home Guard, General Sir Henry Pownall said, "If we stand firm as we did in 1940, all will be well". This is a clear championship of the spirit of the Home Guard during the dark days of that dramatic period in our history. He seems to have realised that this remarkable force, which was not like the Army, nevertheless could show great resolve in the face of national emergency.

The Home Guard must have been pleased to learn that the Battle of Britain had been won, and with the longer winter nights ahead, many anticipated their hours of duty would be shortened. However, their importance and the need for continuing vigilance, was underlined by Churchill, during a speech he made in December. He spoke of "the highest value and importance of the Home Guard". He added that a country where, "every street and village bristles with resolute armed men", is one which will overthrow tactics which had earlier in the year crushed the Dutch so decisively. He warned the Home Guard, that although the danger to Britain had disappeared for a time, they should not make the mistake of believing it had passed away.

The Eastern Daily Press reminded its readers that whether invasion was imminent or not, only a few miles of sea divided us from a well-organised enemy with a vast army and a powerful air force. In Churchill's words, "unremitting vigilance" was essential in the face of the huge German army and its substantial naval resources in all the harbours of the western European seaboard.

Few could have any doubt at the end of 1940, that there would be many real dangers ahead, and that the Home Guard still had a very important role to play. In the "Home Guard Training Manual", published in December of 1940, men were reminded that, "they were not a spare wheel kept in readiness if anything goes wrong with the others ... but an essential part of the machinery with which Britain is being defended".

CHAPTER 3

1941 New Problems but a Big Step Forward

For many of the original volunteers who formed the first LDV units in Norfolk during the early summer of 1940, nothing would be quite the same again. These men had been involved in a unique and unforgettable experience and their spirit was unquenchable. Now, with the War Office exerting ever more control over the Home Guard, it was only natural that some of them would find certain changes hard to take. However, at a time when Hitler's attention was turning to the Balkans and North Africa, and the immediate threat of an invasion seemed to have receded, (albeit for a time only), the Home Guard took some important steps towards becoming a fully-equipped and professionally trained force. Along the way it experienced fresh problems and new challenges.

ARGUMENTS OVER THE SOCIAL STATUS OF HOME GUARD OFFICERS

In April, 1941 the national press had published names of many of the newly appointed commissioned officers, pointing out that there were very few "Misters", and stressing the large numbers of knights, baronets and peers appearing on the list.

The issue provoked an ironic letter from a Norfolk Home Guardsman to the local press. He remarked how thrilling it was for the rank and file of "this magnificent force built on the voluntary and patriotic instincts of the common man", to have such distinguished aristocrats as their leaders! He regretted the departure of a Home Guard where things worked harmoniously and men were content with their leaders who ensured units were efficient. The writer of this letter, disapproved of what he perceived as a takeover of officer ranks by "gentlemen", who often had little military experience. Most of all he seemed to fear that the new officers would lack the ability to handle power in an unassuming way, which the Home Guard had been accustomed to and appreciated. He reminded readers that the Home Guard had a democratic system in which every man pulled his weight regardless of rank or station in civil life. This kind of force was essential he felt, "if we are to beat the Nazi savages".

The class issue which had been raised in the national press, was defused in Norfolk by Lord Hastings, who was the CO of No.4 Battalion Norfolk Home Guard, based at Holt. He responded to the letter mentioned above by pointing out that knights, baronets and peers, in common with hundreds of Home Guard leaders throughout Norfolk from all walks of life, had striven in the past 11 months to organise, train and develop the units in their care. Many of the "new leaders" in Norfolk were in fact the old ones who had now been appointed to commissioned rank. Lord Hastings regretted that an unwise journalist had chosen to select a few titled men from a mighty list of officers in the most democratic force ever raised.

This attitude was echoed by other correspondents, serving Home Guardsmen, who stressed that they were too busy to be concerned with the trivial jealousy of social status. They reminded readers that all sorts, classes and occupations made up the Home Guard, and that patriotism was unconnected to class.

RECRUITMENT PROBLEMS

Though the spirit of the men could not be questioned, there was clearly a concern that numbers in the force should be maintained. In March, the War Office announced that boys approaching 17 years of age could join the Home Guard, to compensate for the expected departure of some Guardsmen as a result of "call-up" to the regulars. Other losses from Home Guard ranks could be expected following the proposal to reduce the number of "reserved" occupations.

However, would these young men respond? An article in the Eastern Daily Press suggested that farm workers be exempt military service, but should be compelled to join the Home Guard. The views of a platoon commander who wrote to the paper, implied support for such an idea. He said that many young farm labourers had refused to join, despite the example set by their older colleagues.

He knew of one village in his area where at least 12 men had refused to join, even though they were exempt military service by virtue of their occupation. Whether it was typical of the rest of the county, as he alleged, it is difficult to say. However, as a platoon commander he felt that the shortfall of men in the Home Guard resulting from call-up, should be made up by new recruits. In the situation, he said, "I'm prepared to disregard the old adage – 'One volunteer is worth three pressed men'".

Another Home Guardsman writing to the Eastern Daily Press expressed the same concern. Apparently, he was travelling through a village and stopped at the "local", where he noticed eight strong young men in civvies playing cards! Outside however, he saw some older men in Home Guard uniform doing weapon training. He added that in his experience, it was mostly the older ranks who regularly attended parades and training. Like the platoon commander, he felt that compulsory membership was essential. He reminded readers that the danger of invasion had not gone away and it was vital that each Home Guard unit was up to strength, so that "hearths and homes" could be effectively protected.

Despite the pessimism expressed by some, perhaps things were not as bad as they feared. The Norfolk Chronicle reported in June 1941, that the strength of the Home Guard was being maintained, and that Cadet Units of youths from the age of 17 had been formed. These volunteers were being trained to take the places of the men who were being called up. However, in Wymondham there were problems, as indicated by a local Home Guardsman, who wrote that the "deplorably low" strength of the Wymondham platoon was due to the "call-up". He believed that if there was to be a committee to deal with the problem of recruiting "idle young men", then Wymondham Home Guardsmen should be on it! He was clearly anxious to check the steady reduction of numbers in Wymondham though the issue of conscription was not mentioned.

The problem of recruitment continued throughout the year. In November, a member of the Home Guard appealed for volunteers in the Diss Express. He claimed that local rural workers were failing in their duty to defend their hearths and homes against invasion by a barbarous aggressor. He felt that many able-bodied men were doing no more than they would if there had been no war on! The typical spirit of 1940 was reflected in his claim that if the invader did come he would be wiped out. However, he added that if rural workers put aside their complacency and the idea that the other nations would win the war for us, an enemy attacker would be defeated more quickly, because the local Home Guard would be at full strength.

Other letters in the Diss Express supported these views and suggested that conscription into the Home Guard would be justifiable, especially at a time when women were due to be conscripted into the services. Clearly the feeling was growing at the end of 1941, that the reliance of the Home Guard on volunteers might not be enough. At Dickleburgh, a meeting about the sadly depleted numbers of the local Home Guard and the Civil Defence caused by the call-up, echoed the concern about the shortage of volunteers, even though able-bodied men existed. As a result, the meeting felt that a system of compulsion should be introduced. A resolution was passed to that effect and copies were sent to the local MP Mr. J.A. Christie and the Prime Minister.

In October, as a result of the shortfall in volunteers, the Wymondham Urban District Council received a letter from the CO of the 9th Battalion Home Guard, asking for its co-operation in helping him to obtain more recruits for the local battalion. The council considered that a public meeting would not obtain the desired result! Instead, it was decided to make a personal appeal to all those men who were not at that time doing any form of Civil Defence work. A sub-committee was then appointed to meet the Home Guard CO and other guardsmen with a good knowledge of the town! On 4 November, the sub-committee met the Home Guard representatives, who included Col. Back and Mr. Fryer, and drew up a list of people to whom a personal appeal would be sent. A letter was accordingly prepared. The response to this appeal is not known! But that such efforts were being made in Wymondham to boost Home Guard numbers demonstrates the determination of the local unit to get up to full strength.

In Stoke Holy Cross there was a similar concern. The minute book of the village Invasion Committee tells us that the voters list was scrutinized for men who might be persuaded to join the Home Guard. On 10 June, through the Parish Council, a letter was sent to appeal for volunteers. Again the evidence is unavailable regarding the success of this appeal.

It is clear that there was real concern in many parts of the county about the depleted ranks of the Home Guard. Although some fresh volunteers appeared, these were insufficient, and the government decided at the end of the year that some form of compulsory service, would have to be introduced in the future.

The Invasion Committees and The Home Guard

Early in 1941 the Government ordered Invasion Committees to be set up in every area of the country. Sir William Spens, the Regional Commissioner, began to implement the instruction in Norfolk and other counties in the region immediately. He reported later in the year that such committees had been set up in most parishes and that they were taking up their duties energetically. He warned that though the threat of invasion may have temporarily receded, it had not disappeared and the risk of an invasion was, if anything, increasing. Therefore plans to prepare for an invasion should be continually overhauled and brought up to date.

The Home Guard was of course much involved in the co-ordinating of Invasion Committee plans, and in many cases military exercises which took place with regularity now proved the value of such committees. Some were set up very rapidly; others took longer to get off the ground. In June, it was claimed that nearly every parish in mid-Norfolk had an Invasion Committee. The slogan of the time was "The invasion prepared; can't be scared!" In September, Col. Cubitt, CO of East Zone, Norfolk Home Guard, wrote to the Eastern Daily Press to say that the Home Guard was anxious to co-operate with and co-ordinate all aspects of the Invasion Committees. He emphasized that there was a need for local initiative to ensure maximum efficiency of local defence arrangements.

New Tactics and Role Suggested for The Home Guard

In April 1941, Hugh Slater's book "The Home Guard for Victory" was reviewed in the Norfolk Chronicle. Slater was an expert on guerrilla warfare with experience in the Spanish Civil War. The book was very popular with the Home Guard because it put forward the view that the force should be stimulating intelligence, resourcefulness, imagination and originality rather than drilling! He urged the Home Guard to be trained in anti-aircraft musketry, bomb throwing, map reading and camouflage and said that these skills should be incorporated in field exercises. Among the many points made in the review, was that Observation Posts should always be in communication with church towers, from which the signal of local invasion would be given.

Home Guard commanders were urged to read the book more than once! The reviewer, clearly convinced of its merits concluded: "Perhaps the most important thing for the Home Guard is the grave and glorious responsibility they carry in the defence of their homes and country, and that life under Hitler would be what he has promised – 'Blood and tears which as a punishment will reduce the British population to degradation and poverty' ".

HOW TO DEAL WITH A PARACHUTIST

On a lighter note, Hugh Wansey Bayly, military correspondent of the Norfolk Chronicle, gave the following advice to the Home Guard when confronted by a parachutist:-

"Examine him from behind with his hands up! Be careful not to harm Canadian, American or other friendly parachutists! If you are not sure about his accent and he speaks English, have a sentence in block capitals on a piece of paper, and make him read it out loud! Foreigners have difficulty with "W", "TH", "SH", and "H". A suitable sentence would be:-

A peaceful village with Home Guard training in the surrounding fields.
IWM D4859   *Photo with kind permission of The Imperial War Museum*

*"THEODORE SHOULD SHAKE HALF THE HALO WITH
WENDELL WILKIE"*
A German parachutist is worth more alive than DEAD!"

HOME GUARDS ON EXERCISES – ENTHUSIASTIC AND CONFIDENT

This was the year when military exercises became a regular part
of Home Guard life, usually at the weekends! In late June many
Norfolk units were involved in a huge exercise in Eastern England
together with 170,000 regulars. For good measure, tanks,
parachutists and Fifth Columnists were included too! The exercise
took place in an area of 2,000 square miles and covered three
counties.

Norfolk units had to defend a medieval castle, which they did
in a lively encounter, until driven from the battlements by sheer
weight of "enemy" numbers! However, earlier in the day,
according to an observer, they had wiped out the first batch of
paras! Unfortunately, just as they thought they had the situation
under control, a police van, hooter screaming, rushed through the

King's Lynn Home Guard in a street fighting exercise.
Photo with kind permission of Mr. C.W. Scott

44

castle gates, concealing more paras inside, who then jumped out "Trojan Horse" style and completely overwhelmed the brave Home Guards. All was not fair in military exercises!

The street fighting in another part of the same exercise was very realistic! One paratrooper ended up with two black eyes, which he claimed were due to his knees hitting his head accidentally! However, a Home Guard commander told the press he knew this was not true!

Regular staff officers were delighted with the performance of Home Guard units, especially in small villages, where they held up convoys and made them easy targets for friendly aircraft. A high ranking Norwegian officer said that the Home Guard had worked with remarkable efficiency. But perhaps the most interesting compliment came from an experienced member of the Parachute Regiment, who said that: "I have the greatest respect for the beribboned "old timers" in the Home Guard, and I was also struck by the great enthusiasm of the 17-18 year olds!". Clearly every member of the units involved that weekend rose to the occasion and passed with flying colours.

In one exercise in a market town, a small party of four Guardsmen, two women and four messenger boys, surprised and put out of action three light tanks!! The enthusiasm of those involved is particularly shown in an incident when a woman, the wife of a local ARP man, crept towards a tank, hurling into it a newspaper wrapped round a stone, shouting: "You are killed – that was a Molotov bomb!" The astonished tank officer said, "Look here Madam, I'm not fighting women!" The woman's reply was, "But I'm dealing with an invader". The umpire at the exercise ruled that the woman had done very well! Later in the day, the same group of Home Guards inflicted 20 casualties on the Somerset Regiment who were stationed in the area at the time. They also captured an "enemy agent" who had located the defender's position and strength.

Perhaps the most significant feature of these exercises was their variety and the contrast with the usual Home Guard duties. A senior Home Guard officer commented how welcome it was for the men to be able to show enterprise and movement in an offensive manner, because so much of their time was concerned with a static role, involving hours of watching and waiting.

Weapons and Training

Apart from the first months of improvisation in 1940, the armoury of the Home Guard was not as haphazard as is sometimes suggested. However, after Dunkirk, whilst the Home Guard was rich in enthusiastic manpower, weapons *were* in short supply and it was some time before all members of Norfolk's units were adequately equipped with rifles and ammunition.

In the early days a major concern was how to knock out a tank. The accepted anti-tank weapon was the Molotov Cocktail and many of these improvised weapons must have been made in 1940. Their effectiveness was variable, but the Home Guard must have been cheered by a newspaper report that these weapons had proved of value in the Tobruk campaign in North Africa (1941), where several German and Italian tanks had been destroyed by these devices.

By early 1941, all units were in possession of rifles and ammunition, though the latter was often in only limited supply. In June, the Norfolk Chronicle's military correspondent, reported that the difficulty over rifles had been overcome. Furthermore, the Home Guard now had its own light and medium machine guns, some Tommy guns and several types of grenades. The report also mentioned that more new weapons had recently been perfected to deal with tanks, presumably a reference to the artillery devices such as Northover Projectors.

The Norfolk Home Guard undoubtedly benefited from the programme of training, military exercises and an improved weaponry situation which took place during the year. The press continued to sing the praises of the force. One paper was convinced that with its exact local knowledge, and growing military skills honed by regular practice, even the smallest unit would provide formidable opposition against an enemy which would be facing the Home Guard on its own ground.

Further developments for some men included anti-aircraft duties, especially along the Norfolk coast, and anti-gas training at the Army's Gas School. Many units appointed Intelligence Officers, who were sent on courses at Army Intelligence Centres. Some units had to provide men to help in the protection of aerodromes, with guard duties and patrols. Members of the Norfolk Home Guard were certainly kept very busy!

The weapons situation improved.
One Home Guard with a Tommy Gun and one with a Bren.
IWM H5840   *Photo with kind permission of The Imperial War Museum*

CONCERN OVER STANDARDS

There had been some public criticism in the national press of the quality of some officers and the training. This was echoed in the Norfolk Chronicle, where the military correspondent, a supporter of guerrilla fighting and scouting, suggested that some of the officers lacked the relevant experience and ability. He believed that the best volunteers were probably those who had formerly served in the International Brigade in the Spanish Civil War. He estimated that between 10 and 20 per cent of the men might be slackers, in that they failed to attend for instruction sessions, field exercises, rifle and grenade practice. While there may be some substance in certain of these criticisms, it is impossible to be sure about the degree of slackness that had appeared by this time. What is clear is that the spirit of the Home Guard remained very strong and the sense of national duty proved powerful motivation. On 30 June, 1,000 members of the Norfolk Home Guard attended a parade in Tombland in Norwich, where the Director General of the Home Guard, Major-General Lord Bridgeman, commended the men on their discipline.

LESSONS OF THE RECENT HOME GUARD EXERCISES

In August the Home Guard was reminded that it was different from the Regular Forces, in that it was practising for only one battle – the one to be fought on its own ground. Thus it was essential to keep practising so that its role was second nature. The recent exercises in the county and eastern region had shown that good training and keenness was evident. In co-operation with the regulars, the Home Guard were told that they would be particularly useful in harassing the enemy and obstructing his progress, thus keeping him "looking over his shoulder". The force was also told that proper construction of defensive positions was essential, and that although digging was not very popular, it should remember Lord Gort's adage, "Sweat saves blood".

On a lighter note, it was reported in the Diss Express, that during Home Guard exercises in an East Anglian town in August, a Quisling came along disguised as a clergyman. Unfortunately he was still wearing army boots! In another incident, a "time bomb" left in an office, turned out to be an orange! It was the first the defenders had seen for some time!

Sometimes Naval units took part in Home Guard exercises and were able to provide valuable experience.
IWM H 12126   *Photo with kind permission of The Imperial War Museum*

CONFIDENCE IN THE HOME GUARD'S KEY ROLE

In October, Churchill had again stressed the Home Guard's importance, as integral to our defences, designed to throw the Germans back into the sea. The Norfolk Chronicle took up the theme with this comment:– "If the Home Guard is called upon to prove itself in action in the coming year, it is confidently expected that it will prove its mettle, showing itself fit "to fight, on the beaches, in the fields, in the streets", as long as a single enemy remains on British soil". Such sentiments indicate the spirit which the Home Guard had always symbolized.

SNAPSHOTS OF TWO HOME GUARD UNITS IN 1941

At this point it is perhaps worth looking at two units in a little detail. Surviving documentary evidence, particularly from Salle, near Reepham, allows glimpses into the organization, activities and problems of units at this period of Home Guard history. Some of the issues discussed earlier, are revealed in the papers of the Salle unit.

Salle Home Guard (part of the Reepham Platoon)

On 19 January, 12 members of the Salle section went for shooting practice at Swaffham. They were issued 5 rounds of ammunition each and the Lewis Machine gun group received 45 rounds. It seems a paltry amount but resources had to be rationed. Doubtless the men concentrated particularly carefully!

Attendance at Home Guard lectures and drills was of course, voluntary and some men clearly did not attend on a regular basis. In March, a member of the Salle unit received a letter from the platoon commander, noting with regret, his absence from drills and lectures for "a very long while". The absentee was asked whether he wished to continue service in the Home Guard, "which may mean defence of your own home and family". The appeal to patriotism seems to have fallen on deaf ears in this case, because the man resigned from the Home Guard two days later. He was immediately asked to return all his equipment and send his identity card for amendment.

Transport was in short supply at this time, and the Home Guard was empowered to earmark certain vehicles in the area for use in the event of "ACTION STATIONS". The platoon commander at Reepham, asked the agent of Sir Dymoke White, MP, for particulars of his big Morris, and then informed the MP of the situation.

Platoon Orders These instructions for the week were issued regularly by the platoon commander to the sections under his command. Their contents reveal the wide range of activities which were laid on for local units as well as testifying to the administrative grip the Home Guard had established. Sunday parades were a regular feature as were drills, though attendance at these activities was not always popular! Other more exciting activities included, explosives classes, range days and exercises. Special events were also organized, such as the Divisional Circus, held at Reepham Drill Hall, where the men were instructed in the use of Tommy guns and grenades. There was also a Brigade Circus, at which the Harvey Flame Thrower and the Northover Projector were demonstrated. Special parades were held for the first birthday of the Home Guard and during War Weapons Week in May, when the platoon was inspected in Reepham by Brig-Gen Sterling, DSO MC.

The orders display a remarkable attention to detail, such as what type of equipment the men should bring to the various activities, the dress they should wear and any extra items they would need. On one range practice at Weybourne, the Salle section were told to bring rifles and respirators, but "on no account are bayonets to be carried". Furthermore, the men were advised that, "they should all carry haversacks in case they are late getting home". Every effort seems to have been made to achieve and maintain high standards in the platoon. For the church parade during War Weapons Week, the dress was very specific:- "Walking out with side arms. Respirators and tin hats to be carried. Tin hats slung on the respirator haversacks". The platoon commander told all units that "special effort should be made by all ranks to attend this parade".

On one occasion when a range practice had been planned at Cawston, the men were told to meet at the Salle Guard Room at 1200 hours one Sunday in April. Any men who were unable to attend owing to pressure of work, were told that they could report to the range at any time before 4pm, when every effort would be made to let them shoot. They would however, have to provide their own transport to the range!

It is worth noting that at this time members of the unit were known as Volunteers, not Privates. However, when a volunteer was promoted, and details were given in platoon orders, he would become a Lance Corporal. The Reepham platoon showed real awareness of the fact that the men *were* volunteers, as indicated in the previous paragraph. Another example was shown in the preparations for a special parade, when the platoon commander told section leaders that they could arrange "any evening convenient to the men", to practice marching, saluting, etc.

On 18 April the Salle section leader received a Secret Memo from the platoon commander telling him that the Battalion Adjutant wished all ranks to be aware that "a blue car, occupant of which is asking questions re crashed aircraft and refusing to produce identity card, should be detained, and Civil Police and Zone informed immediately". It was the kind of challenge the Home Guard would relish, but there is unfortunately, no record of any arrest being made!

Departures from the Salle Home Guard There were inevitably some fluctuations in the strength of the unit resulting from old age, recruitment into the regular forces and perhaps, loss of interest in some cases. However, every effort was made to maintain the unit's full strength, and when someone did resign, he was reminded that his equipment was government property, and "urgently required for other recruits". A deadline for the return of equipment was given, followed by a threat that "action will be taken in the matter" if the former Home Guardsman did not respond! In July two men were given 14 days notice to terminate their service in the Home Guard. This was because of their continued absence from the unit's activities. One of these men received a strong letter from his platoon commander pointing out that as he had not attended Home Guard duties for the past 6 months, the company commander had said that he must leave the force. Another volunteer left the Salle section in November. He too received a letter from the company commander, who had been informed of his non-attendance at drills for a long time. Accordingly his resignation was politely requested, together with the return of his equipment "at your convenience, during the next few days". In this case the volunteer's son seems to have taken his father's place in the Salle section.

In April 1941, there were officially 28 men registered in the Salle unit. A letter from the company commander at this time, notes that the company, of which Salle section was only a part, held the following items of equipment in excess of its needs. This must reflect the gradual loss of personnel at this time throughout the company. The items which had to be called in were:-

23 Great Coats	24 Belts
16 pairs Boots	12 Haversacks
5 Caps	19 Respirators
16 Armlets	

In May, the Salle unit were issued with .300 rifles and ammunition and had to return their .303 rifles to the Guard Room. Only one man failed to do this promptly and consequently received a stiff note from a highly organized platoon commander!

A Platoon Commander's many concerns Among the various responsibilities of the platoon commander, were inspecting boots and arranging for repair, arranging for anti-tetanus inoculation, organizing feeding of the Home Guard when they were mustered for operational duty. He also co-ordinated security with the company commander by ensuring that the national registration identity numbers of men in his charge were accurate and passed to higher authority.

Of the 28 men in the Salle section of the Home Guard, two operated the Lewis Machine gun and the remainder had rifles. By 1941, they were all kitted out with the full range of uniform and military accessories. They were part of a well-organized company, commanded by Major Gurney whose many memos had as his official address, c/o Barclay's Bank, Bank Plain, Norwich. The platoon commander was Lt. Stimpson, who operated from his home in Salle, and whose occupation was a grain merchant. The Salle section leader was a Sergeant Allen, who appears from all the available evidence to have been a reliable, loyal and competent NCO. In due course, both Gurney and Stimpson were promoted to the positions of CO and 2 i/c respectively, of the 17th Battalion Norfolk Home Guard, formed in 1943 and based at Reepham. Gurney became a Lt. Colonel and Ben Stimpson a Major.

The commitment of these men to their responsibilities cannot be faulted. They gave much of their time and energy freely, while at the same time holding down full time jobs during the day. Such men ensured that the units under their command, were proficient and that the highest possible standards were maintained at all times. They were typical of so many other commanders throughout

Norfolk, and their leadership explains in part, why the spirit in the Norfolk Home Guard was so positive, a mixture of common sense, competence and comradely good-humour. Of course there were units and some men, who did not reach or aspire to exacting standards. But in 1941, at a time when Hitler's main objective was the defeat of Russia, if the Salle and Reepham examples are typical, the Home Guard in Norfolk was settling down and turning itself into a real military defence force, much better equipped than 1940 and with improved training. Yet it was still a force based on volunteers!

A NORWICH HOME GUARD COMPANY

The following comments are based on a study of the surviving documentary evidence of No.5 Company, of the 10th Battalion of the Norfolk Home Guard, based in Norwich. The company orders offer a useful glimpse into the life of a large unit based in the city. The evidence reveals that a full and wide ranging programme of activities was laid on by the company. In March of 1941, all ranks were thanked for their splendid bearing and discipline at a church parade, as were the large number who attended the Monday evening parade at Carrow Works.

An interesting reference is to complaints from various railway authorities, who alleged that interference with lights, particularly signal lights, could be traced to military sentries and patrols, including Home Guard men. The company commander concluded that an "excess of zeal" was the main explanation!

If one week's programme in April was typical of the company, then it is clear that every effort was made to maintain a proficient unit. On the Sunday there was a full dress parade in Palace Plain, followed by an exercise on Mousehold Heath. On the Monday evening there was a training class and conference for NCOs to which officers were also invited. Platoon commanders were to make their own training arrangements on Tuesday and Wednesday. On the Thursday, there was an Officer's and NCO's conference at the company HQ. Friday seemed to be a free night for the men! However, on Saturday, the company paraded again in Palace Plain and this was followed by a route march and combined tactical exercise.

However it is clear also, that attendance at some of these activities left something to be desired! The company commander noted that a large number of the men were confining their Home Guard activities to guard duties and were not attending parades and some of the exercises. He told the men that this attitude was not helping to improve the efficiency of their platoon or the company as a whole. However, he did seem to adopt a common sense compromise by saying that, whilst the men were not expected to attend *every* event organised by the Company, they were expected to be present at a reasonable number of parades and exercises. It was this flexible approach to the issue of attendance by men who were essentially volunteers, which ensured that the excellent spirit, which was characteristic of the Home Guard, was maintained.

In May, company orders announced that Zone HQ had given a ruling for subsistence allowances for out-of-pocket expenses. Such allowances could apply only to men who manned posts nightly, by order of the Section commander. These posts were, Battalion HQ, Company HQ, LNER Railway Control Room, the City Station, RAF North Walsham and the Telephone Exchange in Unthank Road.

A final fragment of the company's orders underlines the variety of life. It announces the award of commissions to four lieutenants, details of an officer's dinner, arrangements for boot repair, an NCOs training class and of course, the usual Sunday parade.

SOME HOME GUARD POETS – THE PEN IS MIGHTY LIKE THE RIFLE!

The Diss Express published this poem in February 1941 from a Home Guardsman who lived in Eye.

> *On lonely hill the Home Guard stands,*
> *His rifle ready in his hand.*
> *He's ready to defend or die,*
> *Should Hitler's Nazis come nearby.*

> *The moon is lovely to behold,*
> *The night is nippy, bitter cold.*
> *But brave, undaunted, still he stands*
> *The rifle ready in his hand.*

For freedom he's prepared to fight,
And Right shall conquer Hitler's might.
Should Hitler's hosts decide to land,
His rifle ready in his hand.

A few months later, the same newspaper reported that the Home Guard in Harleston, were entertained to a supper in the Railway Tavern. The evening included some topical lines by a Mr. T. Aldous whose poem captures the camaraderie of the Home Guard and the range of "characters" to be found in this, and surely many other units.

The Huns talked of invasion,
The Harleston men got raw,
They formed a band of fighting men,
And now they're right for war.

They are led by Major Taylor,
The name that's held most dear,
By all Harleston's population,
And those who've drunk his beer!

We hear that Captain Foulsham,
Is loved by all his crowd,
And now I've made it public,
Of this we hope he's proud.

Next on our list is Mr. Wainwright,
A Lieutenant now is he,
"Quick rise" did I hear you say,
He got "pipped" in the ARP.

Now Alex is the CSM,
And a good old boy is he,
He's given us all some useful hints,
So as good, we'll try to be.

Our Quarter Master Sergeant,
A real ole scrounger he,
But can you wonder at it,
After the years he's spent at sea!

Now Sergeant Henery and his Corporals,
Are good men, we'll give a cheer,
Not so much for their proficiency,
But the way they mop their beer!

There's one for special mention,
He dodges all parades,
And never does a Duty,
'Case his little tummy fades!

Of course you know the little man,
Perfect is not his name,
Now should his cash be 6d short,
He has himself to blame.

And now we come to Rookies,
Who do all the dirty work,
There's a good lot of fellows,
And their duties never shirk.

There's Warren, Scoones and Avey,
The Bank Squad we call them,
They'll be handy when we're short of cash,
Before pay days' just dawning.

And Youngs you know, the builder chap,
He spends his dough like water,
Ask John Perfitt what I mean,
Or perhaps I didn't oughter!

Now these few lines are all in fun,
So I hope that none will mind,
For a leg-pull here and another there,
Helps one on the road you'll find.

Now here's good health and luck to all,
And when you meet the Huns,
Shoot straight and shoot to Hell you boys,
Good Germans are dead Huns!

HOME GUARD PROFICIENCY CERTIFICATES

As part of the drive towards improving skills, Home Guard Proficiency Certificates were introduced in April 1941. Holders would wear a diamond-shaped red badge on their sleeve. A more difficult certificate examination started in 1943. Holders of this wore a diamond and a bar.

The proficiency badges and certificates did encourage a high standard of training and ensured that the men who wore the badges did possess a good standard in the various military skills. These could vary from rifle shooting and grenade throwing to battlecraft, bomb disposal, coastal artillery, heavy AA battery work, map reading, military transport and first aid. The certificate was of considerable value to those members of the Home Guard who joined the regular forces, who appreciated the skill and knowledge they had acquired. The COs and platoon commanders were made responsible for the training and preparing of the men under their command for the proficiency tests. Examining boards consisted of both regular and Home Guard officers of senior rank.

EXPANSION OF THE NORFOLK HOME GUARD

Although eleven battalions had been formed as early as August 1940, the increased importance attached to the Home Guard, together with the steady increase in membership, necessitated constant reorganization. By 1943, six more battalions had been formed, and there were over 32,000 men involved altogether.

			Commanding Officer
No.12	Brancaster	1940	Lt. Col. Leslie, DSO, MC
No.13	Sheringham	1941	Lt. Col. Spurrell
No.14	Hapton	1941	Lt. Col. R.J. Read
No.15	Downham Market	1941	Lt. Col. H. Buchanan
No.16	Norwich	1943	Lt. Col. H.N. Morgan, MC
No.17	Reepham	1943	Lt. Col. Q.E. Gurney, TD

The year indicates the time that the battalion was started. There were then, 17 battalions in all for the county of Norfolk.

Membership of the units varied in size from between 1,200 and 2,500 men. Each battalion was organised into companies and platoons, which represented the various communities within the

O.S. - ped Slender

A.F.W 4026

Certificate of Proficiency
HOME GUARD

On arrival at the Training Establishment, Primary Training Centre or Recruit Training Centre, the holder must produce this Certificate at once for the officer commanding, together with Certificate A if gained in the Junior Training Corps or Army Cadet Force.

T.R.K.K : 130/1.

PART I. I hereby certify that (Rank) Ple. (Name and initials) MANN John

of __1__ Battery / Company __13__ Regiment / Battalion HOME GUARD has qualified
in the Proficiency Badge tests as laid down in the pamphlet "Qualifications for, and Conditions governing the Award of the Home Guard Proficiency Badges and Certificates" for the following subjects:

	Subject		Date	Initials
1.	General knowledge (all candidates)	.. ..	1942	O.S
2.	Rifle	.. .. ..	1942	O.S
3.	36 M Grenade	..	22/2/44	K.M.
*4.	(a) Other weapon STEN		20/6/44	R.R.
	(b) Signalling			
*5.	(a) Battlecraft, (b) Coast Artillery, (c) Heavy A.A. Bty. work, (d) "Z" A.A. Battery work, (e) Bomb Disposal, (f) Watermanship, (g) M.T.	..	30/5/44	E.W.B
*6.	(a) Map Reading, (b) Field works, (c) First Aid	..	1942	O.S.

Date 1 July 1943. Signature O. S.
* President or Member of the Board.

Date 21 JUN 44 194__ Signature _Chas H Walsh_ Major
* President or Member of the Board. 2nd in Command 13 Battalion (E) Norfolk Home Guard

Date 194__ Signature
* President or Member of the Board.

Date 194__ Signature
* President or Member of the Board.

Date 194__ Signature
* President or Member of the Board.

PART II. I certify that (Rank) Ple. (Name and initials) MANN John.
of __1__ Battery / Company __13__ Regiment / Battalion HOME GUARD, having duly passed the Proficiency tests in the subjects detailed above in accordance with the pamphlet and is hereby authorized to wear the Proficiency Badge as laid down in Regulations for the Home Guard, Vol. 1, 1942, para. 41d.

Date 1 July 1943. Signature _Chas H Walsh_ Major for
Commanding O.C., 13th BN. (E) NORFOLK H.G. H.G.

PART III. If the holder joins H.M. Forces, his Company or equivalent Commander will record below any particulars which he considers useful in assessing the man's value on arrival at the T.E., P.T.C., R.T.C., e.g. service, rank, duties on which employed, power of leadership, etc.

Date 194__ Signature
* Delete where not applicable. O.C.

58

geographical area covered by the battalion. In view of the huge difficulties facing Britain at this time, the creation of such an organization dependent on volunteers, who had full time jobs to hold down as well, was a major achievement.

AN ASSESSMENT OF THE NORFOLK HOME GUARD AT THE END OF 1941

Despite continuing problems, the Norfolk Home Guard had achieved much of which it could be proud. It was an accepted part of public life in the county and, in the eyes of the military, it was playing a valuable part in the region's defences. It was better armed and equipped, subject to regular tactical training and exercises, and now relishing a new role in the defensive scheme, namely the "nodal point", a strongly defended village, small town or important road junction, to which the Home Guard would retreat and then hold until overwhelmed. It is important to remember that the part-time soldiers in Norfolk and throughout the country, ensured that every acre of this island was defended by trained men. The regulars alone could not have provided the defence in

Throwing grenades on exercise.

IWM D9272   *Photo with kind permission of The Imperial War Museum*

depth all over the country. The role of the Home Guard enabled the regular forces to be deployed rapidly at the point of greatest danger, while our factories could keep busy producing arms, ammunition and equipment together with all manner of goods, and our farmers could grow and harvest the crops vital to our national survival.

However, despite the great progress made by the Home Guard in 1941 and the widespread recognition of its important role, it was increasingly apparent that numbers were falling. There simply were not enough volunteers coming forward anymore. To combat this problem, the government introduced, in December, the National Service Bill, which required anyone between the ages of 18 and 60 to undertake some form of national service. There were reservations about including the Home Guard, which had always been a voluntary organization. It was felt that its essential character would change and morale would suffer. Nevertheless, it was decided, mainly perhaps because of Churchill's belief that the force must be kept up to strength, to conscript men into the Home Guard for the first time.

CHAPTER 4

1942 Conscription, Exercises and a Changing Role

A NEW YEAR AND A NEW LAW

Why were the numbers of the original volunteer force falling? There were a number of contributory factors. Firstly, the young men in the Home Guard were being called up into the regular forces. Some of the original volunteers were old men. Age, ill health and the increasing hours of civilian work, all took their toll. Attendance was certainly suffering in many of the units in Norfolk as elsewhere in the country. A number of the veteran LDV members resigned because they resented the element of compulsion and were understandably nostalgic about the spirit of the Home Guard during its volunteer phase. The main volunteers now were young lads of 17 (the minimum age for entry), but their presence did not significantly help the situation because within a year they would be called-up. Another point was that some men were actually expelled from the Home Guard because they failed to live up to the high standards of the force!

Churchill had always sung the praises of the Home Guard and he had said in a speech in December 1941, that "this great bulwark of our safety" must not be allowed to deteriorate. It seems then, that it was the Prime Minister who ensured that the National Service Act, which became law in February 1942, would empower authorities to compel men to join the Home Guard in those areas where it was necessary to boost numbers. Men conscripted in this way would be required to serve 48 hours per month and be expected to attend the various drills, exercises and training. However, a reasonable cause for non-attendance, such as illness would always be considered fairly by the Home Guard commanders.

The Impact of Conscription in Norfolk

It seems that there were many units in the Norfolk Home Guard, as in other parts of the country, which were below strength. The Norfolk Chronicle reported in January that the Fakenham Company needed strengthening and optimistically hoped that volunteers would come forward. The same newspaper also quoted Sir William Spens, the Regional Commissioner, who said that "untrained and unorganized resistance is of little use", and that "the Home Guard is not as strong as it should be".

On 23 January the Eastern Daily Press reported that compulsory service in the Home Guard was to be introduced. Existing members would not be able to resign after 16th February. However, men would still be able to apply for discharge on grounds of age, medical or other hardship. For the first time in the history of the Home Guard though, men who absented themselves from parade or duty, without reasonable excuse could be fined or even imprisoned! Furthermore, in the event of an actual or imminent invasion, they would be required to serve continuously and live away from home when their platoon was mustered.

Despite the impending conscription, efforts were still made to encourage voluntary recruitment. At a meeting in Wroxham, Col. Medlicott, MP, said that the invasion danger was ever present. Consequently he hoped that everyone who could possibly do so, would join the Home Guard.

What the Old Volunteers Thought About The Prospect of Conscription

Opinion seems to have been divided about the issue. Many resented the plan to enforce membership of the Home Guard and attendance at its various activities. One correspondent to the Eastern Daily Press who signed himself "An Old Volunteer", said that he and others were considering resignation because of the power of officers to enforce attendance. He pointed out that most of his section were over 50 and that up till now they had worked with a good spirit and as far as age, family and health permitted. Now he feared that this spirit would be threatened by War Office rules!

Other veteran Home Guardsmen did not share these fears and one wrote in response to the letter discussed in the previous paragraph. Signing himself "Another Old Volunteer", he played down the fears expressed. Furthermore, he added robustly, "if invasion comes many will be killed; surely it is better to die with a rifle in your hands and be regularly in training, than to be shot against a wall". Churchill would surely have applauded such sentiments! On another point, the writer expressed regret at the end of the title "Volunteer", which would now become "Member" he assumed. He believed that the title "Comrade" was more appropriate to men who had banded together to protect their homes, family and country. Such a view is a true echo of the LDV spirit which is inseparably linked with the birth and early months of the force.

The Norfolk Chronicle struck an optimistic note about this issue. It reported in February, that though conscription had come to the Home Guard, the voluntary tradition would be maintained. It hoped that the new and old would work together and maintain the great reputation which the volunteers had built up since 1940. The same newspaper was pleased to report in May that although compulsory enrolment had now become a fact of life, voluntary recruitment had not come to an end, as 17 year olds from the ACF were swelling the ranks.

In March, the War Office had begun to implement the new law by announcing that where voluntary recruitment was insufficient, it was urgent that numbers be brought up to strength through conscription. It was anticipated that 19 counties would be affected. A few days after this news was reported, a parish councillor wrote to the Eastern Daily Press expressing the hope that "conscription would be introduced in these parts". He alleged that in many parishes, there were able-bodied men who were not involved in any form of national service. In one village he knew of with a population of 900, where there were 100 men under 60 years old, only 12 men from the parish were in the Home Guard. He believed that this was not untypical and appealed to conscience and patriotism among those men who had not yet joined the Home Guard.

ENFORCING ATTENDANCE AT PARADE

In February 1942, optional resignation from the Home Guard was no longer allowed, and volunteers, like "directed men", had to stay in the force until victory in the war or they became too

A big parade of No.7 Battalion in Tuesday Market Place, King's Lynn in 1942.
Photo with kind permission of Mr. C.W. Scott

Church Parade.
IWM D4257   Photo with kind permission of The Imperial War Museum

old. Conscription did involve more work for local commanders and NCOs. They had to organise parades, training and exercises for men who were sometimes less than enthusiastic! Attendance registers were kept and absentees noted and reported, though exemption from a particular activity would always be granted on reasonable grounds.

In a rural county like Norfolk, the rival claims of farm workers and Home Guard duties inevitably conflicted. It was felt that milkmen and stockmen could not be expected to attend all the parades in view of their very long hours of work, including Sundays. At harvest time of course, it was particularly difficult for farm workers to fulfil their Home Guard duties. Commanders were flexible and understanding of this situation. Even so, this did not mean that men would be permanently excused duties in the Home Guard however busy they were on the farm or elsewhere! Both the needs of farming and the Home Guard were of great importance in these dangerous times and the vast majority of men who were conscripted accepted the situation and did their best, ensuring that the excellent spirit of the force was not threatened in any way.

In August, the Eastern Daily Press highlighted the issue with a headline, "Harvest must come first". It reported that Home Guard commanders must contact the War Agricultural Executive before arranging protracted exercises and that farmers and labourers could only do Home Guard duties that would not interfere with the harvesting of crops. However, the same report said that Norfolk did not subscribe to the view – "Food or Home Guard". Instead, it recognised that minimal duties could be expected for the next few weeks when life on the farms was especially hectic. This sensible compromise satisfied the vast majority of all concerned. However, there were always going to be some who objected. In November the Norfolk Chronicle reported the case of a man before the Cromer magistrates under the headline, "Can't Serve Two Masters". He was before the bench because he would not co-operate and do his Home Guard duties and told the magistrate that, "If I can't help to feed the nation, I'll go and fight for it". Presumably he planned to join the Army and give up his farming job! This case was one of a very small number of court cases which resulted from conscription. Those in the next section illustrate the issue and underline the spirit of the times.

Home Guard Men In Court

In August 1942 a 17 year old from Wells was before the Walsingham magistrates for "making fun" of the Home Guard. He had apparently appeared in civilian clothes on the Buttlands and had been so provocative to the Sergeant instructor, that he was forced to dismiss the parade. There was foul language and the police had been called. In court he was fined five shillings and obliged to pay four shillings costs. The chairman told him that it was a particularly disgraceful episode for someone who was actually a member of the Home Guard. He added, "that if the man had been in the army he would have been shot!". This was perhaps a little extreme! However it serves to underline the fact that the magistrates did all they could to back up the Home Guard. We need to remember that for most people, the Home Guard existed to defend homes, families and country and should not be trifled with by rebellious youths!

In November, the Norfolk Chronicle carried the following headline:– "Home Guards and Parades – They Must Attend Even When Employer Refuses Release". The case was believed to be the first of its kind in the country. Two Home Guardsmen, who worked 72 hours a week for a firm employed by the Ministry of War Transport and the Ministry of Agriculture, had absented themselves from Home Guard parades. They said that their employer would not release them for Home Guard duty. Furthermore, their employer had appealed to the court for the men to be exempt from the Home Guard on the grounds that they were involved in war work which he said came before the Home Guard! In spite of this the men were fined £2 each with costs, for being absent "without reasonable excuse". They were told that they could not shelter themselves under the wing of their employer and despite the difficult position they must attend all Home Guard parades! The decision was regarded as one of the utmost importance to the Home Guard and employers alike.

What is clear from these cases is that service in the Home Guard was of great importance and attendance at parades and other activities was expected. Very few excuses for absence would be accepted as reasonable, as this final case illustrates. It concerned a Walsingham old soldier, aged 48 and one of the "Old Contemptibles" who had served in the First World War. He had vehemently refused to be enrolled in the Home Guard, saying that he had been in the Army once and was not going to "play at soldiers". Furthermore, he worked 70 hours a week as a plate-layer for the LNER and was working when he should have reported to the Home Guard. He told the court that he had three sons in the Army and was willing to work for the Civil Defence. Despite this plea, the magistrate quietly told the man that he was very sorry to see an old soldier before the bench, but that nevertheless, he must arrange to join the Home Guard as required by law.

Once instructions had been issued by local authorities about compulsory enrolment in the Home Guard, most men who were eligible accepted the inevitable and joined what had once been a volunteer force with good grace ensuring each battalion was kept up to strength. Even mortuary staff were not excused. It was difficult to recruit and maintain mortuary workers and their manager assumed that his men would not be pressed to enrol. However, documentary evidence exists to confirm that a cemetery worker was instructed to enrol in the Home Guard in June 1942. Thus the Home Guard acquired all sorts and conditions of men, including grave diggers!

HOME GUARD SUMMER CAMP – AUGUST 1942 (SOMEWHERE IN MID-NORFOLK!)

Over 2,000 men of the Norfolk Home Guard drawn from units all over the county assembled for some intensive training in mid-August. A military correspondent of the local press thought that, judging by this camp, the Norfolk Home Guard was becoming as self-contained an organization as it was possible to be. There was plenty of evidence of both the progress made by the force and its spirit. All the instructors were local men and many of those present had devoted their spare time from farms, offices and shops to win commissions and stripes, having attended special courses of military study. Many men wore ribbons of the First World War; one of these veterans who wore the Mons Star, had no illusions however, about the relevance of that experience and said, "I'm not sure that World War I ribbons count for a lot these days – warfare has changed so much over 25 years".

On one day of the camp, training covered nine different subjects including, rifle training, grenade throwing, gas drill, camouflage, and mortar firing. The reporter watched a Spigot Mortar display and concluded that the Home Guard were rivalling the regulars.

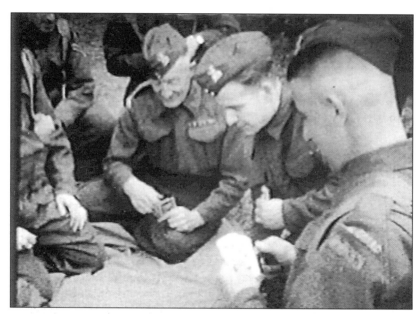

Relaxing during a break in a Summer Camp near King's Lynn, 1943.
Photo with kind permission of Mr. C.W. Scott

King's Lynn Home Guard on the march in West Norfolk.
Photo with kind permission of Mr. C.W. Scott

He saw wheels knocked off a moving target with one shot and the vehicle wrecked with a second!

In another part of the camp, a fieldcraft exercise was taking place. One squad had a man from Costessey enacting the role of rear-gunner. He was limping badly as a result of an injury received in World War One. However, the reporter described him as "the gamest Home Guard in the camp". It was this kind of spirit which had always distinguished so much of the Home Guard story.

The view that the presence of conscripts in the Home Guard would alter the character of the force, is not borne out by the evidence of men on this camp. The reporter discovered that in some Norfolk units, men had "dug deep into their own pockets to add to the efficiency of their own unit". The excellent spirit of the Home Guard in Norfolk was further underlined by Lord Walsingham, the CO of the camp. He told the military correspondent of the Eastern Daily Press that he had great admiration for the men. "Many had left the harvest fields on Saturday, donned their uniform without waiting for a meal, and travelled long distances in unpleasant conditions in order to spend the night under canvas".

King's Lynn Home Guard practising with bayonets.
Photo with kind permission of Mr. C.W. Scott.

HOME GUARD EXERCISES

During 1942, training was intensified and many exercises were organised. Two of these are referred to below:–

Dereham Invasion Exercise

This took place in March and after it was over, there was some criticism of the Home Guard personnel, some of whom were told that they needed to be more efficient. It was pointed out by a press reporter, that dive bombers and the enemy ground attack broke through the Home Guard defences in the town! This criticism provoked a letter to the Eastern Daily Press from an irate despatch rider in the Dereham Home Guard. The claim that the town had been "captured" was totally rejected and it was pointed out that Dereham's defences had not been penetrated. Furthermore, he told readers that the chief umpire at the exercise, told the CO of the Dereham Home Guard that his men were, "far too good for the enemy". He went on with considerable feeling to add that the original report was a damaging statement to the prestige of the Home Guard, pointing out that on two previous exercises, Dereham had not been "captured" either, and that the War Office had commended the Home Guard of the town! He ended by saying that the recent exercise saw a third "victory" for the Home Guard, and that the Dereham unit was fast becoming one of the most enthusiastic, well trained and disciplined forces in the county! The writer said that the whole of the Dereham Home Guard were indignant over the original inaccurate report. Much of the pride and spirit of the Home Guard is revealed in this episode.

Holt Invasion Exercise

In this exercise, Civil Defence personnel, armed with grenades and rifles, assisted the Home Guard. Clearly Holt Home Guard was below strength at this point (March 1942) and the use of CD men reflected the government's policy, announced in February, that in districts where there was a temporary shortfall of Home Guard, the training of CD personnel should take place.

During the exercise, the Eastern Daily Press reporter, suspected of being a "Fifth Columnist", was taken to a Home Guard sergeant! Having shown his ID card he was released with an apology. Meanwhile, despite stout resistance, the numerically stronger attackers reached the centre of Holt. The umpire praised the Home Guard for a "good show", considering they were outnumbered ten to one. Holt Home Guard clearly needed more recruits and the coming of conscription would help to solve this local problem.

THE PROBLEM OF WEAPONS

In early February 1942, a Home Guard employed by the LNER was awoken at 4am by the sound of foreign voices. Believing them to be Germans, he grabbed a poker and confronted the enemy! What he discovered was not Germans, but six Polish airmen who had been forced down by a Wellington bomber! Presumably, the Home Guard in this incident had no rifle. The story is included to emphasize the fact that there was still a shortage of weapons in some Home Guard units in early 1942.

The lack of weapons was the main cause of discontent in the early months and it continued to cause bad feeling among some units as late as 1942. In the letter columns of the Eastern Daily Press, there was a lively debate about the merits of shotguns compared with military weaponry. Some correspondents favoured the idea of a "Sportsmen's Corps" or shotgun guerrilla groups in each village which they believed, would be most effective in combating an invader. One champion of the 12 bore, said that it was endorsed by big game hunters and was more deadly than any crackshot rifle. In any case, it was argued, such guns would be a useful support to the Home Guard and the military.

One correspondent said that every village should have a "guerrilla band", whose intimate knowledge of the local terrain, could be exploited to kill or put out of action invaders. Little did he, or anyone else at the time know, that there was already in place a "Secret Army" of highly organised and well armed resistance groups, whose role was to sabotage and disrupt enemy forces.

The shortage of weapons among the Home Guard was also illustrated by a letter, from a well-to-do lady, who complained that a policeman wanted to see her licence for being in possession of firearms. She said that she had been treated like a criminal because she had lent some rifles to the local Home Guard in Ditchingham! She found the attitude of the authorities rather odd in view of Churchill's view that, in case of invasion, "we are to fight to the last ditch with every available weapon". But even with the help of people like this good lady, the Home Guard were still lacking sufficient weapons.

THE WAR OFFICE OFFERS TO ARM THE HOME GUARD WITH PIKES!

As early as June 1940, Churchill had wanted every Home Guard to have a weapon of some kind ("everyone, can kill a Hun!"). Initially the War Office issued some units with truncheons! In mid 1941, it was decided that a large number of pikes should be manufactured. These were long metal tubes with surplus bayonet blades welded into one end! By early 1942, this plan had become public news in Norfolk. In February, the Eastern Daily Press reported a debate in the House of Lords, in which Lord Croft, Under Secretary of War, urged the Home Guard to adopt the pike as one of its official weapons.

It was, Lord Croft said, a silent but effective weapon! He went on to say that pikes and grenades would be much more useful than rifles in close fighting during an invasion! In the meantime, the Home Guard were asked to be patient and promised more rifles as soon as possible. The suggestion that the Home Guard should be armed with pikes, was greeted with disbelief throughout the country and many members thought they were being insulted.

WHAT THE NORFOLK HOME GUARD THOUGHT OF THE PIKE!

The Norfolk Home Guard greeted the idea of being armed with pikes as absurd. The feelings of the men were heartfelt, but also laced with irony and good humour as a letter to the Eastern Daily Press from a Home Guard "Major", shows:

THE HOME GUARD PIKE

Sir – High authority having seen nothing humorous in the solemn public announcement of the new terror in store for marauding invaders, lesser mortals need no longer fear to expose their own cherished devices for the discomfiture of the enemy.

I therefore propose immediately to embark my command upon an intensive course of training in the production and use of the weapons specified below. I need hardly state my fervent belief that the mere publication of this intention will involve a readjustment of the enemy plans for invasion, if not their total abandonment.

1. *A pair of disused scythe blades sharpened and securely fastened (edge foremost) at right angles to the wheel of an ordinary cycle will, when that vehicle is propelled at a speed to be determined by experiment, mow down considerable bodies of infantry, whose approaching reserves will prefer to lay down their arms rather than their legs.*
2. *The despised safety razor blade, suitably mounted on a 3-foot platinum handle, can be employed in numerous ways in the task of cutting up any normal division.*
3. *Discarded pruning shears (long-handled model with distant control), when wielded by determined experts, would lay low the scions of full many a noble Prussian House (N.B. In the absence of suitable scions this weapon could nip in the bud almost any offensive movement and at an extremity could even sever the cords of descending parachutes, thus causing severe falls to the occupants).*
4. *Fish manure, cleverly sited on a menaced flank, might well divert the most serious threat by denying that approach to the enemy.*

The foregoing by no means exhausts the list of simple and inexpensive ruses de guerre, and a further list may be had on application. Meanwhile I would rather have rifles and ammunition. – Yours faithfully,

MAJOR.

A few days later, the Eastern Daily Press received another letter from a Home Guard challenging Lord Croft to a duel – the noble lord with a pike and the writer with a service Webley, which had not been used in anger since 1918! He offered to meet the Minister anywhere and anytime, suggesting Wembley on a Saturday and that the proceeds from spectators could go to the Red Cross! He pointed out that, the expenses would be the lowest on record as only one round of revolver ammunition would be needed!

A third letter on the pike issue came from an interesting and amusing lady. She pulled no punches, and said that in the light of the suggestion that Home Guardsmen should be equipped with a pike, it seemed that Rip Van Winkle had awoken once more and entered the Government, thereby making it "the laughing stock of the Hun". The concluding paragraph of her letter merits quoting in full: "PIKES ?!?! What are we to do with them? Prod the Hun in the pants if we get the chance before we're shot I presume! I think that I'll rely on a toasting fork – it has at least got **FOUR** prongs!" It was fighting talk and reminded readers that the Home Guard was still in need of more weapons. Pikes apart however, the lady's spirited language would have surely commended itself to Prime Minister Churchill.

PROGRESS DESPITE THE PIKES!

The irritation among Home Guardsmen caused by the government's proposal to supply them with pikes, is understandable, particularly because, at the same time it was stressing the key role of the force in the nation's defences. Furthermore, the War Office said it would be most unwise to think that the danger of invasion had passed.

In fact, the weapon situation continued to improve throughout 1942. In January, the Norfolk Chronicle reported that the Home Guard in the county were being trained to use many different types

The Home Guard in a bayonet charge.

IWM D4259   *Photo with kind permission of The Imperial War Museum*

of weapons. Some were learning to use anti aircraft guns, others were practising with various anti-tank guns. The Thompson machine gun, or "Tommy", together with the Browning automatic were also being more widely distributed among Home Guard units. Then there was the Northover Projector, which fired heavy grenades or incendiaries at tanks. It claimed to be able to destroy light tanks and damage heavy ones, provided the aimer scored a direct hit! There is no doubt that units in Norfolk were being provided with a variety of weapons. Many must have relished the opportunity to work on the AA batteries. In February, the Eastern Daily Press ran a headline, "Home Guard for AA Guns". A senior officer of AA Command was quoted as saying, "There's no better occupation for the Home Guard than to shoot down an enemy who is bombing his home". Such sentiments echoed the spirit of the force from its LDV days.

INVASION PROCEDURE – FARMERS MUSTER LAST!

Mention has already been made of the clashing interests of the Home Guard and the farming community. In general, difficulties in the county were resolved sensibly and flexibly. It was of course, widely recognised that farming was a vital industry and maximum food production in wartime was essential. The farm workers did more than their bit for the country and the Home Guard.

However, early in 1942, the Ministry of Agriculture issued the procedure to be followed if invasion was imminent or actual. The Eastern Daily Press reported the matter in February. While all were expected to do their duty in such circumstances, there were some qualifications! The Ministry was quoted as follows:– "Many will muster, but some are engaged on essential work and will not be available until a later stage and in the last resort (i.e. farm workers). Others can well be spared for mustering in such a national emergency as invasion. In deciding each man's position, the Home Guard Company Commander will consult the man and his employer. If there is still doubt, the Company Commander will consult the Manager of the Local Employment Exchange, who will in turn ask the advice of the County's War Agriculture Committee. When giving advice, the Committee will take into account the man's job and the general circumstances of the farm".

It is a masterpiece of wartime bureaucracy and it is gratifying to learn that in the face of imminent national danger, the Ministry of Agriculture was leaving nothing to chance! Incidentally, when men were mustered, there was no limit to the time they could be used by their commanders. However, in the event of a real emergency, there is little doubt that the majority of Home Guards would have responded promptly regardless of the "circumstances of the farm".

WYMONDHAM INVASION EXERCISE – SEPTEMBER 1942

Like towns and villages throughout the county, Wymondham formed its Invasion Committee. The town authorities chaired by Edwin Gooch, together with the military and the Home Guard drew up a defence plan to be implemented in the event of invasion. The civil authority's HQ would be the Council Offices in Middleton Street and the military and the Home Guard adopted the new Drill Hall in Pople Street as their HQ. Wymondham's plan was a very ambitious one which was designed to involve all the services in a co-operative effort.

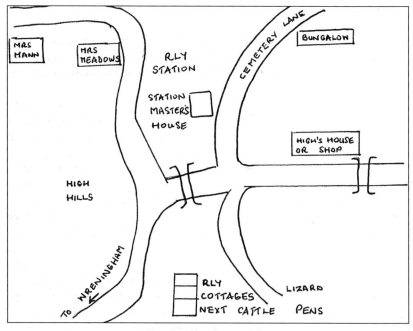

Wartime sketchmap of the
"Railway Station as a defended area with houses to be evacuated".
Wymondham Town Archives

It was decided to test the scheme which the Invasion Committee had drawn up by involving the Home Guard, Civil Defence, Fire Service, Police, Rest Centres and Billeting officer. Locally based regular troops would be the "enemy". The exercise was to be code-named "Harvest". As can be seen from the poster advertising the exercise, everyone was expected to co-operate cheerfully!

In early September, there was a meeting of the Emergency Committee which was attended by the senior military officer for the district, Major Fryer of the local Home Guard. Major Fryer is remembered by his son, going about his Home Guard duties. He particularly recalls his father practising his motor cycling skills in the garden of Browick Hall! One of Major Fryer's duties in the exercise, was to liaise with the medical authorities over expected casualties. In a later meeting, six days before the exercise was due to start, Major Fryer gave details of the military plan to defend Wymondham. He told the committee the locations of the defended areas or "keeps", such as the railway station and gave details of where road blocks would be erected. He said that his men would also guard the telephone exchange and the Report and Control Centre. The feeding of his men, Major Fryer said, would have to be done by civilians from their supplies as far as possible. For this purpose, he wanted to use the Methodist schoolroom canteen. He promised to inform the committee of all military warnings as they were received.

The "invasion" of Wymondham began on 17th and 18th September (1942), when the "enemy" established a bridgehead on the North Norfolk coast. Mobile columns of the enemy passed through Dereham and were reported near Thetford on 19th September. It was reported that gas was being used and that high altitude bombing had dislocated the telephone service around Wymondham. The situation now became confused! However, Home Guard patrols had made contact with enemy paratroopers around villages near Wymondham, though the outcome of these engagements was unclear.

During the night of 19th/20th September, Wymondham was "bombed" causing much damage. Though all fires were put out by 9.30am, a number of people had been made homeless. After such a dramatic build-up, the real excitement was still to come! Despite fierce resistance by the Home Guard they were clearly overwhelmed by sheer force and weight of numbers. After it was over, all the town's services met to discuss the lessons that they

People of Wymondham !

WE are in the FOURTH Year of War.

A Wicked and Ruthless Enemy seeks to Destroy this Country.

The Peoples of the Occupied Countries— People like You, who lived in Towns like Yours—are Paying a Terrible Price because they were UNPREPARED FOR INVASION.

ANTI-INVASION Measures are intended to Protect the People.

BUT EVERYONE Must Know what to do if INVASION Comes.

It will be TOO LATE to Learn once the Enemy has Landed.

Those who could have Instructed you will be otherwise employed.

IT IS YOUR DUTY to Learn all you can about Anti-Invasion Measures NOW !

On September 20th

An *INVASION EXERCISE*

will be held in Wymondham.

This will be a rehearsal of what to do if the enemy lands.

Everyone MUST CO-OPERATE to the best of their ability so that the exercise will be a success.

We hope you will CO-OPERATE CHEER-FULLY.

GEO. R. REEVE, MODEL PRESS, WYMONDHAM, NORFOLK.

had learned. For an account of the final day of the exercise, there follows a list of the messages received by the Council at Invasion Committee HQ, a unique insight into "Wymondham at War"!

THE DAY THE GERMANS CAPTURED WYMONDHAM!
20 SEPTEMBER 1942

MESSAGES HANDED IN TO COUNCIL OR INVASION COMMITTEE HEADQUARTERS

10.00 *1,356 Homeless and Refugees already billeted on basis of one per room of existing accommodation.*
Decision now made to billet two per room of existing accommodation.
(This information sent to Mrs. L.A.Crowe, Billeting Officer)

10.00 *Report & Control Centre requested to supply information of urgent importance as soon as possible after incidents and a brief situation report every half-hour.*

10.00 *Decided to reserve St. Thomas-a-Becketts Hall as alternative accommodation with use of telephone at Green Dragon due to Co-op Shop fire and U.X. at Police Station.*

10.00 *5th Columnists reported to have spread rumour in town during night of food shortage. Police asked to co-operate and notice issued contradicting rumour.*

10.20 *Message received from Fire Station:*
"Suspected Mustard Bomb opposite telephone exchange. All messages to Fire Station by Chain Entry and Back Entrance".
Surveyor & Home Guard informed.

10.40 *Message from Report & Control Centre:*
"Whitehorse Street blocked – Briton Brush burnt down. All traffic diverted at Handkerchief Corner via Bradham's Land, Cavick and Town Green. Time of origin 10.40.
Surveyor and Home Guard informed.

10.55 Message from Report & Control Centre:
"Unexploded Bomb Police Station yard, Norwich Road and Browick Road blocked. Police in charge.

10.45 Reported to Home Guard:
Enemy approaching North along Kimberley Road. Seen at 10.29 on Spratt's footpath and Right-Up Lane. Fire and Surveyor informed.

11.03 Casualty, Fire and Surveyor informed that Home Guard were about to erect road blocks.

11.15 Home Guard report Drill Hall, Pople Street blown up. No information of casualties. Telephonist known to have escaped. (5th columnists?)

11.15 Report & Control Centre Reports:
"One batch of enemy troops approaching by Spratt's footpath another batch coming by main road".
"U.X.B. Feathers Public House Yard. Necessary action taken".
Surveyor & Fire informed.
"Mustard Gas suspected opposite Old Post Office, Market St. 4 casualties. Go via Queen Street, Chandler's Hill and Damgate".

11.18 From Home Guard:
Enemy N.E. Barford Road.

11.20 Water Officer reported that Fairland Street water main repaired, but Church Street at present cut off. This also puts Middleton Street Water Main out of action. Inhabitants using alternative supply of wells.

11.30 Food D/C Squad required Old Post Office, Market Street. Mustard Gas confirmed. From Report & Control Centre. Surveyor and Fire Service informed.

11.40 Home Guard report:
"Enemy attacking Brick Yard post, Melton Road".
Surveyor and Fire Service informed.

11.45   Military attacking Melton Road area (junction of Barnham Broom Road). Instructions sent to casualty services and also to Rest Centre to restrict movement of casualties and to refrain from billeting in this area.

11.47   Home Guard Reports:
"Have to leave Defence Sub-Quarters and Sentries & Guard withdrawn"
Defence & Invasion Committee requested Police to provide Special Constables to act as Sentries.
Mr. F. Clarke a member of Invasion Committee sent to keep as Civil Co-ordinator's representative.

11.50   A bomb dropped on the roof of the Invasion Committee's Headquarters, but as damage was slight the Committee decided to remain and carry on. All C.D. services informed also Home Guard.

11.54   Surveyor asked Police if road closed as result of U.X. at Feathers, Town Green, and if so when it would be opened.

11.56   Fire Service reports:
"Market Street clear of gas"
Surveyor and Home Guard informed.

12.00   Home Guard Sentries having been withdrawn, Mr. H.E. Clarke (Member of Defence Committee) with additional staff took over Sentry duty. At 12.05 the Police staff arrived and took over Sentry duties.

12.03   Reports Centre reports:
"5th Columnist arrested. Later was released by the Umpire.
Fire reported Friarscroft Lane. 4 casualties.
250 H.E. fallen near Council Buildings, partly demolished, 3 casualties on upper floor. Rescue squad despatched.
U.X.B. outside Senior School, Norwich Road. Traffic diverted. Immediately vicinity being evacuated".

12.06   From Post Office service:
"All telephones out of action. Communicated fact to Fire and other services. Carrying on with Messengers.

12.20 From Home Guard:
       "H.E. demolished Rudlings, Howes Stores, Damgate and
       Peacocks Stores, Market Street. Roads passable??

12.25 Report received that Report & Control Centre demolished
       by bomb. Decided to provide them with Room on
       downstairs floor of Council Offices. All local services
       informed of change of address.

12.36 From Police:
       Senior School, Norwich Road out of action. U.X.B.
       Reserve Centre now Baptist's School Room.
       Necessary crockery were requisitioned also Cooking
       Stoves. Rest Officer and Food Officer at once informed.

12.37 Report from Police:
       Further Phosgene Bomb dropped Middleton Street,
       Wymondham between Post Office and Damgate Corner. 2
       persons injured; require attention.
       Necessary services at once informed.

12.50 Surveyor reported that Wardens reported that Damgate was
       badly damaged and could not be used by traffic. In view
       of the Military position and presence of enemy in town, the
       Invasion Committee decided to close the road for all traffic.

12.55 In answer to enquiry from Defence Committee the Food
       Officer reports:
       "Food situation well in hand. Assist Divisional Food
       Officer, Cambridge, present to supervise arrangements and
       considers position very satisfactory".

13.00 Committee being anxious as to Military position and
       having heard nothing from them since they retired to the
       "Keep" a messenger was despatched to seek information
       from them.
       Posters as to emergency Water Supplies have been posted
       up in Districts concerned.

13.16 Home Guard reports:
       "Enemy attacks in vicinity of C.W.S. Brush Works and Drill
       Hall, Strength unknown. Some enemy Station Road.

13.35 *From report & Control Centre:*
"*H.E. Town Green. 7 dead. Middleton Street and Town Green blocked*".
In view of proximity of enemy, decided to do nothing.

13.45 *Police reported 2 enemy troops wearing steel helmets seen in town.*

13.53 *Enemy troops seen in street outside Headquarters.*

13.56 *Enemy troops seen making enquiries of Council's outside staff.*

13.56 *Defence Committee decided to remain sitting and take enemy instructions.*

14.04 *Enemy Officer enters H/Q with armed guard and make the following requests:-*
£10,000 Cash. All bank balances. All books of account. Petrol Supplies. Food stocks. A list of all motor vehicles complete with rota arms &c. Hotels to be put out of bounds. List of all policemen. The personal attendance of the chief of Police. Keys to town and police cells. The billeting of 200 troops of the 3rd Reich with meal of the best of food. Anyone obstructing would be shot.
Orders from now on to be taken from Commandant of Town. No one to leave the room.

The requests to be complied with within 15 minutes.

The Defence Committee thereupon met and prepared the following replies:-

Banks already evacuated and taken all available money. Thought £2,000 could be found.
Petrol supplies destroyed.
Food supplies dispersed.
No record of cars kept. We are not the authority.
No police records. As no one was allowed to leave the chief of Police had not been sent for.
No keys to Town. Police keys with chief.

Billets for 200 would be arranged but troops would have
to eat what food as had been left.
Hotels would be ordered out of bounds.
Committee willing to take orders from Commandant.

The Officer expressing dissatisfaction with the replies order
the members present to be held as hostages pending better
arrangements. The Chairman to be used to put over to the
public the instructions of the Commandant.

Wymondham Defeated But Not Dishonoured

And so at the end of it all, Wymondham was occupied by the
"enemy". However, it is gratifying to note that the authorities in
the town had removed most of the money, destroyed the petrol
supplies and left very little food for their conquerors to enjoy!
The surrender was a dignified affair and the chief umpire, Lt. Col.
H.W. Back, CO of No.9 Battalion Norfolk Home Guard, must have
been pleased with that, even though the Home Guard had been
defeated.

As a footnote, it is worth recording, that during the exercise,
the "enemy" wore steel helmets, while "our" troops were identified
by their soft caps! Finally, in planning the exercise, one of the
minutes of the many meetings reads, "Lunch will not be provided"!

Action Stations and Feeding The Home Guard

Earlier in the year the military authorities had issued
instructions to be followed during military operations in which the
Home Guard were involved. They are set out below:–

"Each man will take a 24 hour ration from his house to
the Home post.

A 48 hour emergency pack ration would be issued
consisting of,

10 ounces of canned roll
12 ounces of hard biscuit
8 ounces of chocolate

plus, a supplement of 1 ounce of tea and 1½ ounces of
sugar.

The chocolate will not be touched for 24 hours, and then only if no other supplies are available!

Reserve Rations will be sent to village shops or the Home Guard post".

It is not known if Wymondham Home Guard had to cope with these instructions during the invasion exercise.

Two Years Old This Month – Home Guard Birthday May 1942

The Eastern Daily Press reported the Prime Minister's tribute to the Home Guard with the headline, "Invaders would fall into a hornet's nest". Churchill had warned that an airborne invasion was an increasing possibility. He referred back to the dark days of 1940 when only little clusters of men, armed mainly with shotguns, gathered round searchlights to resist the Nazis. Now he was pleased that whenever or wherever he comes, the enemy would face in the Home Guard, determined, resolute men whose aim was to kill the enemy or force his surrender.

There were no ceremonial parades on this second birthday as training had to be the priority, so that within another year the Home Guard would be fit to take over the defences of Britain from the Army. This process was already under way as has been shown, with the use of Home Guardsmen on AA batteries, thus relieving regulars for overseas service. The steady improvement in the weapon situation underlined the government's belief that the force would have a vital role in the years ahead.

There was also an announcement by King George VI that he would be Colonel-in-Chief of the Home Guard. He boosted morale by referring to the fact that many of the original volunteers had left, because of age or transfer to the regular service, but that they had left a great tradition of service and comradeship to inspire new recruits to enrol in the defence of their country. He also said that he knew that the Home Guard would offer the fiercest resistance to an enemy and be unsparing in their efforts to be ready for the invader. The King's message was greeted by units in Norfolk, as elsewhere, with pride and pleasure.

Tribute by the GOC Eastern Command – June 1942

An interesting speech was reported in the Eastern Daily Press by the GOC Eastern Command when he visited Cambridgeshire. He said that, "We depend on the Home Guard, and we want our citizen army to use its wits, and have no use for parade ground soldiers who obeyed orders without understanding". Those members of the Norfolk Home Guard who disliked parades, (and there were a number!) would have welcomed this. However, the general did stress that discipline was essential!

The general also remarked on how the Home Guard had grown in numbers, arms, skill and confidence since 1940. He then pointed out that, without the Home Guard, it would be impossible for us to stage an attack on Europe. Concluding his address, he said that anyone foolish enough to suggest that the Home Guard was not wanted, "will get a rocket!"

With tributes like these few could doubt the continuing importance of the Home Guard. It is appropriate at this point to discuss its changing role as the war situation also changed.

The Changing Role of The Home Guard

Initially, the role of the Home Guard had been to "observe and harass" the enemy, and then retire in the face of superior numbers. By 1941, the force was being introduced to a new scheme which involved the creation of "nodal points", such as defensive positions built round villages or important road junctions. To these the Home Guard would retreat and fight it out until they were overwhelmed. Thus the role of the Home Guard was changing from one of static defence, never popular with those men who wanted to "have a go" at the enemy, to one involving tactical mobility. During 1942, many helped on the AA and searchlight batteries and with coastal defences. Some also guarded the American Air Force bases in their area.

By the Autumn of 1942, German forces were getting bogged down in Russia, whose invasion proved to be one of Hitler's errors. Later in the year, Rommel's Afrika Corps was defeated in the battle of El Alamein in North Africa. With these setbacks to German ambitions, the invasion threat to Britain, seemed a very remote prospect. Hence some men began to question the need for the continued existence of the Home Guard.

Diss water tower will not be captured!
Noel Madgett, Mr. Voss (?), Albert Green of the Diss Home Guard.
Photo with kind permission of Miss J. Green

However, the government warned that it would be very unwise to relax our guard. The Germans could still try one final desperate gamble. Vigilance was essential the Home Guard were told. To reinforce the point, Lord Croft, Under Secretary for War visited the region to speak to Home Guard commanders from Norfolk and other counties. He told them that it would be most unwise to think of the invasion being "written off". The message for the Home Guard at the end of the year, was that while Britain may not be in the front line in the next campaign against Hitler, we would be the advance base for the western front, and enemy counter-attacks and raids must be expected. Therefore the Home Guard's responsibility for the defence of the country would increase, as the allies widened their offensive against the enemy.

MANY OTHER DUTIES FOR THE HOME GUARD TOO

Apart from the main role outlined above, the Home Guard were expected to support the Civil Defence and the Police. In Norwich they helped both and the Fire fighters who had to deal with the air attacks on the city in 1942.

Finally, the Eastern Daily Press reported that the War Office had underlined the Home Guard's traditional role while on duty and in uniform. They were entitled to search civilian vehicles and premises, stop and question anyone and request an ID and their reason for being in a particular place. If they had reason to believe that someone was a danger to the public safety or the defence of the realm, Home Guards could arrest without a warrant! So, the force still had plenty to think about and do!

THE POSITION OF THE HOME GUARD BY THE END OF 1942

By this time, the Home Guard had made remarkable progress. It was now better armed, better equipped and better trained and it was an integral part of the active home defence. As many as 7,000 men manned the coastal artillery defences, many in Norfolk, thereby releasing regulars for service overseas. The year ended on a positive and purposeful note and the Norfolk Home Guard could be justifiably proud of its work and achievements.

CHAPTER 5

1943 - The Work Of The Home Guard Must Still Go On.

The usual round of parades, patrols and training continued in the new year. However, the Home Guard also became involved in a variety of other activities. One of these was reported in the Diss Express in January. A company of the 9th Battalion, which covered Attleborough, Old and New Buckenham, Banham, Hargham, Wilby, Besthorpe, Great and Little Ellingham and Rocklands, raised £1250 for the Prisoners of War Fund. The Company Commander, Major Russell said that "such a magnificent effort speaks well for the loyalty and teamwork of the men".

The Home Guard also made a big contribution to the development and expansion of the ACF (Army Cadet Force) in the county. As a result of its efforts, the cadet organization had sub-units in many villages and towns throughout Norfolk. The enthusiasm and support of local Home Guard units for the ACF helped to increase the pool of youths who would join the defence forces when they were old enough.

KEY FIGURES IN AA COMMAND

Some Home Guardsmen had begun to be part of the AA batteries and coastal defences in 1942. This trend would continue in 1943. In March, the Eastern Daily Press reported a statement by the GOC AA Command in which he told the Home Guard that they would be mainly responsible for manning the batteries before the war was ended. He stressed that, their skill and training would be vital to the safety of people's lives. "We've not seen the end of the Luftwaffe yet," he told them.

A month after this speech, the Norfolk Chronicle reported an episode that illustrated the role of the Home Guard in the AA batteries. During a raid over a town in the area, four enemy planes were successfully picked out by the searchlight team, enabling the AA batteries to send up "a terrific barrage". It was noted that many of the AA guns were manned by men from the Home Guard.

THE HOME GUARD'S THIRD BIRTHDAY - 14TH MAY 1943

In his message to the Home Guard in May, the King drew attention to the work it was doing in the AA and in coastal defence. He told the force that he knew that the Army appreciated its contribution in this particular area. Further, he underlined what a number of military figures had been saying for some time, namely, that as the Army moved increasingly on to the offensive, the Home Guard's responsibility for the defence of the country grew heavier. The King spoke too of the high standard of proficiency in the force and its tradition of service and devotion. It was well deserved praise and both the King, the Prime Minister and others underlined the debt that was owed to the Home Guard by the nation.

PROWLING IN THE LION'S DEN!

No one could underline the importance of the Home Guard like Churchill. He was one of its greatest champions from the earliest days, and in his birthday tribute, he produced typically colourful language. The Eastern Daily Press reported the speech which included the following memorable passage:- "If the Nazi villains drop down upon us, either by paratroop raid or bombs on our factories, you (the Home Guard), will make it clear to them that they have not alighted in a poultry run, or in a rabbit farm or even a sheepfold, but that they have come down in the lion's den!"

Elsewhere in the speech Churchill spelt out that the Home Guard must now be capable of taking on the full burden of home defence themselves. This would set free the bulk of our troops for the "deadly grapple" with the strongholds of Nazi power. He also complimented the men for manning the coastal defences, AA batteries and motor transport units, and thanked the employers who had made it possible for the men to do their duties. The farm owners and managers in Norfolk must have appreciated that!

Women were not forgotten as he paid tribute to the wives and mothers who had made service in the Home Guard easier. Voluntary women helpers in the Home Guard, would receive a badge in recognition of their important service.

Finally, he emphasized that the danger of invasion would never pass away until Hitlerism was defeated. He told the men that the sense of imminent emergency, "which inspires the long routine of drills and musters, after the hard day's work is done, is the reality of your work".

THE NORFOLK HOME GUARD CELEBRATES ITS BIRTHDAY

There were a host of parades, services, lectures and demonstrations throughout the county. The occasion was reported in the local press. The Norwich battalions were a "great credit" said the Eastern Daily Press, which enthused about "our great citizen army", which was clearly well equipped, disciplined and proficient in its weaponry display. The paper also commented on the degree of public confidence in the force, which had grown as its numbers had increased, with a consequent rise in proficiency. The inspecting officer of the Norwich parade, said that it could be the *sixth* birthday he was so impressed. There clearly was a great contrast with the LDV days. Spectators were reminded of those times as some of the men wore LDV armlets on civilian clothes, while others were dressed in denims and soft caps (the first "uniform").

However, the most striking feature of the celebrations was the sight of a whole range of weapons:- rifles, Tommy and Sten guns, camouflaged mobile Spigot Mortars, Northover Projectors, etc. Also on display were signal sections, wireless operators, dispatch riders and flame throwers.

What the spectators saw that day, was a completely self-sufficient civilian army trained by its own officers, not just in static defence, but also in mobile offensive tactics. Battle platoons were in the parade and No.10 Battalion laid on a big demonstration in Chapel Field Gardens, in which Home Guard units attacked an "enemy" strongpoint manned by men wearing German uniforms taken from prisoners of war! Meanwhile, another big crowd was being entertained near Mile Cross by No.16 Battalion, who put on a display of accurate Spigot Mortar firing.

The Eastern Daily Press reporter said that buildings in Chapel Field Road and Northumberland Street, which had been damaged by the German air attacks on the city, made excellent vantage points for the public watching the street fighting demonstration. It seems that there were a variety of fighting tactics proudly on display in Norwich on that day.

But similar activities were taking place throughout the county. Virtually every town in Norfolk was the scene of some appropriate Home Guard display, exercise or demonstration. For example, at Reepham, No.17 Battalion, the newest of the Home Guard Battalions, commanded by Lt. Col. Gurney, paraded proudly and then demonstrated its weapons and tactics. Later in the day the battalion paraded at Bawdeswell Hall, where the salute was taken by Lord Ironside, formerly the C in C Home Forces. He was then to witness a display of live ammunition firing, after which he complimented the men on their discipline and fighting efficiency.

WHY HOME GUARD EFFICIENCY WAS SO IMPORTANT

At Fakenham, during the "Wings for Victory" week, No.4 Battalion demonstrated its strength and efficiency. The unit's CO, Lt. Col. Hastings praised the men and his views were echoed by a visiting brigadier who inspected the battle platoons. The Norfolk Chronicle quoted him as saying, "The greater the efficiency of each individual Home Guard, the greater the number of regular troops it will be possible to send overseas". The same point was emphasised by Lt. Gen. Franklyn, C in C Home Forces, in a letter he sent to Norfolk Home Guard units. A copy of the letter has survived in some papers relating to No.12 Battalion, based at Brancaster. The General spoke of "a well armed, well trained force, fit for those duties of local defence which have become the more important as the Field Army prepares to go overseas".

No one who witnessed the birthday displays could doubt the commitment of Norfolk's Home Guard or the obvious efficiency of many units. The belief in a continuing role at home as attention turned increasingly overseas, sustained the spirit and morale of the men during 1943.

LATE 1943 - CAN THE HOME GUARD RELAX NOW?

In November, Walter Citrine, General Secretary of the TUC made a speech in which he criticized some aspects of the Home Guard. As an invasion was less and less likely, he argued that it was time to relax things. He thought there was no need for irrelevant drills and that harsh penalties for absence should be relaxed. It is true that things were not going well for the Germans at this point in the war. Defeated in North Africa and in Russia, and on the defensive in Italy, it could be argued that the last thing they would be considering was an attack on Britain. Citrine's comments however, produced a flurry of correspondents to the Eastern Daily Press, following a leading article which argued that it would be folly to view the Home Guard as no longer necessary.

The same article reminded readers of Churchill's attitude to the Germans, that the German army was still very strong and therefore we should not relax our guard.

SOME NORFOLK VIEWS ON WHETHER THE HOME GUARD COULD RELAX

Judging by some of the letters to the Eastern Daily Press however, there was some support for the view that things could be made easier for men in the Home Guard. One writer complained of Sunday duties following a hard week's work. It was also pointed out that men didn't need training to keep fit, because most were fit as a result of the nature of their work (farming again). They were also proficient in their weapons. Because farm workers were excused parades during harvest when they worked from dawn to dusk, this did not mean they weren't capable of being called out to stop the Germans in the unlikely event of an invasion!

An extreme view was that the Home Guard could now be safely disbanded! One correspondent rejected this idea, but suggested that men with 200 parades behind them, were adequately trained, put on "reserve" and called up occasionally for refresher courses. The same writer was harsh about some of his colleagues. Those unlikely to make efficient soldiers he believed, should be discharged!

The main concern however, was that weekends should be free. One correspondent thought that after three and a half years of training the Home Guard *should* be able to relax. He added that as invasion was unlikely due to the fact that German resources were incapable of supporting such a project, then occasional Sundays off seemed reasonable.

An LDV Veteran Speaks Out On The Issue

In December, the Eastern Daily Press published a letter from an LDV veteran. He wrote that he was in a "reserved" occupation, worked 60 hours per week, and roundly condemned the majority of letters which had supported the idea of relaxing the Home Guard. In his view, these letters should be signed "Dodgers!" He then proceeded to invoke the spirit of 1940, when he and thousands like him, trained once a week, also did an all night guard duty and trained again on Sunday! He told readers that he too worked long hours but could always attend parades, etc. without excessive fatigue. His experience was that Home Guard commanders always arranged parades and training to suit their men. He ended his letter with an emotional appeal:- "What must the Eighth Army and other units think as they toil in the front line, while some Home Guard grumble about duties!!" Such robust sentiments must have brought "three cheers" from many parts of Norfolk!

It is fair to say that throughout Norfolk, local Home Guard commanders were sensitive to reducing parades wherever this was possible, while at the same time ensuring their units remained in a high state of readiness. As someone who wrote to the Eastern Daily Press at the time of this debate said, "there are *some* grumblers and bad soldiers in the Home Guard, but most are loyal and patriotic, and Citrine was doing a disservice to the Allied cause", by playing down the Home Guard's importance.

Women In The Home Guard

At the beginning of the crisis in 1940, women had come forward to serve in the Home Guard. In Parliament, Dr. Summerskill had asked why women could not be part of the force. However, the government had consistently refused permission for women to be enrolled.

Nevertheless, by 1943, with the progress of the war, the manpower problem increased, and the total strength of many battalions began to decline. In his tribute to the Home Guard on its third birthday, Churchill had also spelt out the important contribution women were making to the war effort. In June, women auxiliaries were enrolled for the first time in Norfolk. Some of them took over certain duties which were being performed by men, who could then be released for more specialist active training. They were trained in the usual way and took on a variety of duties - telephone operators, drivers, orderlies, clerks, etc.

By 1944, there were 32,000 women enrolled in the Home Guard nationwide. At the end of the war they received a badge as recognition of their important service. A tribute was paid to Norfolk women by a Home Guard major, reported in the Chronicle in June. He underlined their importance and said that, "their consideration is one of the great efforts of the war".

Women were naturally very concerned about the safety of their menfolk in the Home Guard. In particular they wanted a pension if their husband was killed while on duty. They were pleased to hear in June 1943, that pension rights were to apply to the Home Guard on the same basis as for regular servicemen.

SECURITY ARRANGEMENTS AT SYDERSTONE CHURCH

The CO of the Syderstone platoon was the local rector. Among his papers, deposited in the Norfolk Record Office along with the usual church records, were documents relating to the local Home Guard. One of these was a notice he produced for display outside the church. It read, "In compliance with a request by the military authorities, this church is at present kept locked. The key may be obtained by parishioners and visitors on enquiry at the Rectory. In normal times the church is always open". There may have been a war on, but this commander was determined to preserve ancient custom about church access within the military constraints of the time.

CHAPTER 6

1944 – Final Phase – The long watch Ends

By the end of 1943, the Home Guard in the county had built a considerable reputation and it was ready for the increased responsibilities at home, which an allied offensive on Europe would necessitate.

EARLY 1944 – STILL BUSY

In February, Stafford Cripps, Minister of Aircraft Production, was reported in the Eastern Daily Press as saying that the Home Guard was as important to the country now as ever it was. Home Guardsmen's work was invaluable, because they worked much more than normal hours, when their duties and training were added to their daytime jobs. In March, the same newspaper, ran a headline, "Home Guard Gunners get night raiders". This referred to an air attack over parts of London and East Anglia, including Norfolk. During the incidents, five of the ten enemy planes were brought down, several being being held very effectively in searchlights. Among the men operating the AA batteries and rocket guns were men from the Norfolk Home Guard.

In May, there was a "Salute the Soldier Week" and Home Guard units throughout the county took an active part. Various social and fund raising events were held, including at Reepham, a football match between a regimental team and one from the Home Guard. It seems that the regulars had a sprinkling of professionals playing for them and not surprisingly, the Home Guard team were defeated! The Norfolk Chronicle reported parades and services attended by the Home Guard in most north Norfolk towns.

TWO NORFOLK HOME GUARDS AWARDED BEM FOR GALLANTRY

The first of these was for a farm worker, Ernest William Bowman, who, assisted by a police sergeant, rescued a gunner from a crashed American plane at Shipdham. Mr Bowman, aged 27, was in his garden at the time, and he ran to the blazing aircraft and pulled the airman clear. He had joined the Home Guard when it was known as the LDV in 1940, and was still an active member of his unit in 1944. The second award of the BEM was to George Mutimer, of Westwick. He was a lieutenant in his local Home Guard and at the time of the incident was in bed! He heard the sound of a plane coming down; jumping up and partially dressing, he ran to the blazing aircraft. He displayed exceptional gallantry in the face of great personal danger, and succeeded in rescuing all three members of the crew.

NUMBER 5 BATTALION HOME GUARD, READY FOR ACTION

In the papers of the 5th Battalion (North Walsham), located in the Norfolk Record Office, we are reminded of the state of readiness of a typical Home Guard unit in the Spring of 1944. Among the documents are detailed operational instructions for anti-aircraft measures, together with what are termed "X Day Plans", which refer to appropriate action when enemy raiders are reported to have landed. There is also a secret memo which gives the most favourable conditions for a combined sea and air attack on the Norfolk coast, bearing in mind the moon, wind, sea and tides. Two dates were thought specially favourable for the enemy, 1st May and 15th August. Also set out in the memo were the specific objectives of the enemy, together with key places which the 5th Battalion was assigned to defend . These were the radar stations at Trimingham and Happisburgh, and the RAF station at Mundesley. If the enemy did land in this area, the battalion had a clear role which was to engage and destroy it! The existence of the "Action Stations" plans serves to remind us that the role of each Home Guard unit was specific and an integral part of the region's defences. A list of the towns and villages within the geographical limits of the 5th Battalion, gives an idea of the extensive area for which a Home Guard battalion could be responsible. The places concerned were:– North Walsham, Thorpe Market, Neatishead, Aylsham, Stalham, Mundesley, Cromer,

Trimingham, Palling, Happisburgh, Witton, Lessingham, Waxham, Swanton Abbott, Tunstead, Smallburgh, Worstead, Sloley, Westwick, Wroxham, Horning, Wayford and Ashmanaugh. The administration of such a large area presented considerable challenges and it is a tribute to those responsible that it was carried out with such enthusiasm and efficiency.

4TH BIRTHDAY TRIBUTES BY THE LOCAL PRESS

As one would expect, all the county's newspapers praised the work of the Home Guard and took the opportunity to underline the importance of its achievements and continuing role.

The Eastern Daily Press argued that although a large scale counter-attack by the Germans was unlikely, following the imminent allied assault on Europe, they would attempt sabotage airborne raids to disrupt communications here, and in any way possible upset our invasion schedule. For such an eventuality, the Home Guard would have to be on its mettle. However, the paper continued, if no such enemy raids took place, the waiting and training by the Home Guard, would not be in vain. It had become an "army, in being", and had performed the functions of an army, not remaining idle. By performing a range of jobs like manning coastal defence batteries and many other tasks normally carried out by the regulars, these men could be released for overseas service or specialist training in readiness for what became known as D Day. The Home Guard's role in supporting the Civil Defence services was also stressed, as these were likely to be stretched if the enemy resorted to pilotless planes and rocket guns to attack Britain in the event of our assault on occupied Europe.

The Eastern Daily Press also challenged the view that the Home Guard was no longer the enthusiastic body it had been when thousands joined the Local Defence Volunteers. It told its readers that those in the best position to judge on this matter, namely long serving officers and NCOs, had no fear on this score. It accepted that while enthusiasm was difficult to keep at fever heat over four years of waiting for the enemy, in its place was an "esprit de corps" and a complete confidence that it could do its job. Such a view of the Home Guard was fair and positive. Despite the unpopularity of conscription, the vast majority of men in the force contributed to the high standard of efficiency and their attitude was a credit to themselves and their commanders. The Norfolk

Chronicle was also very complimentary about how competent, well trained and equipped the Home Guard had become. It too appreciated the fact that the Home Guard had not had the opportunity of showing its prowess in battle. However, the paper pointed out the importance of the force in the wider context of the war. It told readers that the Home Guard had a big place in the allied victories in Africa, and in the successful invasion of Sicily and Italy, (1942–43). Had it not been for the fact that the Home Guard stood behind the Regular Army, reinforcements could not have been sent to the Middle East in time to drive Hitler's great general Rommel, out of Africa. Now "the greatest ever amateur army" was waiting alongside the regular forces for the Second Front.

D Day in Europe – The Home Guard Ready for Anything

It was made very clear to Home Guard units, that as the great offensive in Europe which would hopefully lead to the final destruction of Nazi power drew near, much would depend on them to maintain the safety of the country. The defence of the main base of the allied armies as they began the difficult task of dislodging the Germans from north west Europe, rested almost totally on the shoulders of the Home Guard. Of course the dangers of an effective counter attack were exaggerated, but for a time the Home Guard could feel part of the grand strategy to destroy Hitler.

In September, 1944, Lt. General Schreiber, GOC South Eastern Command, sent a message of thanks to the Home Guard for its work at the time of D Day. He wrote, "I want to thank all ranks of the Home Guard under my command for the splendid way in which they assumed the operational responsibility of keeping watch and ward over the command during the successful crossing of the Channel by the Allied Expeditionary Force". While some members of the Home Guard may have thought that their job was as good as over, many of the Norfolk units would surely have appreciated the fact that their role was still taken seriously at this stage of the war.

The Difficulty of Maintaining Interest in the Home Guard

Despite all the public pronouncements about the importance of the Home Guard and its morale, in Norfolk, as elsewhere in the country, many members were less and less willing to be involved. By the late summer of 1944, invasion seemed highly unlikely, and the relevance of the force was increasingly questioned. During July and August, morale in some units suffered, as men became less and less convinced of the arguments in favour of continuing the force. A Government poster showing Hitler patting a Home Guard shirker on the back as "Mein Pal", which was designed to check the increasing trend towards absenteeism, merely caused anger. However, absenteeism continued to be a problem for commanders.

According to the cases of absenteeism by Norfolk Home Guards, which ended up in court and were then reported in the press, the customary excuses were long hours of work, particularly for farm workers, and the difficulty of getting to parade as a result.

However, magistrates continued to impose fines on such offenders though in exceptional cases they recommended a man be exempt from continued Home Guard membership. Judging by the evidence of those cases that did come to court, it seems that by this stage of the war, absence from Home Guard parades could be quite prolonged, before any decisive action was taken by long suffering commanders. For instance, one man who appeared before the bench in August 1944, had only attended nine parades since July 1943, according to the sergeant of his unit.

The vast majority of the Home Guard however, fulfilled their obligations conscientiously during this period and any suggestion that they were shirkers was deeply disliked. At the time of the government poster, mentioned earlier in this section, Colonel Medlicott, MP for East Norfolk, told the Secretary for War that the poster was resented by many members of the Norfolk Home Guard.

Time to relax in the Home Guard?

However, by late August 1944, with the allied offensive against Germany in Europe going well, any possibility of an attack by the enemy seemed unrealistic. A letter to the Eastern Daily Press scorned the idea that Hitler could now attack us and then added that it was time for the Home Guard to relax. After the harvest was in, the writer thought they should have an easy time.

Another letter from someone who described himself as a "tired Home Guard", took a similar line. He pointed out that some men had served four years, with enlistment in some cases. In lighter vein he wrote that "our wives are suspicious of our movements on *night operations*". On a more serious note he argued that although some unit commanders had given relief to their men, it should apply to all units. He suggested "surely one Sunday to ourselves and our family is not too much to ask". At this stage of the war, three Sundays a month and one weekday parade was a reasonable compromise. The writer of this letter pointed out that the men were always available for action in the event of an emergency such as an air raid anyway. His concluding remarks may have expressed the feelings of many of his colleagues. He wrote, "We don't mind work, but we're getting browned off by degrees. Loyalty can be stretched too far and it would be a great pity if the old spirit is finally destroyed, and I fear it will unless some relief is soon given". These fears were not borne out however. As the Home Guard reached its final months, there was a progressive reduction of routine duties in most units.

WYMONDHAM HOME GUARD COMPANY STILL SHOOTING!

However, the enthusiasm which had marked the Home Guard in Norfolk from its inception, was still in evidence in the Wymondham area in the late Summer and early Autumn of 1944. Major Fryer, Commander of the 5th Company, No. 9 Battalion was busy organizing his company's shooting teams for various competitions at Thetford and Garboldisham in August and October. Ammunition was collected from the Wymondham Drill Hall and transport picked up his men from Wymondham, Spooner Row, Wreningham, Braconash and Top Row. These events, together with the battalion's eliminating competition held at Thetford Range, were followed by several final practices by Major Fryer's company in October. It seems this was all in readiness for the grand final of the 9th Battalion's Shooting Competition, which was held at Garboldisham on 22nd October, 1944.

Here, 15 teams representing the five companies of the battalion which involved 90 men took part. It is pleasing to note that the "A" Team from Major Fryer's company won the competition. Its

A Home Guard group from the Wymondham and Attleborough area involved in transport duties.

Back row: Harry Clarke, "Shrimp" Watson, Sid Hurrell (a baker), Mr. Spinks (of Friarscroft lane, a bus driver), Mr. Webster, Lenny Sturman, Charlie Fox (All of Attleborough), Bob Roy.

Second row: W. Corston, ?, "Spat" Chamberlain, G. Burn?, ?, Aubrey Royall, ? George Mabbutt, ?, ?, George Duffield.

Front row seated: Mr. Wade, Cecil Havers, Charlie Daniels, ?, ?, Bill Burroughs (worked in a bank), Billy Squires, Arthur Daniels, ?, Harry Tooke.

Seated on ground: Mr. Lord?, Bert Hadley (signalman, Ketteringham signalbox), Leslie Payne (bus driver, Wreningham), ?, ?, W. Andrews, ?

Photo with kind permission of Mrs. J. Clarke

102

captain was Lt. A D Howlett of Wreningham, whose son kindly loaned me relevant documents. Throughout the county however, similar events were being organized by other battalions.

The Beginning of the End – Plans for Stand Down

In September, the War Office announced plans to "Stand Down" the Home Guard. The Eastern Daily Press covered the story in the leading article, which was a tribute to "a well armed, battle worthy force". It referred to its enthusiasm and loyalty and argued that though it had not seen action, this did not "detract from the honour it has won as a reserve line of defence, in the years when our assurance of ultimate victory was based on the strength of human morale, of which it was so striking a symbol". The article also emphasized that the Home Guard had provided "efficient protection" at the time of potential enemy interference, when the regular forces had left the country. Home Guard units throughout Norfolk would have been pleased with this tribute.

"Stand at Ease"

On the 11th September, the Home Guard once again became a voluntary body. It wasn't quite "Stand Easy" or "Dismiss". The War Office announced that call-up for the Home Guard was suspended and that duties henceforth, would be on a voluntary basis. Many hoped that total disbandment would not take place and that the movement would long continue. In Morley, the local Platoon so enjoyed the comradeship of the Home Guard experience, that they continued to meet long after the war had finished! They finally "Stood Down" in 1972!

"Stand Down" is Official – November 1944

There were over 31,500 men in the Home Guard at "Stand Down". One of the first units to have a "Farewell Supper" was "C" Company, of No.11 Battalion, based in Yarmouth. The company was addressed by the Battalion CO Lt. Col. Hayward who told the men they "had put up a good show". "Stand Down", when it came, was difficult for some men to adjust to. For example, many men in the Norwich units continued to practice their shooting. No.10 Battalion put the miniature range at the Drill Hall

In the years when our Country

was in mortal danger

RONALD WILLIAM EDWARDS

who served   10th May 1942 - 31st December 1944.

gave generously of his time and

powers to make himself ready

for her defence by force of arms

and with his life if need be.

George R.I.

THE HOME GUARD

Certificate from King.
With kind permission of Mrs. Margaret Edwards.

in Chapel Field Road at the disposal of these men. On 26th November, the Eastern Daily Press reported that Home Guards were still keeping their eye in at the Horsford Range.

The Norfolk Chronicle paid its tribute on 3rd November, saying that the country owed a debt of gratitude to the force for its devotion to duty. It also reported that the King had approved the issue of a Certificate of Service to all Home Guardsmen, which would recognize their service to the nation.

THE FINAL PARADES AND OFFICERS TRIBUTES

Each battalion had a parade to mark the "Stand Down". One of the first, was No. 6 Battalion *(Norwich),* which paraded at Britannia Barracks. The men were officially thanked by Lord Ironside (formerly C in C Home Forces), and their CO, Col. Taylor bade them farewell. Companies of the battalion were drawn from an area between Aylsham, Ringland and Reedham. The Norfolk Chronicle reported that Lord Ironside told the men that, "the response of the Home Guard turned the balance against an invasion of England". He also thanked them for their work and for the training of younger men who had since passed into the Regular Army, "imbued with the spirit of the Royal Norfolk Regiment".

In early December, the Eastern Daily Press reported the big parade in London, where it took 42 minutes for a march past of six men abreast, before one of the capital's biggest wartime crowds. Though a few members of the Norfolk Home Guard may have made the journey south, the vast majority took part in local parades in the county.

One of these was in *Norwich* city centre where 4,000 men paraded. There were representatives from various battalions and companies. The salute was taken by Colonel Parry, MBE, MC, and the mayor and other civic dignitaries were present. The men then marched to cinemas, where they were addressed by Colonel Morgan, MC, who spoke of their unselfishness and goodwill, which he believed they would carry into civilian life. The King's message was read to them and among the many tributes was this one from Colonel Bassett, who said, "When the Field Army marched to its appointed task abroad, (ie D Day), and left the defence of this country to you, they paid you the greatest compliment in military history". Meanwhile other parades symbolized the end of a unique period in Norfolk's history. No.14

Battalion, based at Hapton, held four parades at *Long Stratton, Diss, Bunwell* and *Harleston.* Their CO, Colonel Read told the men that the local Home Guard had been run with the minimum of friction throughout the war, and echoing other senior officers, he hoped that this spirit would continue in peacetime. At Melton Constable Hall, 200 men from No. 4 Battalion, based at *Holt,* paraded to take farewell of Lord Hastings, their CO. Also present was the Lord Lieutenant, the Earl of Leicester, who told the men that if it had not been for the Home Guard, the invasion of Europe could not have taken place.

Elsewhere in the county men took part in their last Home Guard parade. At *Yarmouth,* six companies of No.11 Battalion were addressed by Colonel Harward at the Royal Aquarium Theatre. At *Thetford* the local units paraded in the market place, where they were addressed by the mayor and Colonel Buxton who spoke of their loyalty and support over four years. In *Dereham* market place, 600 men of No.1 Battalion paraded and the salute was taken by Lt. Col. Barclay, who complimented the men and hoped that the spirit of service would continue. At *North Walsham,* the 4th Company of No.5 Battalion, held its final parade in the quad of Paston Grammar School, where the Battalion CO, Brigadier W A Blake thanked the men and echoed the views of many at this time, that the spirit of comradeship would continue after the peace. Over at *Reepham,* the 17th Battalion paraded in the market place, under the command of Major Ben Stimpson. After what one reporter described as "an imposing muster," the men marched to the two churches in the town, where the rector addressed them, speaking of their sacrifice and devotion to duty. There was also a collection for the Red Cross POW Fund. Finally, Lieutenant Colonel Gurney, the Battalion CO, carried out a last inspection and then thanked the men for loyalty to their officers.

At *Fakenham* Central School, Lord Hastings addressed the men and read the King's message. Major Scholey, a company commander, told the parade that he had been one of those who believed that the day might come when the Home Guard would be called upon to fight. This was why he had been so keen on training and discipline, and he was delighted that, though a voluntary body, no one had resented it.

At *Diss,* 300 officers and men met at the Corn Hall. In his address Lt. Col. Read, referred to the comradeship of the men and their ability to understand the other man's point of view, which he thought had been created by a common cause. He was convinced that the influence of the Home Guard would be of lasting benefit to the country. He closed by saying that there were two main curses in the world – jealousy and selfishness, but he believed that the men of the Home Guard had learnt to dispel the one and avoid the other.

THE FINAL TRIBUTES

These were paid all over the country in early December 1944. The King's radio broadcast was referred to in the leading article in the Eastern Daily Press, which endorsed the point that, "to have relaxed while the danger continued, would have been a betrayal of all we owe to our fathers and to our sons". The paper captured the public mood by arguing that the time for the Home Guard to stand down had come, and that it had earned its rest and deserved the thanks of the nation expressed in the highest quarters.

Churchill was, as he had always been very generous in his final tribute. He wrote of the Home Guard's devotion, comradeship, hard work and patriotic service, and was in no doubt as to the vitally important part it had played in the nation's struggle for freedom.

THE HOME GUARD KEEPS ITS UNIFORM

It was Churchill again who ensured that the Home Guard would retain their boots and uniform after "Stand Down". Because of the general clothing shortage at the time, some felt that Home Guard uniforms should be handed in. However, Churchill recognised that such action towards volunteers who had served their country loyally, was unacceptable. So the War Office announced that the Home Guard would be able to keep all the clothing issued.

THE FAREWELL DINNERS – VIVID MEMORIES

Throughout Norfolk, Home Guard units held dinners and social gatherings to commemorate their years in the force. Judging by the newspaper reports, they were enjoyable occasions with plenty of toasts, tributes and happy memories. Common to all these events was the spirit of comradeship. As men recalled the Home Guard experience over four years, they remembered with pride, their challenges and achievements, and of course the amusing moments. The teamwork and co-operation of the men is a lasting impression of the Home Guard. It is clear that between the officers, NCOs and the men there was a mutual respect and confidence in each other as a group of people working for a common objective.

Among the recurring themes which were the subject of speeches at farewell dinners, was the vivid memory of the LDV days, in May to July 1940. In the words of one speaker at Diss, "they rose as one man to fight for freedom from the greatest tyrannical power the world had known, even be it only with their bare hands!" In those early months, one officer recalled that his unit had six rifles and six uniforms. Some who had served from the very beginning of the LDV, confessed to the fact that they had not realised the demands that would be made on them, but they had just got on with things to the best of their ability.

A factor which does help to explain the success of the Norfolk Home Guard, was that many of the officers did show a good understanding of "Norfolk character", and a readiness to make allowances for genuine difficulties which many men experienced in coping with the demands of the force. One speaker wistfully recalled that at the start, there were no officers or NCOs, and everyone was equal. However, the coming of ranks and proper military structures, was accepted in good spirit by the men, who were in most cases only too glad that the extra burdens of responsibility would be assumed by others. One CO of a battalion recalled the day he was asked to assume command. The dialogue between himself and a senior officer was as follows:– "Will you take over the battalion?" YES. "Can you do it?" YES. "Any questions?" NO!

Several speakers recalled that one of the many benefits of the Home Guard, was that they got to know people in their local community very well and in neighbouring villages. There was much organization and running about involved in being a Home Guard officer. One adjutant apologized in his speech for not seeing men often enough. The trouble was that he was responsible for 68 sections in his battalion! Many speeches were laced with humorous anecdotes, as in the case of a company commander recalling the enthusiasm of the ammunition officer. "We are all grateful we are able to tell the tale – he had done his best to blow us up at times"! However, the main feature of these farewell gatherings was a genuine pride in what had been accomplished in very difficult circumstances. One officer felt that the influence of the Home Guard would be of lasting benefit to the country. Certainly, men from a wide variety of backgrounds and occupations, with full time jobs, had come together, contributed to, and benefited from, the unique experience of the Home Guard. Many were optimistic that this experience would be invaluable in the future. The sentiments expressed in speech after speech at these farewell dinners, testify to the enduring qualities of comradeship , loyalty and patriotism, which are inseparably linked with Norfolk Home Guard.

Home Guard Reunion at Diss.
Photo with kind permission of Mr. C. Pursehouse

A VERY LATE STAND DOWN BY THE MORLEY HOME GUARD

In 1972, nearly 40 old Home Guard comrades arrived in Morley from all over Norfolk for the final muster in the village hall. They had all been in the Morley Platoon which had paraded and waited for the enemy over thirty years before.

Their CO was Jack Norton, by then aged 74. He and his men enjoyed an evening of reminiscences and surprises. Most members of the unit were particularly surprised to find Mr. Thornton Pigg, by then aged 95, the oldest member of the Morley unit, still alive and kicking. In fact he lived on until he was 99 years of age.

During the evening, the men had a convivial time and a fine meal paid for, from the remnants of their old comrades' association fund. The final toast to the Queen by the "Morley lot", meant that the village Home Guard had finally "Stood Down".

THE 17 HOME GUARD BATTALIONS – EACH HAD A JOB TO DO

Although detailed evidence of many of the battalions is scarce and fragmentary, each had a role in the defence of the county. What follows is largely based on an article in the 1946 edition of the Britannia Magazine, the journal of the Royal Norfolk Regiment.

No.1 Bn. HQ at Dereham Its tasks were the defence of important road and rail junctions and assisting with the defence of local airfields. Later in the war, its mobile platoons were ready to deal with any measures the enemy might take to hamper our operations in Europe after D Day.

No.2 Bn. HQ at Downham Market Covered all Norfolk west of the Great Ouse and the south west, excluding Swaffham and Thetford. It regularly tested the defence of 4 airfields in the area.

No.3 Bn. HQ at Harleston Initially there were 4 companies of volunteers to watch for parachutists in Brooke, Poringland, Diss, Harleston, Loddon, Hethersett, Long Stratton and Bixby. Later in the war, the emphasis shifted from static defence to mobile platoons to combat any airborne landings.

No.4 Bn. HQ at Holt Formed on 17th May by Lord Hastings, its CO for the whole war. It was a very large unit, prided itself on its high level of proficiency, and contributed to the general defence of north Norfolk.

No.5 Bn. HQ at North Walsham Its main operational role was coastal defence. Later in the war, some of its men manned the heavy coastal batteries at Mundesley and Cromer.

No.6 Bn HQ at Norwich One of 3 Battalions covering the city and surrounding areas, but, its main area was north east Norwich. The spirit of 1940 is displayed by the fact that one of its first volunteers, a World War One veteran and well over the upper age limit, travelled from South Africa at his own expense to offer his service to the battalion.

No.7 Bn. HQ at King's Lynn Two members of the battalion received the BEM for rescuing crews of crashed RAF planes. Another invented a mobile mounting device for the Spigot Mortar, an anti-tank gun which was much admired by the military. Another invention was an anti-aircraft mounting device for the light machine gun which was used to defend various vulnerable targets in King's Lynn. The battalion was assigned special duties with the ARP providing good service during the air raids.

No.8 Bn. HQ at Swaffham This unit covered Necton, Bradenham, Watton, Feltwell, Mundford, Swaffham and Stanford Battle Area. The latter was a constant concern because its wooded terrain was ideal for parachutists.

No.9 Bn. HQ at Wymondham Apart from Wymondham, the unit included Eaton, Hethersett, New Buckenham, South Lopham, East Harling, Attleborough and Hingham. In 1940, a corporal extinguished an incendiary bomb at the Angel Inn, Hingham. At Banham, the battalion helped to rescue friendly airmen who had bailed out of a damaged plane.

No.10 Bn. HQ at Norwich By 20 May, 1940, 500 men had enrolled at Chapel Field Drill Hall and from 21 May there were nightly patrols and guards throughout the garrison area. There was also a stretcher-bearer unit which was very active during air raids. During German air attacks on Norwich, members of the battalion manned anti-aircraft posts, scoring a number of hits on enemy planes. During the Blitz, the battalion worked closely with the ARP. A bomb disposal squad was very successful and an unarmed combat squad provided regular demonstrations in the city as well as at the Battle School at Cambridge.

No.11 Bn. HQ at Great Yarmouth The first job of the battalion was to hold the immediate locality as an anti-invasion task. In due course it was allocated an AA battery for the use in its fixed role on the coast. Training for the battery was provided by the regulars and in time the battalion provided teams of gunners for the coastal batteries at Winterton and North Denes. It was also responsible for coastal patrols from Sea Palling to the Suffolk border. Later in the war, it was given a more mobile role and by the time of D Day, its mobile platoons were ready to combat enemy counter-measures.

No.12 Bn. HQ at Brancaster Formed in June 1940 to cover north west Norfolk, its main role was coastal defence. The CO, a veteran of the First World War, formed an armoured car unit to give fire power and mobility in coastal defence duties. The vehicles were high powered second-hand cars which were fitted with armour.

No.13 Bn. HQ at Sheringham Created out of sub units of other battalions based at Dereham, Holt and North Walsham. The Sheringham Platoon trained to work on the coastal artillery. It later took over a battery of naval guns.

No.14 Bn. HQ at Hapton Formed in 1941, it took over the western part of No. 3 Battalion, which included Diss and Newton Flotman. Its main role was the ground defence of local American airfields. Close working relations were established with the Americans. On one occasion members of the battalion searched 500 acres of ground in darkness and brought in injured crewmen from a crashed plane.

No.15 Bn. HQ at Downham Market Created in 1941 because No. 2 Battalion was too large. It was responsible for the area west of the Ouse and the defence of the crossing of the Ouse. It also helped in defending Sutton Bridge airfield. Its patrols successfully rescued a friendly airman who had baled out, and also arrested the crew of a Junkers 88 which had crash-landed.

No.16 Bn. HQ at Norwich The third battalion in the city, formed in 1943 to cover the western part of Norwich. It worked successfully with Civil Defence authorities in helping the civilian population during the air attacks on the city. Stretcher squads were formed to help the hospitals deal with casualties.

No.17 Bn. HQ at Reepham The most junior battalion, formed in June 1943 out of parts of the 1st and 13th Battalions based at Dereham and Sheringham. However, it successfully integrated platoons from other units into the new one which helped in the defence of north Norfolk.

POSTSCRIPT

The vast majority of members served the Home Guard loyally and worked very hard. Hundreds received recognition in various ways such as Certificates for Good or Meritorious Service. There were also awards for many of the Commanders. Nine members of the Norfolk Home Guard received the MBE and two were awarded the OBE. Another four received the BEM and one man was awarded the GM.

COMMEMORATING HOME GUARD LINKS WITH THE ROYAL NORFOLK REGIMENT

Over 6,000 men in Norwich had served in the Home Guard. Most of them had a relative or a friend in the Norfolk Regiment, while many younger members of the Home Guard eventually passed into that regiment. This strengthened the bond which existed between the two organizations. As a result of this happy partnership, the Home Guard Club was formed. Former comrades could continue to meet at Colman House, Pottergate, which opened in 1945.

The 10th and 16th Norwich Home Guard Battalions decided to commemorate the close association between themselves and the Norfolk Regiment with another gesture. They gave a cheque and the title deeds to a plot of land on Mousehold Lane to the Norfolk Regiment. On this land were built the Memorial Cottages in memory of the 2,025 men of the Norfolk Regiment who had fallen in the war. A stone memorial tablet at the entrance to the site where the cottages stand, is a reminder of the Norwich Home Guard's contribution to the creation of the Memorial Cottages, opened in 1951 for the benefit of disabled soldiers of the Royal Norfolk Regiment.

The site of these Second World War Memorial Cottages in Norwich was presented by the Norwich Home Guard.

113

CHAPTER 7

Memories of Life in the Norfolk Home Guard

Mr. M.J. Mann,
Sheringham.

My late father, John Mann, was a member of 1st Company 13th
Battalion, Norfolk Home Guard. He was a member of the section
at West Beckham where we lived. This section later joined up with
Sheringham. I can remember them all parading on one of the local
farmer's fields on the first Sunday morning that the section was
formed. They looked a rather ramshackle collection! Some had
uniform tops and no trousers (that is, uniform trousers!). Of
course, none of them had any weapons, but they all proudly
displayed the LDV armband.

Of course, later it all got more serious and they were issued
with proper uniforms and rifles. My father's rifle was a
Winchester, and it used to stand in the corner of our sitting room
with his 4.10 shotgun. He was also a member of the Lewis gun
team; his friend was NCO in charge of the Lewis gun and he used
to keep the weapon at his home. Us boys used to have great fun
seeing if we could strip and assemble the gun quicker than they
could. Of course, there was no ammunition!

One night, there was great excitement in the village when it was
reported that German paratroopers had been seen landing. It was
very hectic getting father ready for battle. I can remember cleaning
his overcoat buttons! What good was that? Perhaps shiny buttons
would blind the enemy! Anyway, it all turned out to be a false
alarm. Still, it was a good talking point for us boys at school the
next day. They were exciting times for us lads and I don't think
we realised how serious the situation really was.

We used to follow the Home Guard wherever we could, all
wishing that we were old enough to join in. I remember that they
had a firing range in the woodland by the side of Lodge Hill, just
out of Upper Sheringham on the Cromer-Holt road. The Regular

Army used to send instructors down there and fire Bren guns on a fixed field of fire, and the Home Guard had to crawl through undergrowth under fire from the Brens which was all good training for them.

Mr. J. Baldwin,
Fakenham.

My father was in one of the two companies of the Fakenham Home Guard. He was not inclined to tell me anything about it except that the man in charge was a —- Bank Manager! When I started work in the town, I became friends with many older workmates who were in the Home Guard and have fond memories of them and their tales. My father-in-law was in the Home Guard at Dunton, and I recall him saying that he got his first ammunition around the time of D DAY 1944!

Fakenham has a fine market place and for many years the town pump graced the centre of its eastern end. By August 1939 the pump had been removed by the military under the direction of Lord Hastings. It was to be replaced by a blockhouse or pillbox to be used by the Fakenham Home Guard.

The blockhouse itself was of the usual pillbox type with gun windows on each of the four sides. One pointed up Norwich Street, another pointed across the market place, one pointed into the front door of The Red Lion Inn and the fourth pointed directly at the Crown Inn! But here the similarity to other pillboxes ended. This one had been designed by Oliver Messel, the well known stage designer. He was running a Camouflage School as part of the war effort and he had disguised the pillbox as a statue of Justicia! Local legend has it that the statue was not fully acceptable and a local builder was contracted to mix a match of plaster and cover up the naughty bits.

Other features of Fakenham's defensive structure were the Home Guard roadblocks, concrete movable bollards. These were put across the roads leading into the town.

Mr. T. Bevan,
Attleborough.

It was my father who started the Local Defence Volunteers in **Horningtoft,** and I can remember quite well the day the armbands arrived together with two boxes of twelve bore cartridges. These cartridges were for use in normal shotguns and instead of having several small lead pellets, each one had one large lead ball. Shortly afterwards an army officer delivered a box of Molotov cocktails. There were 24 bottles in the box. A hole was dug in the garden and a metal plate placed over the top before returning the soil.

I helped my father to make a lookout post on top of a two storey building in his farmyard. It was accessible by a ladder and the viewing area was about six feet by four feet, with sides about three feet high; it also had a top over it supported by a post at each corner. Six people would be on duty overnight – two in the lookout post and four resting. A portable bungalow that had been used by his in-laws, was situated in the garden at Brancaster House and this was divided into two rooms. One was used as a rest room and the other a games room, with billiard table for those not on lookout.

Shortly after the LDV was changed to the Home Guard, my father became an ARP Lecturer and the section was taken over by Mr. F. Allen. The billiard table went to his house, but the cartridges remained, as we had by then, been fitted out with rifles (they were old army issue) as did the Molotov cocktails.

Horningtoft Home Guard section was under the command of Capt. Allen who had as his Sergeant a Mr. Collinson, a World War I veteran. Our section was part of the 1st Norfolks and formed part of an area controlled by Major Chapman (a retired army major) who lived just outside North Elmham. As the war progressed, the number on duty overnight was reduced to two and lookout was only kept when an air raid was in progress. Training was on a weekly basis, Sunday mornings in Horningtoft. We were also taken to Cockley Cley for rifle shooting at the butts there.

Being a teenager at the time, I was told that it was my duty in the event of German tanks travelling through the village, to get a Molotov cocktail and run up to a tank (as if inviting the enemy with open arms!), and pop it through any opening I could find.

Every night two of us used to stand guard and watch the skyline to see if any German parachutists tried to land. I shall always recall one harvest when my body ached from top to toe. The weather was very hot and after getting up to milk the cows at 6am, then working laboriously in the fields getting the harvest in until 10pm, doing my overnight stint on guard and again working until 10pm the following day, I was all in. Forty hours without sleep and throwing sheaves of corn about for two long days was too much for me.

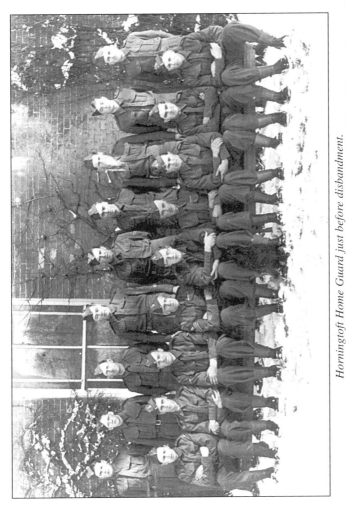

Horningtoft Home Guard just before disbandment.
Back Row; Left to Right: Arthur Bailey, Thomas Bevan (youngest member of the section), Cyril Creed, George Brown, Walter Mitchell, Russell Thetford, Ben Thurston (lived in one of the farm cottages at The Manor), Aubrey Bailey.
Front Row: Sidney Green, Ernie Colman, Bloy Baker, ? Collinson (lived in the other cottage at The Manor), Francis Allen, Fred Thurlow, Kenny Hammond, Clifford Hammond, Algie Hammond.
Photo with kind permission of Mr. T. Bevan

When the war was over, an army officer called to collect the "cocktails" and while we were digging them up from the garden, my father enquired if they were really any good, as they looked like any glass bottle filled with liquid. The officer advised him that they were very effective and if he liked, he would report that one of them had leaked and exploded one. He threw one with force against the stone and mortar wall of our neighbours' barn. It instantly burst into flames and a cloud of black smoke rose into the sky. We noticed over the next winter a dull look over the area where the "cocktail" had burnt, and in the following year an incident happened that brings a smile to my face even today. One evening, when I was in the garden, there was a rumble, and looking up, I saw a circle of the wall had fallen out where the "cocktail" had burnt all those years ago! But the most amusing thing was the expression on Billy Annison's face framed in the hole, as he was milking a cow on the other side of the wall!

In the war years, the Home Guard was a great morale booster for our country, and thankfully, the TV "Dad's Army" series has given a lot of pleasure over the years.

Mrs. C. Pye,
Caston.

One story always remains in my mind, probably because I now live in the house where it took place.

In the early hours of the morning, George was woken up by the sound of gravel thrown against his window pane. He lifted the sash and asked what was the matter William, the Home Guard sergeant, was down below and said, "There's an imaginary bomb crater in the village green and all of us have to turn out and fill it in. "Well," said George, "Imagine I'm there"! With that, he pulled down the window and went back to bed!

(Mrs. Pye is certain that this exchange took place in more colourful language than printed here!)

Mr. S. Saunders,
Watton.

While on our milk round, an Air Defence Corps man asked me if I would deliver a pint of milk to their sentry post placed in a road which had been closed when the Watton Camp was built. One morning when I arrived, the sentry seemed rather agitated, and I asked him what was wrong. "I'm still getting over a fright I had last night", he said. "It was pitch black and I was on guard duty; suddenly, there was a movement in the hedge over there (pointing). I shouted 'advance and be recognised'. Silence. I gave the order again. Silence. My hair now felt as if it would lift my cap off, so I put one up the spout. The noise of the rifle must have startled a black horse, for he let out a terrific snort, which really shook me as I had never heard anything quite like it before. Anyway, one of my mates came out to say it was only a horse, not a German invader"! I felt sorry for any lad who might be placed in such a dark and lonely place as that.

On another occasion, I was talking to the sentry, when the telephone rang in the pillbox. Seconds later he came running out shouting, "Action Stations, enemy aircraft overhead at 20,000 feet". I quickly decided that this was no place for me. I whipped the pony, because the ammunition dump was only 400 yards away, and made a rapid getaway!

One day, while I was rabbiting with a ferret not far from RAF Watton, a friend and I heard a plane approaching, which we realised was not British. It dropped 12 bombs on the camp and we ducked behind a bank to avoid being seen. That same evening, I was on Home Guard duty, acting as a runner to carry messages if needed, from Scoulton searchlight station. Some of the men seemed a bit upset. They too, had seen the Jerry plane that afternoon and had it in their gun sights. However, they'd been ordered to hold fire because the officer saw the plane lower its wheels and thought it was going to land. In fact, it shot straight over them and got away. The men were mad, because the German plane had been a sitting duck for a few seconds.

One evening, a Jerry plane hit a free range hen emplacement of about 12 large huts full of hens roosting for the night. I was quite near when the plane had come over close to Scoulton Camp, and had taken cover while the attack on the chicken huts occurred. Next day I was told that a Lord Haw Haw broadcast from Germany, had said that a military camp had been hit in Norfolk. Next morning there was a headline in the Eastern Daily Press which read, "Hundreds of Casualties"!

Mr. Hubert Dawson,
Dereham.

While I was in the Home Guard, a few things do stick in the memory. The first one was when we were on parade one day early in the war. In front of me was a chap who stood a head higher than the others and he was wearing a tunic with an oversize collar. Instead of an army shirt, he had a white one with a semi-stiff collar and a bright red necktie which really stood out!

On occasions I went to Santon Downham to collect ammunition. It was one big ammunition dump there. On the way we used to call at a little pub which used to be between "The Flintknappers"

Major Northover, the inventor of the Northover Projector, sighting his gun.
IWM 8 H12679   Photo with kind permission of The Imperial War Museum

and the present new pub "The Forest". There were only about five pint mugs in the pub with the regulars' names painted on the side of the mugs! The shelves behind the bar were full of one and two pound jam jars!

One day, we had another issue of Sten guns which had to have five magazines fitted to each gun before they were handed out. As armourer, my job was to adjust the guns so they would feed the rounds into the breach properly. If I made a mistake the Sten would squirt the cartridges straight out of the magazine. I had a dummy round to check firing, and a box of live ammunition to test the magazine. Anyway, on one occasion, I had checked the magazine for loading, emptied it again and put in my dummy round, OR SO I THOUGHT! When I fired it into the wall, everyone in the company office rushed outside to see what had happened. You can imagine how I felt!

One Sunday morning we went to Dereham Golf Course to watch a camouflage demonstration by the Regular Army. While we were waiting, two of our chaps had to walk the site with fixed bayonets, picking up rubber goods, probably American! They found enough to cover one of the seats on the golf course, from one end to the other!

In the Home Guard we had an interesting variety of weapons. Early on in the war, we had a few PIKES. These consisted of old bayonets welded into bits of gas piping about four or five feet long. They were kept in the company store and were never actually issued!

One of our so called pieces of artillery was the **Northover Projector** which was a light anti-tank weapon. It fired a No.36 grenade (Mills Bomb), the No.68 Anti-Tank grenade and the SIP or Self Igniting Phosphorous bomb. Another "evil device" was the Sticky Bomb, which could be thrown, but the recommended method was to sneak up on the enemy tank and apply it physically.

Mr. Alec J. Hunt,
Holme Hale, Thetford.

The Holme Hale Home Guard was a unit of 38 men of all ages, many of whom were men employed in agriculture. It was *not* "Dad's Army"! Captain Bunning was in charge and the oldest men were the Red Cross and stretcher party. There was a searchlight at Top Cross and two men from the Home Guard did all night duty to help defend the light, and if required, to call out other members of the Home Guard.

At Scales Drift, a small trench had been dug and two armed members did night duty. One dark night, a little after midnight, some heavy breathing was heard. Frank Hendry shouted, "Stop, or I will shoot," but the heavy breathing continued, so Ray Harmer shouted the same, but with no better result. The two men loaded their rifles and were in quite a fright. They agreed to shoot as soon as the moon gave them light to aim. At last, the moon came out from behind black clouds, and looking down on the two men, was a large white sheep!

My own night duty was on the American aerodrome at North Pickenham. At the time food was in short supply and I often enjoyed a good meal with plenty of everything which the Americans always had. Sometimes I was given a large tin of pork to take home.

Clark Gable, the famous American film star was often at North Pickenham and one night, a member of the USA Air Force shouted to him, "Hi, this guy (me) wants to meet you". Clark was rather short with very high heels on his shoes to make him appear taller. I had a number of meals with him; he was very quiet and but for his American accent, could have been a Norfolk country gentleman.

I was the Intelligence Officer whose job was to look out for spies. In the event of a German landing, I was to report back their numbers, arms, etc. One night there was an exercise in the area. At 1.30am on a cold winter's night, I was picked up by a jeep, given a map reference, and told that the Germans had landed west of Swaffham. I was the guide in an open jeep with at least 30 jeeps behind us. We came to a large heath and the jeeps formed a line; then across the heath we went with these madmen shooting into long grass, trees and bushes. Any moment I expected to be killed by friendly fire! But as it turned out, the Germans had not landed – the whole thing was just an exercise!

Our Home Guards often shot at Cockley Cley butts for cups. Our young men were natural shots, countrymen born with guns in their hands. At 100 yards, they could all hit the bull. These were not town men who had never handled a gun – most of them were born and brought up in villages. Not even the regular guardsmen could get the better of them at shooting. We had about four men who handled the machine gun. Private Bowman, another very good shot was in charge. We also had the anti-tank unit armed with a *Spigot Mortar.* It fired its bomb about a yard above the ground with a range of between 100 and 200 yards. The Spigot Mortar was a deadly weapon, but I cannot help feeling that, if it had ever been fired in anger, we would have had some dead Home Guards!

I recall that the regulars stationed in Norfolk were not too keen on the countryside at night, especially rats and other forms of wild life! In my opinion, the Home Guard, coped as well as the regulars, in the Norfolk countryside which they knew so well.

Mr. Charles J. Brown, Walsingham.

I joined the Melton Constable and Briston Company of the 4th Battalion, Norfolk Home Guard, in about March 1941, at the age of sixteen and a half. The CO was Lt. Col. The Lord Hastings, of Melton Constable Hall, which was the Battalion HQ. The Regimental Sergeant Major was Sergeant Major King. He was a very smart man with a distinguished army record who was now a popular Automobile Association patrolman. Briston and Melton Company was commanded by Captain J.H. Carter, who lived at Crossways Farm, Briston. The Company's NCOs were World War I veterans, as were many of the men. There were also men in "reserved" occupations and some, like me, who were too young to belong to the service units. There was also a Home Guard Band, made up from the defunct Briston Silver Band and other bands in the area.

By the time I joined the Home Guard, most of us had uniform, albeit incomplete and often ill-fitting! I had a battledress, belt and gaiters, but no overcoat or forage cap. We had a P14.300 rifle, American 1914-18 vintage, and 25 rounds of ammunition in a canvas bandolier. We also had a Bren gun, a Spigot Mortar and Molotov cocktails.

We paraded twice a week, mid-week and Sunday mornings. Most of our weapon training was supervised by regular army NCOs who usually came from Holt. We used to parade on the recreation ground using the pavilion, which was also the armoury. There was a nightly patrol of eight men, four on duty and four resting (for about two hours). Of course we had to go to work when we came off duty. Several of us were employed on construction work at Foulsham Airfield and on the land. Our patrol hut was at Crossways Farm. It had a tortoise stove, bunk beds and tea making facilities. The main part of the village was divided in two, and we were supposed to be on the look out for parachutists from enemy aircraft. We did rifle practice on a range at Matlaske. In addition, we had live hand grenade practice at Thursford. In the village and also at Melton Park, we practiced military manoeuvres.

There were some odd things that happened, but not *quite* as depicted on "Dad's Army". We had one man who fired some of his ammunition at rooks and crows! Another member of our unit, simply could not hit the target on the range, until it was discovered that he could not close one eye! He was soon fixed up with an eye patch! We had a few World War I veterans in our unit akin to "Corporal Jones" of "Dad's Army", and like the TV character, they told us stories of the battles they'd been in! There was doubtless some massaging of the truth too!

In 1942, I joined the Royal Marines and during my initial training, I was hospitalized for a few days. I was about to be put back into a squad just joining, but my Home Guard training with a rifle and Bren gun, saved me. Once properly established, which took a couple of years to achieve, I am sure that the Home Guard would have proved itself if it had been called into action.

Mrs Irene Stearman,
Hethersett.

My husband Philip was in the Home Guard when we lived at **Briston** near Melton Constable. I am proud to have his certificate signed by King George VI. I remember him telling me that one night, while he was out on patrol, he jumped over a gate and fell on to a courting couple laying the other side! He said he just ran off as fast as he could! On another occasion, I recall he came home from Home Guard duty looking like a drowned rat.

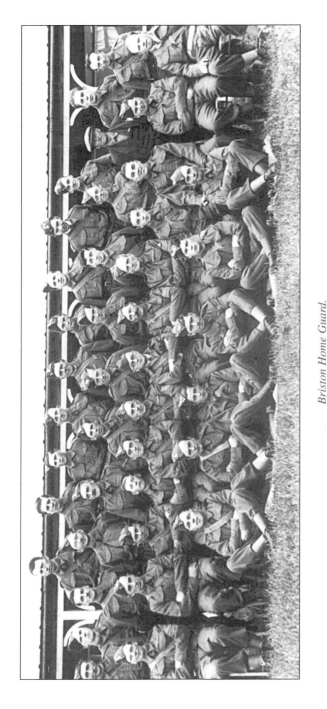

Briston Home Guard.

Back Row: T. Fuller; L. Kingsley, J. Bishop, T. Eggleton, G. Kinsley, D. Bishop, B. Sewell, A. Adams, J. Gemmel.
3rd Row: H. Bishop, B. Fisher, S. Fox, B. Durrant, P. Bunkell, H. Stearman, B. Simmonds, F. Miller, B. Cadler, G. Owens, H. Baxter;
J. Brown, M. Sexton.
2nd Row: A. Partridge, J. Stacy, W. Eggleton, J. Taberham, S. Mears, W. Stimpson, J. Carter, B. Blyth, B. Oliver, G. Newman,
E. Coleman, F. Fisher; G. Reynolds.
Front Row: B. Withers, C. Hagon, R. Barham, W. Fisher; G. Bunkell, ? Neal.
Photo with kind permission of Mrs. M. Race

Apparently he was near Mr. Carter's farm and the vicarage and accidentally fell into a small pond! We had a good laugh at the time — after all, it was all in a good cause!

Mr J. Nichols,
Sheringham

I joined the **Bodham** Home Guard in 1940 when I was 16. Our meetings were held in Bodham Jubilee Hall. I was used to parading, as I was in the Church Lads Brigade at this time. We used to do guard duty in the shepherd's hut belonging to a farmer, Mr Newall, on a small hill at Lower Bodham. Later, our guard position was a small bungalow called Frog's Hall, which was situated on the same farm.

I remember doing guard duty every Friday night with two uncles of mine, Mark Platford (a World War I veteran) and Herbert Whitton. Our Sergeant was Mr Sayer, who used to be landlord of the Red Hart public house in Bodham.

One night when we were on guard, there was a big air raid on Norwich and the planes came directly over Bodham from the coast; in fact we followed their trails to Norwich. We were on the main Holt road (A148) at Bodham, watching with great consternation, when we heard a very loud swishing noise approaching. Suddenly there was a big flash . . . . . it was a barrage balloon which had broken free. The trailing cable had struck the overhead electricity wires, resulting in a huge flash as the barrage balloon exploded in a ball of fire. It was extremely frightening.

One thing about being in the Home Guard was that it gave you a chance to wear a uniform, which allowed us to go to dances in the local WAAF and army camps! So there was some good times — some not so good!

We had a scheme one Saturday when the Regular Army stationed in this area, planned an exercise. They were to attack our Home Guard to see if we could protect our village. We treated this very seriously, digging slit trenches along the main and by-roads. The ladies of the village arranged to feed us all in the village hall; it was a really united effort. Unfortunately, the Army suddenly had orders to move (we learned later that they had gone to France), and the exercise was called off at 11pm! So we had to eat all the supper — rabbit stew and dumplings, swede and potatoes, followed by apple tart. This was very welcome after we had been laying in the trenches for hours in the cold! I joined the

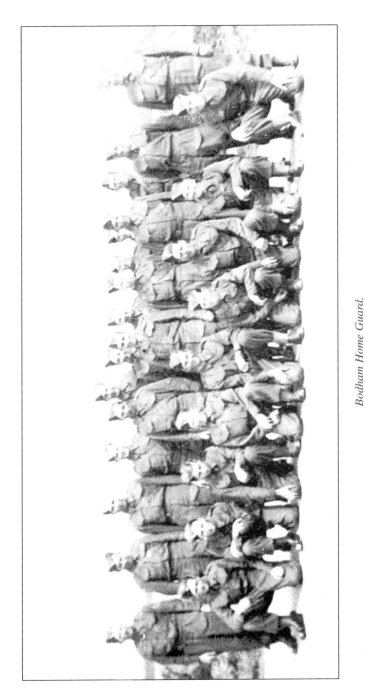

Bodham Home Guard.
Back Row, Standing, Left to right: G. Bumphrey, W. Sayer, L. Cooper, A. Gant, M. Bullimore, F. Sayer, D. Gant, (W. Beeton Lt),
G. Thirtle, G. Wells, G. Cooper, W. Cooper, H. Whitton, A. Digby, Sgt. Oakford, Sgt. A. Sayer.
Front Row: R. Nichols, A. Cooper, G. Coe, H. Holland, G. Cooper, J. Bacon, W. Bullock, S. Nichols, J. Nichols.
Photo with kind permission of Mr. J. Nichols

127

Army in July 1942 (the day after my 18th birthday) at Norwich Barracks. On my second night, there was another bad air raid on Norwich. I was put on the barracks hill with a Bren gun section and was quite frightened in my first real action.

In the Army one of the exercises was attacking the Home Guard at Louth in Lincolnshire. I knew they had their HQ in a local pub, so I managed to get captured quite early on, thereby having a warm afternoon and evening with a nice drink and a good fire. At least, I had learnt that much from being in the Home Guard earlier!

Mr W. J. Wade,
Wicklewood.

My first memories are of when I joined the LDV — Local Defence Volunteers, which was later renamed the Home Guard. We were part of the 9th Battalion, Norfolk Home Guard. When I first joined, I was called a "runner," and on my nights of duty, I had to go to Wicklewood searchlight and sleep in the army hut with the searchlight crew. We were to take messages to our officer in charge.

Our uniform was an armlet with the letters LDV on it, and we had a forage cap. When the Home Guard was formed, we were issued with army uniform battledress, leggings, which were real leather in the raw state — we had to clean them with brown boot polish until they had turned brown. We had a real leather belt and the Norfolk's cap badge, army black boots and a Lee Enfield rifle.

We had one night a week drill which was at Wicklewood village hall. There was a regular army sergeant who used to come from Wymondham for rifle drill and marching — he also gave us instructions on how to clean and fire a rifle. As time went on, we were issued with Sten guns, Bren guns, a Lewis gun and a Spigot Mortar. We had rifle practice at the army range at Kimberley with live ammunition. Sometimes, we had aircraft recognition with models and silhouettes, also grenade practice in some sandpits at Wymondham. We then had gas drill and had to go into a gas chamber with tear gas. There were exercises with the regular army which lasted all weekend — the army were the "enemy," and of course they always won!

Our main duty was guarding bridges. Our bridge was the Warren Hill bridge between Wymondham and Kimberley, on the train line to Dereham, Fakenham and Wells. We had an old gypsy caravan which stood on the verge of the Warren Hill.

There were four of us on duty; two would sleep for two hours while the other two were on guard. We went on duty at dusk and came off at dawn. I used to have to go to work the next morning like everyone else — there was no day off the next day! I can't remember if we got paid or not.

I was 16 years old when I joined the Home Guard in 1940, and was probably the youngest member of the Wicklewood Platoon. There were 41 men in this unit. In 1943 I was called up and served three years in the Royal Navy.

Cecil B. Davey,
Holt.

I clearly remember the days prior to the outbreak of the 1939 War — a war which we thought would never come. However, on the 3rd September 1939, our lives were changed. All those who had left school were directed into work of national importance and everyone had to do something for the war effort, whether it be ARP or the LDV or the Auxiliary Fire Service.

As soon as I was old enough I had to join the Home Guard, which was very interesting at the start. We were taught by regular soldiers who were stationed nearby — first to march correctly and then we did square-bashing drill. We learned to use a rifle, and had arms drill and practice at targets. We were also instructed how to keep everything in good order. My uniform was very smart — the creases were kept in by soaping the insides of the trouser legs and pressing them hard.

Little did we know that in the event of an invasion we were to play a big part in watching at night for paratroopers landing in important places, like railway stations and bridges.

In Wroxham we were one of the few Home Guard Units to have a flotilla of fast launches with a central bollard to take a Lewis gun. God help them if they had been attacked by a German fighter plane or strafed by bullets. They were only wooden, rich men's afternoon teaboats which patrolled the Broads. They were manned by chaps who were ex-skippers of what we called "floating hotels" and a few marine engineers.

There were some lighter sides to the working of the Home Guard. Some men were very frightened, for example, when we were being trained to throw hand grenades at Cawston by the army. We were told to stand in a trench and shown how to lean back with the left arm out, pointing to the direction of the flight, and retaining the pin. A man named Freddie dropped his grenade back into the trench in panic. I picked it up very quickly and threw it as hard as I could. It exploded in the air about 30 feet away. I went over to speak to a friend named Peter when I noticed a hole in his gas mask case. When we took the gas mask out a piece of shrapnel the size of an old halfpenny fell out. He said "Don't you think I was lucky!!" (or words to that effect!!). I cannot quote the words the army sergeant uttered. On the same day we had a machine for firing Molotov bottles when one got stuck in the barrel, so it was not all sweetness and light!

When we became proficient we were attached to a section guarding Wroxham Station. There were two of us by the old water tower next to what the locals called the viaduct (an iron bridge over the river) which is still there. At the same time another pair patrolled the village side, whilst the rest of the men tried to sleep on the waiting room floor on the tower side. One night we were patrolling when we spotted someone/thing moving, coming down from the viaduct end, very low down near the ground. It was a rather steep embankment and my mate Jimmy, who was the senior man asked me what to do. I said, "Challenge him. You know the words. Halt, who goes there?" Jimmy did this three times, but with no response from the person/thing creeping along. Jimmy challenged him/it again and then asked me what he should do. I replied, "Fire a round overhead". Eventually, with much trepidation, he fired his gun. You can imagine the panic in the waiting room when the men heard the shot. They were jumping down on to the railway line crossing over to our side. Meanwhile the person who was creeping up the bank was shouting "Its only me. Don't shoot. I am the new Guard commander testing you out!" He did not do that again. Jimmy was told off for firing but his response was that the man should have called out at the first challenge. The reply to that was, "What if it had been a Jerry paratrooper?"

I have always boasted that I am the only member of the Home Guard to have been court martialled!! I turned up for parade in the Assembly Rooms at Wroxham (not there now). As I entered, my rifle was confiscated by a chap who was to become my brother-in-law. My hat was removed by an old school mate and then two more "friends" marched me through the village (where I had spent all my life), over the water bridge. We passed lots of people whom I knew and who knew me. I heard several ask what I had been up to. I was then asked to meet a Captain — a man who had known me all my life. I was not at all pleased about this and I asked what it was all about. I was told to salute the officer (I could not do so as I had no hat). I was then told to say "Sir", but he still had not told me the reason I was there. I asked him again and by this time I was bending over across his desk, when I spotted my record card lying there. He finally advised me that I had been absent from parade from October to February. I agreed with him and asked him (very politely!) if he could read, whereupon he got very angry and said he would call in the guard. I said, "Before you do so, read what it says on the reverse side of the card". It clearly stated on the back of the card that because I was employed by the Ministry of Agriculture and Fisheries I was exempt from routine parades. With this I walked out and went back to the Assembly Rooms, picked up my hat and rifle and went to the Adjutant's house. He just could not believe my story, but the Captain could not have been nicer after that!!

Mr Ronald High
Old Costessey,

I served in the Ringland Platoon and joined a battle squad. I was very happy in that unit. Many times I had to cycle from Costessey for parade. There were three of us in the firing pit during practice. Sometimes, we had fired our rifles so much, we couldn't hold them, because they got so hot with smoke pouring from the barrels; so we had to wait until they were cool again.

One of my proudest days, was when we were firing the Spigot Mortar. We had six shells and five had missed! So they let me try the last one — yes, I hit the target which went up in the air. A terrific roar went up and I was the hero of that day and didn't have to cycle home!

I was proud of my rifle which I had with me all of the time. I was lucky in having a very good overcoat but my blouse was not a very good fit! We didn't like the Sten gun which seemed a lot of trouble and I wonder if they would have been any good in an emergency.

Britain was in great danger in those days and I'm glad people will learn of the part we played. I remember the many times when our planes returned from bombing raids. Sometimes, they crawled home with one of their engines on fire.

Mr Clem Lond,
Sheringham.

I decided to join the Home Guard instead of the ATC squadron at Bungay Grammar School, in 1943. I was issued with a uniform, rifle and bayonet (Lee Enfield, I believe) and a bandolier of 60 rounds of ammunition. I remember that there were two meetings per week, including Sunday morning. From time to time, our company visited Thetford rifle ranges. We were transported on a 3 ton lorry. There was drill practice and some .22 rifle shooting locally. I did the company notices as spelling was not the sergeant's forte!

Mr Norman Barrie,
Bawburgh.

When I joined the Home Guard or LDV as it was known at the start of the war, we were given a thin overall uniform with an armband, rifle, bandolier and 40 rounds of ammunition. At that time, I had never fired a rifle and realised later, that I would never have hit an enemy! I was away from there before the Home Guard came into being.

The Butts – Wortham Ling.

Mr G. Sturgeon,
Diss.

Though I was at school at the time of the Home Guard, I recall that a large number of Home Guard men came over the county border to **Wortham** for shooting practice. On the **Ling,** over the river from Blooms, Bressingham, there is a hill which I believe was made by Diss Volunteer Corps, commanded by Mr. Gaze, at the beginning of the First World War. Dug into the hill is a concrete butt for targets, which was used by the Home Guard for rifle practice. It still survives to this day!

Mr. R. T. Hines,
Brockdish.

I was in the Needham unit of the Home Guard — there were between 14 and 18 of us. We linked up with other units at Harleston and **Brockdish.**

One day we were all called out at the time the Germans tried to invade us. We were at our posts from midday on Saturday until 8pm Sunday evening. I believed that the Germans *did* try to land and that they were burnt alive on the sea. We certainly had a lot of training with other Home Guard units and the Regular Army, using all kinds of weapons. This training included weekend exercises and summer camps.

Mr H. P. Amies,
Poringland.

I put down my name for the LDV, as the Home Guard was originally called, 10 minutes after the radio announcement of its planned formation. Several weeks before training began, though I was at Poringland, I went to Stoke Holy Cross with Mr Alec Bussey, who became our lieutenant. I suppose I was one of the youngest members of my unit (age 17 years), and I don't think we thought much of spirit or morale. Our training was at the Stoke Scout HQ, and also the Red Lion! We did guard duty at the post office and the telephone exchange. Exercises included gaining entry to a radar installation masts enclosure, with local army and RAF personnel. We also had to guard a crashed Dornier 2172 at West Poringland. Most of us adjourned to the pub after exercises — evenings and Sunday mornings, where we mixed with men from the local sites of searchlight or AA batteries, and of course the WAAFs from the radar stations! Many of my unit were

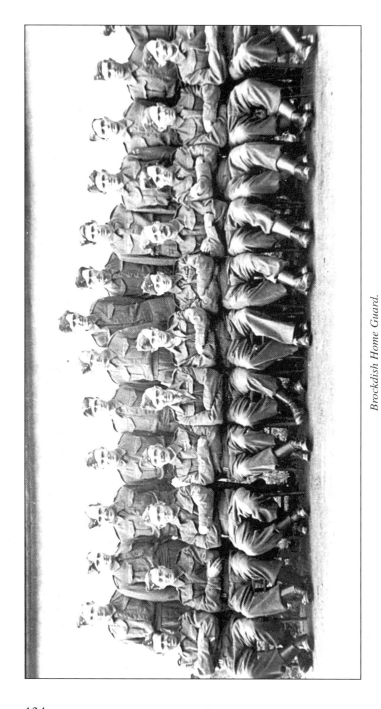

Brockdish Home Guard.

Standing, from left: C. Lord, B. Reader, R. Saunders, B. Lancaster, R.T. Hines, T. Broome, C. Goodwin, W. Reeve.

Seated: N. Flatman, ?, ?, W. Chelves (Sgt), ?, ?, W. Finch, E. Shemming, ?, C. Debenham.

Photo with kind permission of Mr. R.T. Hines

First World War veterans, who told us the inevitable, "Now when I was . . . . . we did it this way!"

It was a job that had to be done as well as working from 8am to 8pm every day and 8am to 4pm on Saturdays. Personally, I did not "feel" we would be invaded, even though we did have to search for parachuting aircraft crews. In fact, a parachute lay about 100 metres from the crashed Dornier and at first it was thought to be one of the crew who had baled out. But it was later identified as a land mine parachute that had been blown away from one of the land mines that were dropped that night in addition to the thousands of incendiaries, all of which "missed" Norwich, which was surrounded by balloons and cables.

I remember that we were taken in army trucks from the depot at Framlingham Earl Hall to the range at Fritton for rifle practice. We also did hand grenade practice in various local gravel pits, with Mills fragmentation bombs, "Sticky" bombs. The idea was that you waited patiently for a passing enemy tank and then stuck it, forcibly, to break the glass, either on to the driver's visor or the track wheels to disable the tank and/or driver! Then, when the crew opened the hatch, you had to lob a 3 second fuse Mills bomb inside! Training had its humorous moments! Actually, "Sticky" bombs would blow a 6 inch hole in ½" thick steel plate. You just had to step aside to avoid the flying handle! The explosive force went towards the surface it was stuck to.

At one point, I was transferred to the Signals section which trained at Framlingham Pigot. We had cross country exercises of flag semaphore signalling and surveyed church towers for this possibility. The signalling we had to learn, both Morse and semaphore, was for me, quite easy as I had learned it as a boy scout a few years earlier. The duties at night were more to my liking as it meant sleeping by the telephone in Kirby Bedon Rectory in the hallway, with a "runner" for assistance.

If any messages came through, in theory they were written on a message pad and the "runner" took it to the CO, Major Moore who lived next door. We started duty at 10pm and finished at 6am. The only message I ever took was that parachutists were seen on Acle Marshes at about 2am. My "runner" had arrived after the pub closed at 11pm! I could not get any sense from him and so took the message myself to the CO's house. Then I couldn't rouse him either! So I used the "old gravel thrown at the window dodge", and a very irate CO appeared at the window asking:

"What . . . . was I playing at?"

"Message from HQ Sir"

"What is it about?"

"HQ suspects 2 parachutists on Yarmouth or Acle marshes, Sir".

"Go back to bed its not our area!!"

He slammed the window shut. I obeyed orders and went back to my camp bed. It seemed that I had only just got to sleep again, when the telephone rang.

"Disregard message of 2am; all units to stand down".

I went back to sleep after I'd written it down and it was still on the pad when I next went on duty.

A few other memories include the fact that for a time, before I was transferred to the Signals section, I was in charge of No. 1, on a Lewis Machine gun, which got me a Lance Corporal's stripe. One night I had a JC88 in the sights of the Lewis gun, but no one gave me an order to "Fire"!

My family were "bombed out" for several weeks, losing the roof of our bungalow in Poringland, while a UXB landed just across the road from us. But the UXB which fell on our Home Guard HQ in Stoke was at the home of our officer, Mr Bussey. Next day we had to move all our ammunition and stores, including phosphorous bombs to safety. The UXB was eventually dug out and exploded harmlessly in a nearby field.

My final memory is of the "Stand Down" parade at the Theatre Royal and the march through the city of Norwich. After this I joined the Royal Observer Corps.

Mr. David Hanner,
Long Stratton.

I belonged to the **Starston** Company of the 14th Battalion Norfolk Home Guard. Our HQ was at the Coach House at the Rectory. We were lucky that we had a few old soldiers from the 1st World War, including our Sergeant Sampson who had been a scout in the desert. He was a canny old soldier, and when we had been on manoeuvres one Sunday morning, attacking an imaginary machine gun post, he led us through ditches and hedgerows on our stomachs and completely surprised the "enemy" (Harleston Home Guard), by coming up from their rear. Their officer said we had cheated coming from behind! But Sarge Sampson pointed out that you don't cheat in war, which got a big laugh and the regular army umpire said we had won.

Starston Home Guard 14th Norfolks, October 1944.

Back Row, Standing Left to Right: W. Mark, A. Hanner, W. Morris, ? Hanner, J. Flemming, F. Newsome, J. Ward, D. Smith, D. Nobbs, F. Smith.

Middle Row, Standing: M. Pilch, A. Adams, C. Snowling, F. Gray, R. Riches, D. Hanner, H. Stocks, Major Gilcrest, C. Lang, W. Meadows.

Third Row, Sitting: L.Cpl. Thurlow, Cpl. Moore, Sgt. Adcock, Sgt. Denny, Maj. Taylor, Sgt. Sampson, Sgt. Gower, Cpl. Goodswen, L.Cpl. Hanner.

Front Row, Sitting: F. Spacman, B.Chapman, C. Musk, W. Peck, K. Leftley, J. Adams.

Photo with kind permission of Mr. David Hanner.

On another occasion Sergeant Adcock was told to take a few men to a certain map reference and defend it from us, who had to attack it. Well, we worked out the map reference, then very carefully encircled it. With bayonets fixed, we moved in. But there was nobody there! It was 9.30pm, so our Corporal said we must have made a mistake and called the exercise off. After we had been dismissed, we decided to go to the Old Starston Gate for a drink. But there sitting in the bar was Sergeant Adcock with his men! He'd been there all evening. The crafty old soldier had altered the map reference!!

One night when we were on guard at Starston Bridge near the church, at about 11pm, we saw what appeared to be a pair of white feet, nothing else, coming up the road! We challenged but got no answer, and the white feet disappeared up the church hill. Naturally, we were both a bit scared and were still discussing what these white feet might be about half an hour later, when they came back down the hill from the church! In the pitch darkness, we challenged again but still got no answer. As we had no ammunition, we ran across to investigate. To our surprise and relief, we found that the feet belonged to the church fire stoker, who was stone deaf!! He had been wearing a dark blue boiler suit and white tennis shoes! I still wonder what would have happened if we had our ammo! This episode happened in the early days of the war before we were fully armed!

One winter's moonlit night after parade, we saw a pheasant up a tree at the top of Starston Church Hill. One of the gang said, "I'll have that bird for Sunday dinner". He put a round in his rifle and killed the pheasant stone dead. But at the other end of the village, Sergeant Sampson, on his way home, heard the shot and recognised it as a rifle. Next Sunday morning, we had an ammo inspection and my mate got into deep trouble. He had to stand and watch us drill like a dunce in school.

Another amusing memory concerned Sergeant Adcock. He always went to parade without an overcoat when it was raining! Then he would go to Major Gilcrest, our Quartermaster, when the parade had finished and ask for an overcoat to go home with! By the end of the war the old soldier had FOUR brand new overcoats!

Mr. William H. Mills,
Norwich.

I was only 14 years old when I joined the Home Guard and I wasn't the only one of that age! I had left school in 1941 at 14 and went to work at Barnard's Factory on the Rackheath Road. While I was there they made parts for aeroplanes, shells and other war munitions. My pay in the office was 12/6d a week, and to get more, I did aircraft spotting about two hours a day from a tower above the office for 2/6d. In charge of us spotters was a Captain Wright of the Home Guard, and he recruited me and at least three other boys.

One Saturday night we had a manoeuvre with the Regular Army from the Nelson and Britannia Barracks. I was the company "runner" and was Captain Wright's man. They gave me a Thompson Sub-Machine gun. I remember that it poured with rain all night. Soldiers wearing capes were lying about over Mousehold Heath. But I was lucky as I was in the dry in a shed with one of the NCOs whose father was landlord of The Brickmakers Arms on Sprowston Road, Norwich. Well, we were drinking tea and whisky for most of the night! When I saw my pal Basil Garner on Sunday morning, he asked me how I had got on the night before. When I told him, he blew his top, as he had got soaked to the skin! Apparently they had called the whole exercise off at midnight and he was stuck down Blue Boar Lane, Wroxham Road, but no one had told him the news!

I must say the drill and the weapon training I received while I was in the Home Guard, helped me a lot when I joined the Regular Army at the age of 17½ years. Before I was 19, I was a Corporal, serving for nearly 2½ years in Palestine and feel proud of what I achieved. I look back on my days in the Home Guard and the army with many happy memories.

Mr. Arthur J. Kirby,
Fakenham.

In 1940 I was working for the LNER at Thorpe Station, Norwich, as a messenger lad. In May or June 1940, I joined the Home Guard, Railway Section. Our platoon consisted of between 40 to 50 men, all of whom were railway employees.

We trained with the Regular Army some weekends at Britannia Barracks and elsewhere. Our platoon was very pleased to have amongst our weapons, one Tommy gun (of which I was the proud owner), one Lewis gun and .303 rifles. Our commander was Captain Laurence Rowbury, who later became a major. Our main duty was to mount guard at Thorpe Junction signal box, which controlled all railway lines in and out of Norwich. This guard was every night from 7pm to 7am the next morning. In 1942 I left the Home Guard and the railway and joined the Royal Marines, seeing service around the world.

Mr. G. Neave,
Norwich.

I served in the Home Guard for about a year in 1944, before joining the Grenadier Guards. The only comparison was the last word "Guards"! I was only 17 years old at the time and very keen. Most of the other chaps in my unit were World War I veterans or farm workers. For the married ones who liked a drink, the Sunday morning and evening parades were a good chance to get out for a drink at the local pub at Neatishead.

I remember one evening we had to report at 10.30pm in Neatishead Street. We then cycled to the radar station, where we had to patrol through some blackcurrant bushes! We had to look for someone, "possibly a spy", who had been flashing a light. Well, the men had been in the White Horse pub most of the evening and they were laughing and shouting! If there had been anyone there he could have heard us leave Neatishead Street! It was more like beating at a pheasant shoot than a proper military patrol!

One Sunday morning, two of us were in a slit trench at Ludham Bridge. An officer came along and asked which area we were covering, so I told him. But when he asked my mate, his answer was "anything that fly over"! He couldn't see out of the trench; I'm 6 feet three but he was about a foot shorter! We went on guard at Ludham Bridge at night and an army lorry picked us up and

Thorpe Railway Station Home Guard.　　　*Photo with kind permission of Mr. A.J. Kirby.*

brought us home the next morning. One morning we were all in the lorry when someone said, "where's Derek?" Well, he was busy pulling up his eel lines which he had laid the previous evening!

Another Sunday while on an exercise we marched down Irstead Road, then we had to lay on the bank and look through a hedge with camouflage on. Well we had to stay there quite a time and one old chap in our unit picked some hogweed for his rabbits! Later, when we got dismissed, Charlie still had the hogweed under his arm! One night two chaps had come off guard and were laying down on their bed. The younger of the two men couldn't get to sleep because the other man, a World War I veteran, kept snoring! Well, the younger man took a mug of cold tea and poured some in the old chap's ear! The old chap jumped up and swore at the other man, whereupon the young man said "Don't talk to me like that, my father is Lord . . . . . .!" The old chap was undeterred and said, "I don't care who he is, he can be the King of England for all I care, but you're not pouring tea down my lugs!!"

While in the building trade, we built **5 *Spigot Mortar*** posts. There is still one on the green at ***Guist*** and another near Ludham Mill. We also built ammunition sheds for the Home Guard and at the Drayton store they had a Smith gun delivered; it was the only anti-tank type gun I ever saw.

Spigot Mortar on Guist Green.

Norwich Home Guard

Jack Church: 1st right standing.

My brother Jack Church died in 1981. He worked at Laurence Scott in Thorpe Road during the war, but we lived in Mount Pleasant, so his group could have been in that area.

Photographs with kind permission of Mrs. Joan Church, Norwich.

Jack Church: Back row, fifth from right.

Barbara Y. C. Smith,
Norwich.

My father was 36 when the Second World War began. He was employed in the highways department of Norfolk County Council, and because of the nature of his job and his age, he was exempt from active service. He therefore enlisted in the Home Guard in 1940 and served in it throughout the war.

I remember the rather tattered snapshot of Dad in his Home Guard uniform and the certificate he received, signed by King George VI. I'm not sure of the name of his unit but one of my sisters thinks that he sometimes went to the old Drill Hall on Chapel Field where the large roundabout is now. One thing that I can remember about dad's Home Guard days, was that he kept his gun in our grandfather clock case.

I remember that he spent a lot of time on Trowse Marshes keeping a watch for enemy planes and particularly anyone parachuting out of one. He told me that he went on a training course near Watton, at the same place as his unit had its initial training. He pointed out the exact field when we were driving one day along the Watton Road from Downham Market. The head of his unit was a Major Buckpit, who lived a few doors from us on Harvey Lane. Also our neighbour, William Dicks served in the same unit as dad. I remember dad telling me that two of the unit died; one got very wet on an exercise when he was already poorly and subsequently developed pneumonia. Another man was tragically killed during bayonet practice.

Mr. A. N. Other,
Diss.

I joined the LDV in 1940 at the time of the fall of France. At this point, there were no rifles for most of us except those few men in our unit who had served in the first World War. Of course, those members who had 12 bore shotguns, brought them along. Our headquarters for the Wilby and Hargham Platoon was at Hall Farm, Hargham, the home of our Lieutenant, George Howlett. We went on duty every three nights; guard would consist of four men who would be on duty from about 9.30pm until 6am the next morning. This was the pattern all year round.

The first rifles we received were Canadian Moss rifles which were very long. We also had a Lewis Machine gun from World

A Norwich Home Guard unit.
Leslie W.H. Smith: Second from left in row sitting on chairs.
Photo with kind permission of Barbara Y.C. Smith

Topcroft, Hardwick and Fritton Home Guard.

Front row: Fred Penn, Lenny Andrews, Ben Hickling, Mr: Chapman, Mr: Holman, Walter Ladbrooke, Mr: Hill, Jack Taylor, Walter Pigg, Charles Ainger.

First row: Alfred Mace, Lennie Rackham, Reg Elvin, Fred Moore, Arthur Reeder, David Potter, Walter Beckett, William Leatherstick, ?, Jack Waddelow.

Second row: Jack Vincent, George Pugney, Fred Vincent (Mrs. Vincent's late husband), ?, George Fairman, Joe Fisher, ?, Albert Tyrell, Clement Mobbs.

Back row: Philip Moore, Alan Catchpole, Sam Long, Charlie Taylor, ?, Jack Reeder, Charlie Dickinson, Spencer Purt, Jimmy Leggett, Frank Alexander.

Photo with kind permission of Mrs. M. Vincent

War I, but it was inclined to jam when fired! We were given some weapon training on the rifle range at Thetford. We also had some training in throwing live hand grenades in a local pit. On one occasion, someone in the company tried to throw the grenade but it hit the bank just in front causing the grenade to fall back under his feet! He was quickly pulled back behind a barrier by our Platoon Lieutenant before the grenade exploded! Regular arms drill was given and we received field training by the regulars. One day we were taken for battle training at Wymondham and were under fire by men of the Grenadier Guards. We had to crawl in gravel pits with machine gun bullets whizzing overhead! In addition to this type of training, we had shooting competitions with the Regular Army, which we generally won.

About a year after joining the Home Guard, we were issued with proper uniforms, tin hat, greatcoat, gas mask and a shorter rifle taking .300 ammunition. At a later date our platoon was issued with a Spigot Mortar which could be used against tanks! Our platoon also took part in a tank recognition test which was held at Cambridge. Our team finished about 9th, which was not bad considering the Home Guard was up against Regular Army teams from all over Eastern Command.

Mr F. W. Hudson,
Aylsham.

When I was in the Home Guard (1942-44), we met at Banningham Reading Room on Sunday mornings and on two nights per week, we went on guard at Roughton. We kept guard in pairs, taking turns to try and get some sleep. Our night duty post was about two miles from Cromer from where we kept watch for an invasion. Most of the foot boards on Cromer Pier were blown up to stop the enemy getting ashore easily. We used to attend the rifle range at West Runton. One Sunday morning, Major Gurney, our CO, bought a 40 gallon drum in an army vehicle to the recreation ground. He then placed a Sticky bomb on the drum and it burst the drum which blew several feet into the air! Then he placed another Sticky bomb on a square piece of iron which was about 2 inches thick — but that never went off! So he then placed another one of these bombs on the other side of the piece of iron. This time the demonstration was successful, as there was a big explosion and the iron was cracked in to several pieces!

Of course we used to go on route marches and do regular drill.

One Saturday night we spent at Fish Tail Woods, Northrepps and then did some more training on Sunday morning. Some Sunday mornings we would have a short service in Banningham Reading Room and Miss Olive Plume (now Mrs Googles), played the piano.

Mr Victor Woods,
Attleborough.

In 1940, I was 31 years old and working as a tree feller and sawmill worker, a "reserved" occupation. I joined the Home Guard as soon as it was formed. Our first task was to watch for parachutists. We had no weapons to start with and I cut a good stick from a hedge! It was fun looking for parachutes but I never saw any! On our first night on guard duty I was issued with a rifle and another man had a 12 bore which had been pinched! I remember that first night because the two of us walked about four miles to the Old Buckenham boundary. We stayed until 4am when it was daylight. Then my mate Taffy said he would show me how to unload a rifle. Well, it went off while he was showing me! As we were very near Taffy's home we went to see if his wife was alright. When we got there we found she had fainted.

Later on when the LDV became the Home Guard, we got some proper training by the Cheshire Regiment, who were stationed at Hargham Hall. We went on courses to set tank mines, detonate hand grenades, fire rifles, etc. I became a first class shot and I had to do all night guard duty at Attleborough Post Office. At the time that invasion was expected, we had orders to shoot people if they didn't stop when we called "HALT". One night a friend, Mr McNaught, had been to the pub and on his way home I told him to "HALT", and because he hesitated, I cocked my gun! McNaught said that when he heard that sound it was "the quickest he had ever been sobered up!" One night a new recruit in our unit was frightened because he heard the sound of boots on cobbles — he thought it was a Nazi! In fact when I said, "Stop you here!", it turned out to be a cat!!

One day we went to Roudham Heath for a demonstration of the Spigot Mortar. The target was a mound with a large sheet of steel to fire at. The weapon was meant to knock out a tank. Well, the steel sheet *was* hit low down and it shot into the air and all us onlookers had to run to get out of the way! As I was a good shot I was taught to operate a two inch mortar and a machine gun as well as land mines and hand grenades. One day we were all day

148

Cartoons of Attleborough Home Guard.
Mr. McNaught is mentioned by Mr. Victor Woods who kindly donated them.

Attleborough Home Guard Cartoons.
Kindly donated by Mr. Victor Woods

150

on the range and I fired about 900 mortars!

I remember on one occasion we were taken to some old stone workings on The Lizard at Wymondham, to train to throw hand grenades. Each man had to clean his own grenade so that it did not stick to his hand. Well, our officer was a schoolmaster, and when he demonstrated how to throw the grenade, it did not go in the right direction! In fact it landed very near other members of the Home Guard! Well, I hit the ground but Bob Brown, another member of my unit froze, so I grabbed him by the back of the neck and pulled him to the ground for safety!

One day, Captain Howlett took us with some new recruits to the butts at Elveden for target practice. They had never held a rifle before and shots were going all over the place and into the trees! One of the men whose nickname was "Spot", had been taken short, and suddenly he came crawling out of the woods where the stray shots had been landing! I remember the day when Gaymers, of Attleborough, was bombed. Well, my wife and some friends were nearby when the enemy plane came over. But they waved to the plane because they thought it was one of ours! The German rear gunner merely waved back, then dropped the bombs on Gaymers!!

We did long hours in the Home Guard. On Sundays we were out from 6.30am till 7.30pm, there was a parade once a week and we had guard duty one night a week. Of course we still had to go to work next day! Then there were the special exercises. We attended the big one at Wymondham and at the end of a tiring day, we were supposed to be picked up by army lorry. But the lorries did not appear and we had to *march* back to Attleborough along the old A11. I remember that they put the men with the longest legs at the front so we would get home more quickly! On another occasion we were out all night in a potato field. So in the morning we took some potatoes back home and had a good fry-up!

The week before D Day 1944, I got called up as a "reserve" on stand-by, as I was a good shot. But I never went to France. We had good old times in the Home Guard and I wasn't frightened of the Germans! I'm not sure how many men there were in my unit, but after stand down in December 1944, there was a special dinner laid on for us. Well, a lot more came to the dinner than ever attended the parade!!

Mr. Fred Tillett seen first left on the back row. He joined the Red Cross in 1943 and is seen here at Sea Palling. Photo with kind permission of Mr. F. Tillett

Mr. H. Kidd,
Cambs.

I was a member of the Southrepps unit of the Home Guard. Two of our senior officers were Major Gurney of Northrepps and Mr Barclay who lived at Trimingham. The "Dad's Army" TV series reminds me of our squad!! I was in charge of the EY rifle. I am now 85 and often smile at the amusing little incidents that happened.

Mr. F. A. Tillett,
Hickling.

I was a stretcher bearer and first aid man in the 11th Battalion of the Norfolk Home Guard and remained in it until the Home Guard was stood down in December 1944. I can remember the first night I was called out to the searchlight. It was snowing hard so I had to walk and push my bike and of course we had no lights. The searchlight was right down East field on the marshes and I lived in a house about half way down that field. A first aider had to be on duty at the searchlight every night. It was very cold some nights, as we were not far from the sea at Sea Palling. Later the searchlight was moved to the playing field which was not so far to go, as I had to cycle six miles to work and then home again after my Home Guard duty, Then we moved again to the corn mill and watched from there — seven Home Guards and one first aider. We used to sleep on the second floor and watch out at the top from where we had a good view all round the mill.

The Regular Army was at Hickling throughout the war and I got to know many of them. Some married local girls and still live in Hickling. As well as the Home Guard, there were units of the ARP, Fire Service and Red Cross based in Hickling. I joined the Red Cross when the Home Guard was stood down in 1944.

Mr. E. F. Cook,
Scole.

Within two hours of the appeal on the radio, my father, H W.Cook, was at the local police station volunteering for the LDV. After a short time, armbands were issued – black LDV on light khaki canvas.

My father was put in charge of the Carleton Rode village unit. A shepherd's hut on wheels, was placed at the top of a rise for the unit's headquarters. From this position, there was a very good view of the surrounding countryside. When the change in name to Home Guard came in, everyone got uniforms and NCOs were appointed, by which time my father carried "pips". The arrival of Canadian rifles, Molotov cocktails and the Northover Projector, meant that the headquarters of the unit had to be moved to the end building of my father's premises, a garage business he had established. Here the weapons and ammunition could be safely stored.

Mr. R. Pitcher,
Saham Toney.

I was in the Home Guard when I was about 17 or 18 years old, before I joined the RAF. At the time I lived in a village called Tottington, which is now in the Stanford Battle area. I remember that we were drilled by a regular army corporal from a searchlight battery in the area. We used to have training on Sunday mornings, which included getting from one field to another without being seen.

One night I was on duty with Tom Spragg, who was a lot older than me. We had an old shepherd's hut on Tuddenham Corner as a base. But there was only room for one person to sleep, so Tom said I could lay down inside, while he would sit on an old upturned pail by the fireplace. Suddenly, there was a clatter! Tom had fallen off the pail and at the same time, the German planes came over to bomb Bodney airfield! So Tom said, "Lets get out of here boy; they may be dropping paratroopers!" Well, we spent about seven or eight hours looking in the woods nearby! "No more sleeping in that hut", said Tom. When we went off duty at 6am next morning, we were pretty tired!

Mr V.C. Fenn,
Swanton Morley.

I was one of 120 men in No.3 Platoon of 17 Battalion from Bintree, County School, Guist and Wood Norton whose first commander was Captain Algy Garrod.

I firmly believe that we would have "done our bit" in resisting an invader, even though in the early days we had very little equipment. Soon after Dunkirk, I remember seeing the Inns of Court regiment (a London territorial regiment), very smartly dressed with plumes in their caps at a parade. They were marching with sticks over their shoulders instead of rifles! I was quite shocked to see this and it showed how short of equipment we were.

Mr. A. Jermany,
Wicklewood.

I was 19 when I joined the LDV in Wicklewood, where Major Jack Youngman was the officer. I remember going to the village hall to volunteer on the day in 1940 that the LDV was announced. To start with, I was not allowed a gun and my job was as a "runner" to take messages to and from the searchlight which was near the waterworks. There were 50 men in the Wicklewood Platoon and we drilled at the old village hall. We trained with the Kimberley unit and in general it was quite enjoyable. Guard duty involved guarding the waterworks and the railway bridge. We had a caravan as a base at the railway bridge and we did two nights guard duty per week. We used to go for rifle practice on the range at the Stanford Battle Area.

It was some time before we all got issued with a rifle, but by 1941 everyone in the platoon had a gun! I was very happy in the Home Guard and had no sense of fear. We enjoyed a good supper while on searchlight duty, and in those days, there were *three* pubs in the village!

From our observation point, we could see the German planes coming over to bomb Coventry and elsewhere. I remember too, seeing bombs dropping on Norwich and near Wymondham station. I was at Gaymers of Attleborough when it was bombed. The planes seem to follow the 8.30 train into the target!

Mr. A. J. Howlett,
Wreningham.

I joined the local unit of the Home Guard in 1942. My father was a lieutenant and in charge of training. I was only in the unit for a year or so before I was conscripted as a regular. However, my Home Guard experience and training was a very good preparation for the Regular Army and my father, who had been in the First World War, made an important contribution to that training. We had regular rifle practice and our company did very well in battalion shooting competitions. We used to shoot at the Watton range and also took part in exercises in which we sometimes put the regulars out of action! In one exercise, we had to pretend that some parachutists had dropped. My role was to be a parachutist and to camouflage myself, hiding in a tree.

Mrs F. Duffield,
Gressenhall.

My husband Fred joined the Home Guard in 1940, and he was in it throughout the war, because he was a farmer and in a "reserved" occupation. They had no weapons to start with but had to attend regular meetings at the Reading Room in Gressenhall. One of his duties was guarding the searchlight at Longham.

Mrs B. Bishop,
Deopham.

I remember that my father, Thomas Percy Davey, was in charge of the **Snetterton** Home Guard. He joined right at the start when it was known as the LDV. He obtained an old fashioned shepherd's hut, where the men did guard duty, two at a time. There were bunk beds and a stove inside and playing cards to while away the time waiting for instructions, etc.

Although the men seemed to have some fun in the Home Guard, there were some old soldiers in the Snetterton unit who took it very seriously.

My father was a very big man — he weighed 23 stone — and at first, they could not get him a pair of trousers which would fit. The HQ of my father's unit of the Home Guard was at the thatched house just past the "Hole in the Wall" in Snetterton. Home Guard meetings used to go on until the small hours on some nights. My father's unit were taken to the rifle range at Thetford, where they

The Old Post Office, Snetterton – HQ of Snetterton Home Guard.

were trained by the regulars. I know that Home Guard ammunition was kept at our house, including Molotov cocktails and phosphorous bombs. At the end of the war, these bombs were buried in our garden!

I remember that there were anti-aircraft guns and a searchlight where the petrol station is today on the A11. There was a base there run by British Army regulars and there were about 20 pillboxes in the area near the A11.

Thomas Percy Davey.
Photo with kind permission of Mrs. B. Bishop

Mr. Sidney Bishop,
Larling.

At the start of the war I was a farm labourer and when I joined the Home Guard, I still had to milk 30 cows before I went on parade! I remember that right at the start, about 20 of us reported to the School House, ***Larling,*** which was the HQ of the Home Guard. The CO was Lt Larwood and our sergeant was known as "Buffy". We received an armband and after about 3 weeks, we were measured for uniform. Early on we went to the rifle range and took whatever guns we had ourselves. It was 12 months before proper rifles arrived! I remember that our unit had rifles, grenades and two pistols! We also got our first ammunition, which was dished out in clips of five cartridges.

The day the rifles arrived, we had to assemble in the road and the CO showed us how to hold, load and fire the guns. In the first practice out went the window of the school house! As I had a problem with one eye, I was given a revolver and I became the unit's "runner".

We had regular training and often had to crawl through bogs at night! We usually managed to finish up at the pub though! On Sundays, we trained for 2 hours in the morning. Then we would stay at the pub until 2pm and after that, I went back to the farm to milk the cows again! However, we ***did*** take the Home Guard seriously and did as we were told. We were always ready for action. I think that the Home Guard reflected the strong sense of community at that time. But it was a relief when the Home Guard was stood down in 1944. We had to hand all of our equipment in except our boots and overcoats!

The HQ Larling Home Guard was the house next to Larling School.

I can still recall some incidents. At Harling railway station there was an old wooden hangar from World War I. One day, two of us were in the field of carrots behind the hangar, when a plane came over, which had followed the train in and hit the hangar! We hit the ground among the carrots!

One Saturday, two of us were guarding Larling bridge, when a message came through that the enemy were approaching! The Regular Army used to test us like this. Actually, it was someone coming from the pub, but we still challenged them in the proper way!

A couple of fields up from the Larling cross roads was a shepherd's hut which was used for fire watching. Nearby lived an old boy who knew everything, and on fire watch duty we would make tea and roast potatoes. One night some of the men locked the old man in the shepherd's hut for a joke and I went up to let him out.

Mr. Ray Allen,
Cley.

I was a member of a regular army assault squad stationed on the Cornish coast. I used to get agricultural leave and when I came back to Cley, the CO of the local Home Guard, asked me if I would help with the training of his men. Well, when I first saw them on parade it was quite something! They had no drill sense and some didn't even have their boots done up! But they were ready enough in their own manner. Their rifles were spotless and they knew every inch of the surrounding countryside. There were no rules in the Cley Home Guard, but they reckoned they knew how to shoot Germans alright! They had all kinds of ambushes to deal with the Germans if they did land. They were very confident and on a particularly windy night, one of them said, "what do you want to go on duty tonight for? — the Germans won't come in this weather!"

I remember that the Home Guard sergeant was a bit like Sgt Wilson on "Dad's Army". During military manoeuvres, he said, "Would you mind doing" . . . etc, no orders were given! One day he *asked* me to man a road block. Well, a couple came up the road and as there was no response to the "Halt" challenge, I put one up the breech! "Get out of the ------ way, I'm attached to the West Yorkshires", one of them said. So I asked him for his paybook, pricked his arse with my bayonet and marched him round to the guard room! Some of the West Yorkshires were manning the beaches at Cley and I recall that there was a POW camp for the Italians next door.

One day there was a competition for all Home Guard units with the Vickers machine gun. They asked me to be in the team and the Cley Home Guard won the competition, though *my* skills played a part! I used to like coming home on leave and going along to the Home Guard with its relaxed atmosphere, though on one occasion it was as well that I was on the alert! It was at hand grenade practice at Blakeney. I noticed that during the demonstration, a lever had come off a grenade, but no one had noticed; there were seven seconds, so I ordered the platoon to "Throw" and explained to the CO afterwards why I had interfered in his grenade demonstration! In fact, I had saved the lives of some members of the Cley Home Guard that day.

There was no fear of an invasion among the men of the Cley unit. One of them was in charge of ringing the church bells if any German did land! Although their methods were rather unorthodox, they were always ready in their own way. They did not waste bullets and if the Germans had landed, the Cley lot would have done more damage than a regiment of soldiers!! Once, an aircraft came down near Blakeney Point and the parachutists landed on the salt marshes and tried to get to Holkham Hall. They were swiftly captured by the Home Guard. On another occasion, the air raid siren went off and we saw one man running down the road with his trousers under his arm. When we asked him where he was going, he replied, "Home!" I'd better say no more about that story!

When the war was over, there was a big street party in Cley. Everyone contributed and there was singing, dancing and free drinks all round! As a regular soldier, I was used to a much stricter and disciplined organization, but I always enjoyed my times with the Cley Home Guard.

Mr. Derek Daniels,
Morley St. Peter.

My dad was a sergeant in the Home Guard. One night the Morley Platoon had orders to guard the railway bridge at Spooner Row, about two miles away. Dad went on sentry duty with two colleagues. When he returned next morning, he was tired, cold, and a little bit annoyed! At breakfast he told us, "I have told Jack (that was dad's CO), I will sit up till the cows come home, defending my wife and family but, I won't go to Spooner Row to spend a night guarding a blooming railway bridge while soldiers less than 200 yards away are sleeping! It was a good job that Tom Lord's cows were in the field next to the railway line — at least I had *some* company".

The Home Guard met in the village hall. I remember the church parades and dad told us about the "square bashing" up Buck Lane, where the platoon would sometimes "go missing" for the best part of the exercise! Perhaps they were having a quick pint in the local or enjoying a "fag". Only the boys in dad's squad know the answer.

Dad loved to tell us about the night they "stormed Morley Hall". It was in 1943 and resident in the Hall was a platoon of Canadians who were linked to the Home Guard by the fact that their CO was also overseeing local units of "Dad's Army". A night exercise was arranged and dad and two others in charge of the local Home Guard prepared for the assault! My dad had served in the First World War, so had a good idea what a military exercise might be like. So on the night, just as he was leaving, he put his heavy duty wire cutters in his greatcoat inside pocket in case they might be needed. This is his account of events:— "The lads divided into three squads and we approached our target from three sides. The night was cold with very little moon as it was cloudy. The twigs and bracken snapped and cracked underfoot as we approached Morley Hall. We hoped to outwit the army and capture the Hall and all its occupants if we could! Suddenly, my scout came back and said, "Jimmy, they've erected a six foot barbed wire fence all round the Hall". Dad said, "Just as I expected, but I'm prepared". The squad looked on as dad produced the massive wire cutters from his coat pocket. "What are they for?" asked a youngster. "You'll see," grinned dad.

Dad continued the story:— "The squad was still and the "enemy" inside the Hall thought they were safe in their stronghold some 250 yards beyond the barbed wire. We snapped the wire slowly; we paused and all was still. After 20 minutes we had a hole in the fence large enough to crawl through. So one by one we made our way into "no-mans-land". Soon all three squads were through the wire. By now the moon was peeping through the clouds. We braced ourselves for the final assault, approaching the Hall cautiously. The Home Guard attack was successful. The "enemy" had been totally surprised when dad arrived at the front door of Morley Hall, opened it and led the platoon in. The Canadian CO immediately surrendered. He admitted that he thought we would take much longer getting through the barbed wire. Dad's wire cutters had been the key to a successful operation".

Mr. L. Clarke,
Morley.

I was a miller in the village and I joined the Home Guard when it started. My job was to be a guide, that is, if there was an invasion, I was to take the defending soldiers where they needed to go. I still have the special light which could not be seen from above by aircraft but which I could use in the dark. I kept it as a souvenir of the war. I remember the village school windows being taped up in case of bomb blast.

Mr. P. L. Bradstreet,
Morley.

I joined the LDV when I was 15 and it was three months before I received any uniform! The age range of men in the Morley Home Guard was 13 years to pensioners! There were some First World War veterans of course. As the years passed, some of the men went into the regular forces, but those of us in "reserved" occupations, stayed in the Home Guard until it was "stood down". We had regular guard duties and were trained by the Regular Army. The guard duties were on the outskirts of the village. We had rifle practice on various ranges in the area, like Hingham, Kimberley and Thetford. Some of us went on a special cadre course held at Morley village hall.

In the early days of the Home Guard, it was all about village defence, but in time, we formed a mobile force. This of course, involved a lot of walking. Those older men who could not cope with this aspect of Home Guard life were given different duties. On one of the exercises we were involved in, we were the Germans and our job was to capture Spooner Row station which was defended by regulars. Well, to get round this little problem, we biked to Attleborough station and came in to Spooner Row on a goods train! The surprise attack certainly succeeded!

In the countryside, most of us had a decent shotgun. We were used to firing a gun and had been doing so since the age of ten. So when we were supplied with rifles by the Home Guard, we adapted to them fairly quickly!

At first, we had a variety of rifles – American, Canadian and some from the 1st World War. We had plenty of training. On one occasion, the whole battalion took part in an exercise at Stanford Battle Area. During this we were told to fire at the sand near the command bunker. Well, we certainly frightened the officers when we fired!

I was on duty two evenings a week plus the cadre. We always went on to the Buck public house afterwards. Pubs were popular with all ranks in the Home Guard. During an intelligence test held at Wicklewood, one man was asked where he would find his CO. "At the Cherry Tree", he replied!

One night when we were on guard duty, an army officer came along, but he had no identification papers. He wanted to know where Kimberley Hall was, but we refused to tell him and my mate Bertie said, "You're not going anywhere without an identity and I've got something which will travel to Kimberley much faster than you anyway"! (He pointed to the bullets in his gun!)

In one of the training exercises, the Morley Platoon had to get through "enemy lines". Well, one of our lot got to the Drill Hall at Attleborough but was captured. They took off his boots and braces to make sure he didn't escape! Well, he asked to go to the toilet and was in there a long time! In fact he had escaped through the window. When they realised what had happened, they went to look for him. But he slipped back inside, collected his boots and braces and then made his getaway!

At Morley, we had a Spigot Mortar mounted on a platform behind a tractor. We also had a Northover Projector with a 10 second fuse. It could pierce a sheet of galvanized steel at 250 yards, but you had to be careful it didn't blow up in your face!

When the Americans came over, many were based in our area and of course the American Hospital (now Wymondham College) was built at Morley. We often met the Americans in the pub. One night, I was at the Buck, when Joe Louis, the world heavyweight boxing champion, appeared. But he would not come into the bar because he didn't want to cause offence to any Southern Yanks who might be in there!

One night we had set up an ambush at Wicklewood. An

American officer with a .45 revolver came along in a jeep. We told him that some POWs had escaped from the hospital grounds at Morley and that some of his men were injured. He went as white as a sheet and was much relieved when he realised that we were only joking! There was a concrete rifle butt in the stonepit at Wicklewood which we used a lot to try and get everyone in the unit up to sniper standard. We would take the "odds & sods" there on Sundays for extra practice.

In the period before D Day, we had special training with the regulars so that we would be fully prepared if there had been a German counter-attack. We were certainly very active at this time and visited Salisbury Plain to do some training there.

Looking back, I remember that our platoon was a very close knit one. There were five men from one farm in it. We were known as Jack Norton's "Private Army", after our platoon officer. I think we had a bit of a reputation! When a regular sergeant said one day that we needed to smarten up and that we were like a flock of sheep, quite a lot of the men made a "baa baa" noise! One Home Guard man from another unit, was threatened with transfer to the Morley Platoon as a punishment! When the Home Guard was "stood down" at the end of the war, the Morley men simply carried on! We enjoyed the comradeship so much that we kept on meeting for years afterwards. We finally "stood down" in 1972 and there was an article and photograph in the local newspaper about that final meeting.

Mr. John Foulsham,
Wymondham.

In 1940, I was 34 years old and working on the railway at **Wymondham.** I joined the LDV with my mates. Our CO was Major Fryer of Browick Hall and our first meetings were at the Drill Hall in Pople Street. I remember that most of the men who were in my unit were 1st World War veterans and they kept us up to the mark alright!

If there had been a German invasion in 1940, we had orders to report to the Drill Hall, but we didn't have rifles at first! I remember that the first bit of uniform was a white armlet with LDV on it! Eventually the .303 rifles arrived and I remember a character called Oldfield who was asked by Major Fryer what he would do if he saw someone in the area that he did not know. Oldfield replied, "Shoot him, Sir". Another comedian in the unit

164

asked Oldfield, "Would you ask who he was afterwards?" Major Fryer said this was not the time or the place for humour!

I think that the Wymondham Battalion was a big one and we didn't get to see a lot of the people except on big exercises. My platoon always met in the Railway Inn and though the officers never came in, relations between us were always good.

Looking back, there were many amusing incidents. In one exercise our Lieutenant said, that our job was to find the enemy quarters. As we got near, he said, that what we could really do with, was some machine gun fire. But as we had no such gun at the time, he ran a stick along a corrugated iron fence! On another occasion, we had to capture enemy HQ at Hingham village hall. But by the time we got there, it had already been captured by other units!

One of our officers was a Lt Hadley, though we used to call him, "Hardley". One day I was just going to "skidaddle", and I said, "has Hardley gone?" Then the lieutenant's voice replied, "I'm hardly here!"

I remember the day that Gaymers of Attleborough was bombed. It was 1941 and I was shunting on the railway, when a German plane machine-gunned and holed the engine tender. After that the plane must have gone on and dropped a bomb on Gaymers.

Life in the Home Guard could be quite tiring at times, going on guard duty two nights a week after a day's work and doing exercises on Sunday mornings. We had no parachutists to deal with! We used to go up Wymondham Abbey tower (lots of steps!) on guard duty. One night, a younger man, my mate, went up first.

Pillbox, Cavick Road, Wymondham.

Well, the top of the tower was a square job with a lead roof. When I got up there, I couldn't see my mate! "Are you all right boy?", I asked. No reply. I shouted down to the other men down below, "My mate ain't up here!". They said, I was daft and that of course he was up there. But there is only a small parapet up that tower, and I thought he had fallen over! However, my mate was very agile and had nipped round one side ahead of me and got downstairs again, where the other men had hidden him under blankets in the bell tower!

One day I was involved in semaphore signalling. The message I was receiving, I later learned, was, "Send up three lorries". Well, by the time the message got to me (via 4 other people), I got, "Send up trees"! When the sergeant came round to hear the message, I said, "They are just going to climb that poplar!!"

I remember the inter-battalion shooting competition. The 1st World War snipers in our unit were very good and Major Fryer was an excellent shot. The shooting team was trained by a Welsh regular and they became very proficient.

Mrs. Marion Leith,
Barford.

My husband Claude, who had served in the First World War as a stretcher bearer, volunteered for the Home Guard when it started in 1940. As a farmer he was in a "reserved" occupation, but he served in the Home Guard throughout the war. He became a Captain and I remember he went on a course for Home Guard officers. He served in an area which included, Lenwade, Swannington, Attlebridge, Lyng and Cawston. He received a petrol allowance to help with the transport problems and was out every night. A particularly busy night was during the German's first air raid on Norwich and I was left on my own.

Mr. Ben Stimpson,
Salle.

When I heard the broadcast that recruitment would start at the police station, I went along the following day to join the LDV. I was 30 years old in 1940 and had an agricultural merchant's business, a "reserved" occupation. I was already in the ARP and had helped put gas masks together in 1938-39, but still wanted to get involved in the LDV.

Captain Leith is on the back row far right in this picture of Home Guard members (with a lady secretary) taken outside Lyng Mill House.

Photo with kind permission of Mrs. M. Leith

Reepham War Weapons Week – May 18th, 1941.
3 Company, 13th Battalion, East Norfolk Home Guard.
Photo with kind permission of Mr. B. Stimpson

I remember that there was a preliminary meeting with Col. Barclay, who was in charge of the area, and I was asked to recruit in Salle, Thurning and Wood Dalling. I collected a few men and set up four OPs (observation posts), which were guarded every night, (two men on and two men off duty). At this very early stage, we used whatever arms the men had got – shotguns, revolvers, rifles. One night we were called out to man all the bridges in the area. In 1940, we patrolled regularly but had limited weaponry and, of course, no heavy guns. I think there were more officers than men at this point. The only uniform initially was the LDV armlet! In time, uniform came, arms arrived and a certain amount of organization developed. The new name of Home Guard gave us more status. Major Winch was in charge of our company which covered, Swannington, Haveringland, Foulsham, Cawston, Heydon, Corpusty, Saxthorpe, Guestwick and Reepham.

In the summer of 1940, after Dunkirk, morale was low and we had little equipment. We were very unprepared for the Germans at this time. Some regulars in the area helped with training. However, we manned our control points every night during that summer. There was a "dummy" aerodrome at Fulmodeston and I remember some bombs dropping; on one occasion I was thrown into a ditch full of nettles! I had many World War I veterans in my unit, some of whom fell asleep on duty! We had to establish standards without sanctions, so discipline was by example, not the orderly room!

Reepham railway bridge was the site of a Spigot Mortar.

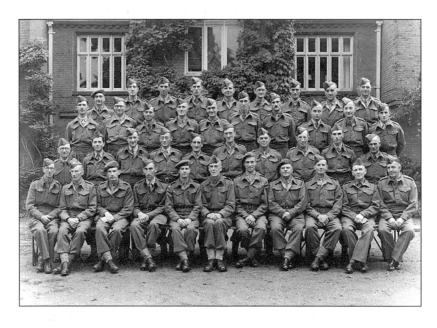

17th Battalion East Norfolk Home Guard.
Officers Photograph, October 1944.

Front row: Lt. C. Dix, Capt. B. Winch, Major P. Sayer, Major T. Sayer,
Capt. R. Cox (adjutant), Lt. Col. Q.E. Gurney (CO), Major B. Stimpson (2i/C),
Capt. W. Hudson (quartermaster), Major S. Simmons, Capt. J. Casburn,
Capt. S. Meanley.

2nd row: Capt. G. Dewing, Lt. A. Burton, Lt. D. Milk, Capt. C. Leith,
Capt. S. Perry-Warnes, Capt. A. Garrod, Lt. W. Jones,
Lt. A. Gibbs, Lt. V. Fenn, 2/Lt. B. Woodhouse.

3rd row: Lt. C. Pye, Lt. S. Buxton, Lt. W. Jarvis, 2/Lt. A. Parfitt, Lt. R. Smith,
Lt. R. Parfitt, 2/Lt. H. Wallis-Hosken, Lt. L. Watts,
Lt. C. Poll, Capt. C. Lane.

Back Row: Lt. A. Elsden, 2/Lt. W. Gaymer, Lt. A. Drummond, 2/Lt. R. Winch,
Lt. G. Sewards, Lt. J. Underwood, 2/Lt. L. Jones,
Lt. V. Joyce, Lt. A. Jones.

Photo with kind permission of Mrs. M. Leith

By 1941 the 13th Battalion was formed and I was a platoon commander with the rank of Lieutenant. Then I became a company commander. Our battalion commander was Col. Spurrell. By this time we had rifles, ammunition and grenades. It was in this year that proficiency tests were introduced. Well, our men did these tests of course, but no one passed unless they knew how to handle a rifle properly and keep it clean! We made the men at Swanton Morley repeat the tests even though they alleged it was arms drill not a proficiency test! In fact the proficiency test was very useful and some men who had passed the test got commissioned soon after they were conscripted into the Regular Army. Possession of these certificates could also help men get into the section of the armed services they most wanted. I had to get Col. Gurney's son through the test before he became a regular. Of course, some of the men had not seen service before. I had been in the OTC (Officer Training Corps) while at Aldenham School.

Life was very hectic in the Home Guard, especially in the early years of the war. We had exercises with the regulars and attended the range weekly. Someone was training every night and all day on Sundays. There were some very good shots in my battalion because there were several rifle clubs in the Reepham area. We were certainly a match for the regulars in shooting competitions! There were very few injuries resulting from accidental fire and no casualties from enemy attacks.

One of our jobs was the defence of local aerodromes, a responsibility we shared with the regulars. Oulton, Foulsham, Haveringland, Weston and Swanton Morley were places we helped to defend. One day I was taken up in a Mosquito in an exercise. The pilot carried out three low level attacks and we were back home in 15 minutes! I was scared stiff! One day, the Americans had got back from a raid over Germany and the Germans followed them in and there was a bit of a panic on and the Americans called me out because they couldn't raise the CO – there was absolute chaos for a time! Actually, we got very tired at the time of the German raids (1940-41). I was running a business and a farm at the time and on top of that of course, there were night guard duties. One night they tried to call me out from Sheringham, but I didn't wake up and a motorbike came over for me!

There was much friendly rivalry between the Home Guard battalions. Bawdeswell had one of the best battle platoons and they often used live ammunition and machine guns in their exercises. In 1942 there was a battle platoon competition at Holkham Marshes. Lord Hastings, CO of No.4 Battalion inspected them before they started. He was a law unto himself! I was at Melton Constable and he told me exactly what he would do if the Germans did actually land! He was extremely confident, fearless and very efficient – a re-assuring presence. On one occasion he told the QM to get us a drink, while he calmly went to bed!

Discipline was very important and generally, morale was very high. After conscription came in, there were some men who did not really want to be involved, go on parade, etc. One man was particularly difficult and I had to refer him to higher authority! I was a stickler for standards and in general tried to lead by example. Of course, we all had our "Captain Mainwarings" and "Corporal Jones"! During one exercise I found a platoon commander in his dressing gown drinking beer! This was not quite the spirit of course, but I found that regular check-ups did help to keep the men up to the mark. I travelled around the battalion area all the time. Fortunately, I had a petrol allowance for my duties and a little two-seater Austin (the company car!).

The Headquarters of 17 Battalion, The Bays, Norwich Road, Reepham.

Looking back on things, I can say that the spirit was excellent, and a rather amateurish group (LDV) was eventually transformed into a very efficient military force. At the beginning, we carried on, without fear, against what seemed overwhelming odds. Later in the war, after the danger of invasion had receded, our people were still motivated and morale was very good. They knew that they still had a job to do here once the D Day landings had begun, and so many regulars would be going overseas.

In my experience the Home Guard always worked closely with the ARP and the civil community had much respect for us – after all, we had come into existence to defend it! We also had a good working relationship with the Regular Army units in our area, and shared with them, the responsibility for defending the locality.

I had been involved in several battalions since 1940, but in 1943 I became 2 i/c No.17 Battalion. I went to The Bays (the HQ of the Battalion in Reepham) every day as part of my duties. We had three women staff and a storeman helping us at HQ. I think that my company was the only one to have a motorbike, a car and a truck! We also had some "armoured vehicles", which were converted vans!

At the end of 1944, came the final "Stand Down" parade, and Col. Gurney took the salute from the Church Institute porch in Reepham. After that my main job was to ensure that the men handed in their rifles and equipment. This took some time!

Being in the Home Guard had been a great challenge. It was fun, it was hard work, but there was a real sense of pride in our achievement. We felt that we had contributed something of which both we and the nation could be proud.

Mrs. J. Lowe (nee Johnson),
Kings Lynn.

When women were allowed to be part of the Home Guard in 1943, I enrolled as a Woman Home Guard Auxiliary. Myself and friends were in the King's Lynn platoons. We did not have any uniforms. There were two of us in the Northend Platoon. We were both at the time in "reserved" occupations. My friend worked for the Dock Company, now ABP, and I was employed at Savages Ltd., Engineering. We used to meet on Thursday evenings and Sunday mornings at a large empty house at Savages. Our duties included office work and help in the stores. We also assisted in the structure of a call-out system for the men in emergencies. Other jobs were, filling Lewis gun pans and giving out 4 x 2, a fine flannel material for cleaning rifles.

At the end of the war we women received a citation and a badge. The photograph was taken at the "Stand Down" held on Tuesday Market Place, King's Lynn. The ladies and officers then adjourned to the Globe Hotel for sherry and goodbyes.

I have received The King's command

to express His Majesty's appreciation

of the loyal service given voluntarily

to her country in a time of grievous danger

by

ℳ. J. JOHNSON

as a Woman Home Guard Auxiliary.

The War Office,
London.

Secretary of State
for War

Women's Auxiliary Home Guard Badge.

Photograph with kind permission of Mr. Lowe

Mr. Alec Rowe,
Reepham.

Little did I think that by the time I was 16 years old I would be in uniform. Mind you, I had to lie about my age as you had to be 17 to join the Home Guard! I think they took me on to help swell the numbers for guard duty, though there did not seem to be much of importance to guard in **Reepham,** except the telephone exchange.

Sometimes an officer from the Royal Norfolk Regiment stationed in Norwich, would come to Reepham to see how things were running. These visits were at night as "Dad's Army" had to work during the day. On one occasion, a young officer arrived and was asked if he would care to inspect the guard. Billy Bishop and Stephen Frankland were on duty and Billy Tubby, one of the sergeants ordered them to "Port Arms" for inspection. This means pulling back the bolt of the rifle and putting the thumb in the breach so the thumb nail would reflect light up the barrel! This was pointless as it was dark, but the officer looked down the barrels and was happy with what he had seen or not seen! The sergeant then ordered the men to "Ease Springs", which meant moving the rifle bolt backwards and forwards several times, closing the bolt and then pulling the trigger... Well, we never did find out which of the two did not do this! But there was an almighty "BANG", and a six foot length of cast iron guttering fell from the top of the bank! Someone had pushed a live one up the spout! The sound of the rifle shot caused such a commotion that the blackout was forgotten as people rushed out of their doors to find out what the noise was about!

Billy Bishop was involved in another mishap, this time involving a bayonet! It was a Sunday morning and we were in an exercise with the RAF Regiment whose men from Oulton Aerodrome were the "enemy" attacking us. Well Billy was on duty at the mouth of Fishers Alley on the Market Square. He heard footsteps running in the alley, so he fixed his bayonet and rushed into the alley to challenge the intruder when, at the bend, an RAF man came charging straight on to Billy's bayonet! Fortunately, it caught him in the left shoulder and not much damage was done. The incident was hushed up pretty well and after this, bayonets were NOT allowed to be fixed unless special orders were given to do so.

In my early days in the Home Guard, most of our weapons were provided by private people. Later I was given a Canadian Long

Reepham Home Guard.
Ptes. B. Read, W. Harvey, J. Harvey, L. Pierce, T. Hall, C. Allen, G. Harvey, L. Alford.
Ptes. J. Rudd, R. Reeve, R. Howes, R. Digby, S. Smith, K. Jarvis, A. Hall, C. Welton, C. Hall.
Bottom Rows? – L/Cpl. W. Frosdick, Cpl. C. Grout, Cpl. J. Cooper, Sgt. J. Cockaday.
Lt. Poll, Cpl. N. Egmore, Cpl. V. Massingham, L/Cpl. D. Duffield, L/Cpl. A. Reeve.
Photo with kind permission of Mr. Alec Rowe.

Ross rifle which stood five inches taller than me! It had a kick like a mule when it was fired. When it came to receiving uniform, I and one other chap were the only two to get fitted out at the start, as they only had size 1. We were very proud to be properly fitted out before all the rest of the unit!

I was very pleased when I was made a despatch rider and given a belt and a pair of .38 Smith & Wesson revolvers. I enjoyed driving the Triumph and delivering messages to various units or to fetch men to guard duty! Often they were at the pub and the "Greyhound" was like the London "Windmill Theatre" – it never closed!

One night I'll never forget. There was the droning noise of Jerry going over, probably on a bombing raid of the Midlands. Suddenly there was the rat-a-tat-tat of German machine gun fire. They were trying to put the searchlight at Jordan, near Bawdeswell, out of action. I was terrified, ran for my Triumph and set off home. Then the searchlight went out and in the sudden darkness, I skidded into a ditch. I managed to get it out and then made straight home to my mum! I was shaking like a leaf and I guess I could have been shot for desertion in the face of the enemy, but at the time I was too terrified to think of that. I was a very new young volunteer at the time and so I hope my CO, Major Ben Stimpson, will forgive me.

Ben Stimpson can recall a time when Reepham did partially get "invaded", which must have been when we young men had been called up by the regular forces. Apparently a charity dance had been laid on by some of the wives of the Reepham Home Guard in the town hall. At some point, a commotion began, caused it seems, by the arrival of a dozen or so American Air Force personnel, who had been attracted by the music. Reepham's special constable, Herbert Wilkin, was trying to stop the Americans coming into the dance! In due course, they were allowed in and as Ben Stimpson said, it was a good move, because with the Yanks' kind of money, the charity did very well out of it, because the "invaders" bought drinks for themselves and everybody else all night!

Finally, one of my mates remembers a football match between Reepham Home Guard and the Jordan Searchlight Battery. The match was rather one-sided, with the searchlight boys winning 13–1. My mate was disappointed at the defeat but later on while the two teams were having a beer, he felt a bit better because it was pointed out that the team they had played was in fact West Ham FC! Apparently, the powers that be had the idea of keeping sporting teams together, in this case as part of a searchlight battery.

Dyker Thew,
King's Lynn.

In 1939, I was a provincial newspaper editor, a job which was classified as a "reserved" occupation during the war, when local papers were seen as important for morale at home.

In 1940, I became editor of the "Lynn News & Advertiser" at King's Lynn. Although I had been in the Royal Observer Corps while I was at my previous job in Wellingborough, it suited my editorial duties to join the Home Guard in King's Lynn. The 7th Battalion Norfolk Home Guard was based in the town, where there were several companies together with those in the surrounding villages.

Loading a Spigot Mortar at King's Lynn.
Photo with kind permission of Mr. C.W. Scott.

We laugh over "Dad's Army" on the TV, but it was nothing like that. Our leading officers and NCOs had all served in World War I and their experience was invaluable. Discipline was strict and they forged us into a real fighting force determined to give a good account of itself. As I had been through an Officers' Training Corps, I knew how to drill with and fire the service .303 rifles issued to us. Then came mass-manufactured automatic Sten guns. My son who was a schoolboy during the war, remembers me keeping my Sten gun in a cupboard under the stairs at our Milton Avenue home. He also says I had a service revolver with ammunition but memory of that entirely eludes me now.

I joined Major Frank Bullen's company with excellent fellows of all ages. Our HQ was a semi-detached house on Gaywood Road which was very handy for off duty refreshment at the Woolpack Inn. We had training sessions on weekday evenings and Sunday mornings and had no trouble with regard to non-attenders or skivers. No sanctions were allowed at this early stage of the war against men who defaulted.

Major Bullen thought my talents would be best employed as an Intelligence Officer for the company, but I only got a sergeant's stripes. One of my friends persisted in putting up his "wings" from flying in World War I, on his tunic. However, authority won in the end and he had to take them down.

I remember doing night time picket duties in the blackout supporting the ARP organization. I was also on a night duty rota at our newspaper offices in Purfleet Street, with a camp bed in reserve. We had sand and water buckets and stirrup pumps for tackling magnesium fire bombs. My hand-wrung bell I used to summon help, I still keep as a wartime souvenir.

King's Lynn was overflown day and night by the RAF and the US Air Force from bases throughout East Anglia. When the Luftwaffe came of course that set the sirens moaning. The worst incident I remember was when a stray bomb hit the Eagle public house in Norfolk Street on a Saturday night, when it was packed with off-duty RAF personnel and civilians. No one survived and the destruction was so great that it was impossible to compile an accurate casualty list. Another incident I recall about this time was when some boys of King Edward School tackled fire bombs in the hall roof and saved the school from destruction. They were truly unsung heroes.

An interesting Home Guard unit at Lynn was the river patrol in motorboats. Its HQ was the Ouse Sailing Club (known as the Ouse Booze Club), and its aim was to prevent Nazi seaplanes landing troops by water.

The Home Guard in the town had tactical training sessions with regular army regiments garrisoned in Lynn and there was much liaison with the US Air Force. One of my most vivid memories was watching from my office window, 1,000 Flying Fortress bombers assembling in the sky between Lynn and Wisbech for a daylight raid on Germany.

Night time air raids on Lynn became frequent and disturbing in 1942, when my daughter was born. My wife decided to sleep with our baby in our dining-room steel table shelter, a Morrison. Jane slept there in a basket for the first three months of her life.

A diversion was the making of some war films at Lynn. The famous "One of our Aircraft is Missing", used the old streets and waterfront to simulate a Dutch town. In the last year of the war I myself had a diversion by going to north west Europe to report back for Associated Newspapers. I saw the liberation of the appalling concentration camp at Belsen, where skeleton bodies were neatly arranged like haystacks. I wore my Home Guard uniform with SHAEF shoulder flashes and had the honorary rank of captain as a war correspondent.

When peace finally came and we celebrated VE day, the Home Guard had a Sunday morning Victory parade in Tuesday Market Place, where about 1,000 men took part. All felt that they had done their duty without having to face the feared German onslaught on the East Coast. As the tallest man in the battalion, I was asked to lead the parade which was a surprise honour. In my smartened up uniform and shining black boots, I proudly led the parade off the square and round the town with bands playing, trying to set a good regulation pace.

The 50th anniversary of that parade was held in 1995. However, to my sorrow and surprise I was the only Home Guard who paraded. I was then 88 years old and must have outlived all my contemporaries. It was left to me to march beside our Royal Norfolk Regiment's hero, Major David Jamieson of Thornham, who won the V.C. in Normandy. He represented all the men who had fought in north west Europe and I those who had held the Home Front.

Diss Home Guard taken behind the Old Grammar School.

Front Row: Sgt. Bob Edwards, Sgt. George Edwards, Sgt. Jack Martin, Fred Westbrook, Jimmy Ives (Officer), H. Pursehouse.
Mr. J. Rice, Eric Pursehoue, Sgt. Major Arthur Fisher, Mr. Flatman, Albert Green, Mr. Downing.
2nd Row: Denny Ward, H. Garnham, ?, Jack Jones, ?, Mr. Voss, ?, Mr. Sussames, ?, Mr. Cobb, ?, ?, ?, Bert Buckle, ?, Mr. Clark, ?.
"Peanut" Hubbard, ?, Mr. Coke, Mr. Pope, ?, Mr. Dye, ?, Mr. Tong.
Back Row: Mr. Lond, ?, Eddie Price, ?, ?, ? Reeve, ?, ?, Mr. Howard, Mr. Howard, Mr. Howard, ?, Alan Morris, ?, C. Rackham.

Photo with kind permission of Mr. Lyn Purling

182

Mr. C. Pursehouse,
Diss.

The HQ of the *Diss* Home Guard was at the British Legion Club in Denmark Street, now the Conservative Club. The weekly parade would form up in the street outside on a Sunday morning. At first, training consisted of map reading and weapon training. They had .303 rifles and I think they eventually got a Bren gun. My father who had served in World War I, had the rank of captain and carried a revolver. RSM Fisher, who had held that rank in the first World War, and took things very seriously, helped to lick the company into shape. He was helped by CSM Jim Rice, another 1st War veteran, employed as a porter at the railway station.

I remember on one occasion when the company was called out to search for an escaped POW in Thetford Forest. It was pouring with rain and the next morning, my father returned to breakfast after a fruitless search saying what a hopeless task it had been, bearing in mind the vast area of forest. I suspect morale was pretty low at that point, as all the men had to go to work after being out all night.

After the war all arms and ammunition were handed in. Much of it was taken in a rowing boat to the middle of the Mere by the police and then dumped.

Diss VE Day Parade, 1945.
The Home Guard follow the Royal Observer Corps.
Photo with kind permission of Mr. Sidney Talbot

183

Guarding Diss water tower.
Left to right: Mr. Downing, Mr. Voss?, Mr. Albert Green.
Photo with kind permission of Miss J. Green

Mrs. L. Purling,
Diss.

I remember going to watch a Home Guard parade in Diss with my sister and mother. My father was in the Home Guard. Suddenly, my mother said, "Well, that soldier who just marched past, winked at me". My sister said, "It's dad!" It was funny to think that my mother did not recognise dad in his uniform!

Mr. Harold Baker,
Scole.

I was a farm worker and so in a "reserved" occupation. I had just got married before the war in April 1939. In 1940 when they asked for volunteers, I joined the LDV and I was in the Home Guard until "Stand Down" in 1944. My first weapon was a broomstick and the only uniform I had at the beginning was an armlet. Our meetings were in the Scole Reading Room and Billingford Church was our OP (observation point). I did searchlight duty at Broome and I remember one night when an enemy plane was very low and near us. We could have shot at it but it crashed near Needham. On another occasion a plane dived into the searchlight beam, but I was able to take cover just in time.

In due course we got rifles and Sten guns and uniform after about 8 months. We didn't get ammunition at first. Training was regular, as were parades. We also had exercises with the army and in one of these I remember that we were given bags of flour to throw at enemy vehicles. If we hit them, then the rule was that the vehicle in question was judged to be out of action for the rest of the exercise. We did shooting practice at the pits on Billingford Common.

One day while I was working in the field, I saw a Spitfire shoot down a German plane, so I threw some muck into the air to celebrate! On another occasion I was nearly killed by some Americans who were out hunting pheasants. I remember one night when two men in our unit went out on duty for the two hour spell before being replaced by others. Well, when they reported back they were covered in barley chaff, which caused a laugh as they couldn't get it off their coats for days!

Being in the Home Guard was hard work on top of your normal job. I worked on the farm for 52 hours a week and was paid 30 shillings. Even at the very busy times of the year like harvest, we still had to attend parade and our other Home Guard duties. When the government introduced compulsory service in the Home Guard, there were some men who really didn't want to be in it at first. However, they all buckled under and did their bit.

Looking back, I think my most vivid memory was one of the nights that Norwich was bombed. It was the third night in a row that the Germans had come over and the sky was full of activity. One plane came so close I could have shot at it, but it fired first.

The spirit and friendliness in our unit was excellent. We were never afraid and had some good times. The pubs in Scole were popular of course, especially the King's Head and the Scole Inn. However, when the time came for us to "Stand Down" in 1944, I was quite relieved that it was all over. We all knew that the King and the Prime Minister appreciated the work we had done during the four years of the Home Guard's life. So now we could enjoy the final parade in Diss and the various reunions which took place afterwards.

The Sergeants of the Diss Home Guard behind what is now the Conservative Club, but what was then The British Legion Club and their Headquarters. Left to right: Albert Green, Bob Edwards, Willy Edwards, Jack Martin, Chuck Flatman.
Photo with kind permission of Mr. L. Purling

Poetic Memories of Diss and Palgrave

THE BATTLE OF DISS, 1942
(Story just released)

Outside the Village School there stood
  Men armed with bow and pike,
The Palgrave Home Guard were out again,
  And at 7 o'clock they would strike.
With blackened faces they waited there,
  Not thinking of comfortable beds,
Some had blackened the whites of their eyes,
  The others the tops of their heads.
The amphibious squad was the first to move,
  They were led by Corporal "Olly",
With Leeder with B.A.R. and Ford with gun,
  Whilst Clarke trailed along with his brolly.
They crossed the River Waveney,
  As the moon rose up in the sky,
They feared not death this little band,
  As long as they kept their feet dry.
Into the heart of the enemy land
  They went, not showing fear,
They pinched a boat on the water's edge,
  And proceeded to cross the Mere.
Brave men they were, as I've said before,
  And three were sensible too,
For these three sat in comfort,
  And made the Corporal row.
No sight of the enemy did they spy,
  As they stormed the slopes that night,
In fact Ford fished on the way across,
  But he didn't get a bite.
Meanwhile the others were on their way,
  Up to their knees in mud,
Pte. Dyer's knees were too near the ground
  So he rode on the shoulders of "Spud".
As they moved along, silent and swift,
  There came a deafening crash,

They looked around, and then stood stunned,
    Smith was killed, by a thunderflash.
Another casualty they had that night,
    Ere the foe they met,
It occurred in the crossing of a stream
    When Websdell got both feet wet.
They searched the streets for the enemy
    For the greater part of the night,
But Diss were waiting somewhere else,
    And didn't get time to fight.
You'd think they were heroes, those gallant men,
    Who'd fought on beneath the full moon,
Not heroes, but cheats instead, said Diss,
    For they'd started a second too soon.

"The Palgrave Poet"
G.E. Clarke, Xmas, 1945.

"THE PASSING OF THE HOME GUARD"
or
"THE DISMISSAL OF A GALLANT BAND"
by George "Shakespeare" Clarke

The Home Guard will parade no more
    Upon the Village Green;
And Palgrave's boys in years to come
    Will speak of what they've seen.

Our Sergeant Sid was very strict,
    With him we dare not trifle,
But now the Home Guard's packing up
    He knows where to put his rifle.

And Cpl. Miller's powerful voice
    Could be heard as far as Diss;
His owl hoots too on night patrol
    Are sounds that we shall miss.

We had some curious weapons,
    Some were very rummy,
But what they thought was our V1
    Was Frank Smith on his tummy.

188

Our firing too on Wortham Ling
  Was heard both far and near.
By far the best we ever saw
  Was when Easto won his beer.

There really were fierce battles,
  Especially at Rose Lane Bend.
The fierceness of a few of these
  Made Dyer's hair stand on end.

In many of their battles
  This gallant little band
Had to use a smoke screen
  From the pipe of Private Bland.

And then there was the seaside trip
  To the East Coast's golden sand.
This outing was a special treat
  For Privates Dyer and Brand.

Lieutenant Cotton's section too
  Can never be passed by.
For when we're asked who won the war
  We'll all say, "It was I".

Whatever faults the Home Guard made
  They were soon all put right;
Not all on the parade ground
  But at Doug's on Saturday night.

No more Cowboys and Indians
  Outside the village School.
We'll have to leave that kind of thing
  To Brian Cattermole.

In France there is a Monument
  To the heroes of Vimy Ridge;
In Palgrave there should be one too
  To the heroes of Rose Lane Bridge.
                                    October 1944.

Poems reproduced by kind permission of the family of the late George E. Clarke.

189

Sir John Mann and the NCOs of the Diss Home Guard
behind the Home Guard Headquarters.
Photo with kind permission of Mrs. C.L. Ives.

In January 1996, a plaque was unveiled on the pillbox which guarded Diss railway station. The wording is reproduced below.

This pillbox was one of some 1800 pillboxes, almost all constructed to War Office designs between June and September 1940, at a time when Winston Churchill MP was Prime Minister and the German armies had reached the coast of Holland some 160 miles from this spot. This plaque is placed here as a reminder of those times, and as a memorial to the Home Guard, formed originally as the Local Defence Volunteers and finally disbanded 50 years ago in May 1945.

I was a member of the Scottow Home Guard and this photograph was taken at "The Three Horseshoes". There are only about three of us left and I am on the back row, third from the left.

Photo with kind permission of Fred Gibbons (Apple Jack) Scottow

Mrs. Julie Fielder,
Wood Dalling.

My father remembers one day when Henry Yarham, a member of the **Wighton** Home Guard, shot through an open kitchen door at a pheasant perching in a nearby tree. He was using his .303 rifle and the blast knocked Henry off his feet, the bullet took a large chunk out of the tree and the pheasant flew away unhurt! Perhaps this was the only time the Home Guard fired "in anger"! There's no telling where the stray bullet went, but hopefully no one on Wells beach at the time was hit!

Mr. Maurice C. Dixon,
Metton, near Cromer.

When the Home Guard was formed, in 1940, I was 19 years old and worked as a cowman, a "reserved" occupation. As I was not eligible for military service, I volunteered for the local Home Guard. I remember that we did various exercises on Sunday mornings, and on Wednesday evenings there was drill in the Gresham Assembly Room. After a hard day's work like threshing or lifting sugar beet, some of us were not too enthusiastic, but we carried on! One chap who did not attend very often, had to explain his absence which he said was because of a back ache. But he had to face a tribunal and as they could not *see* a bad back, he was passed fit.

During the period when they thought the Germans would invade, we were on guard duty all night. There were four of us in my group and we had two hours on and two hours off duty. An officer would sometimes come round during the night.

Some of us were posted on the cliffs as "lookouts". We were taught how to use hand grenades and of course the rifle. We practised shooting at Runton. On some of our duties, we were out all night in case the enemy planes dropped "butterfly bombs" which could set fire to the cornfields. The Regular Army units stationed in the area sent NCOs to instruct and train us on tactics if the Germans had landed. But I really don't know how we would have acted. However, the regulars were nice lads and joined us for a drink after these sessions.

I remember the day when hundreds of planes towing gliders, dropped troops on Arnhem (1944), because our Battalion, No.13, had lots of men on a rifle shoot that Sunday morning in Thetford Forest and saw them go over.

Wighton Home Guard, taken outside the Half Moon at Walsingham.
Back row, left to right, starting in the window: Mr. Beck, B. Allen, S. Dack,
H. Yarman, W. Rowe, H. Fowle, Mr. Frary, J. Temple, J. Savory, Mr. Codman,
R. Dack, ?, Mr. Savory, L. Fowle, Mrs. Rivett (in window, right).
Front Row: S. Smith, S. Claxton, J. Lane, S. Bray, ?, ?, W. Bray, F. Fowle, F. Dack,
P. Ducker, C. Fowle, E. Vincent, C. Bunting, W. Eke, Mr. Savory, A. Buckingham.
Seated: S. Fowle, ?, G. Reynolds.   Seated on ground: R. Lane.
Photo with kind permission of Mrs. J. Fielder.

Looking back, we had our moans and groans, but we also had our laughs. But the main thing is that we saw the job through.

Mr. K. McClure,
Wymondham.

I joined the LDV shortly after the British retreat from Dunkirk in 1940. At the time I was living in Colney Lane, Cringleford and whenever I went out I was always stopped by LDVs in the Colney Road area even though they knew me very well. The river bridge in Cringleford was of course guarded by the LDV and our main meeting place was Patterson's Social Club.

At Wymondham, I remember that there was a Spigot Mortar or Blacker Bombard anti-tank gun sited on the frontage of Cavick House and trained on the Tiffey Bridge near the Abbey.

To deter German gliders or paratroops from landing on the big open expanse of Old Buckenham Common, telegraph poles were "planted" in a staggered fashion across the common.

193

No.3 Platoon, 17th Battalion, East Norfolk Home Guard, showing men from Bintree, County School, Guist and Wood Norton.
Front row: Cpl. T. Mesney, Cpl. W. Wright, Cpl. L. Page Sgt. J. Fuller, 2-Lt. H. Wallis, ? Hosken, Lt. V. Fenn, Sgt. R. Holmes, Sgt. A. Pike, Cpl. E. Barrett, Cpl. A. Hopper, Cpl. J. Field.
Second row: Pte. H. Rutland, Pte. A. Spooner, Cpl. W. Parfitt, Pte. R. Kenny, Cpl. A. Barrett, Pte. E. Wakefield, Pte. R. Harvey, Pte. H. Bray, Pte. R. Shilling, L/Cpl. S. Myhill.
Third row: Pte. R. Prior, Pte. F. Burlingham, Pte. R. Parnell, Pte. R. Wright, Pte. W. Smith, Pte. J. Myhill, Pte. R. Overman, Pte. M. Hudson, Pte. A. Bullock.
Back row: Pte. J. Bell, Pte. G. Hubbard, Pte. G. Oldman, Pte. C. Oldman, Pte. K. Barber, Pte. J. Williamson.
Photo with kind permission of Mr. P.G. Burton

194

Reedham Home Guard taken in 1945 at the Hove in the village.

Top row: Freddy Sparkes, Walter Powles, Mr: Johnson, Fred Howlett, Mr: Flegg, Ben Chase, Fred Cooper; Ted Sales, Chris Race, Mr: Mace, Bunny Edwards, Walter Tovell, George Beck.

Second row: Neville Brown, Bob Howard, Lally Moore, Bob Lake, Harry hunt, Mr: Edwards, Joe Mallett, Billy Ewles, Mr: Dodman. Clem Spalding, Chips Tungate, Ted Nichols, Jack Ewles, Wally Carter.

Seated: Arnold Durrant, Harrold Hall, Victor Wincup, John Ford, Dick Cooper, Frank Collett, Mr: Ray, Tim Hipperson, Billy Walpole, Mr: plummer, Lenny Mutton, Tom Mutton.

Bottom Row: Herbert Walpole, Jimmy Broom, Arthur Taylor, Arthur Haylett, Walter Sharman, Freddy Brown.
Photo with kind permission of Mr: W. Tovell

CHAPTER 8

The Norfolk Home Guard – Some Conclusions

The Norfolk Home Guard was part of a great national movement which represented the impulses of all that was best in British society. There were 32,000 men organised into 17 battalions, part of a nation-wide force which at its peak consisted of over 2 million men and 1200 battalions.

As elsewhere in Britain, the Norfolk Home Guard comprised some of the finest elements in the county, drawn from every walk of life and distributed throughout the entire countryside down to the remotest village. As Churchill had said, "Every village is fortified". In a rural area like Norfolk, many Home Guard units included a significant proportion from the farming community, who of course knew every inch of the surrounding countryside, a useful asset in the context of a possible enemy invasion.

Although no two units were exactly the same – each reflected the quality of its officers and NCOs and the character of the men – they were united in a common cause and proud of their role in a time of great national danger. Above all, they were prepared "to defend their homes and families" in all weathers and for as many hours as it took. When the King said in 1944, "History will say your share in the greatest of all our struggles for freedom was a vitally important one", it was a fully deserved tribute.

Despite the militarization of the Home Guard, the Norfolk force retained its individual, local and civilian identity. It was fortunate to be blessed with many wise and understanding officers and NCOs. In terms of value for money of course, the Home Guard had few peers. The men were not paid, neither did they need to be fed or housed at public expense. The annual budget for the Home Guard constituted a tiny fraction of the cost of the war. In financial terms it could be said, to parody Churchill, "Never had so many received so little and yet achieved so much".

How would the Norfolk platoons have coped had "Operation Sea Lion" been launched and Nazi troops occupied English soil? This is a difficult question to answer. It would depend *when* the enemy had landed. If it had been in early 1940 it would have been no contest, as many Home Guardsmen freely admit. However, we now know that invasion in spring or early summer was very unlikely. Even so Nazi paratroopers and infantry were highly trained, well armed professionals, who would quickly suppress a village platoon however robust the resistance in Norfolk villages would have been. But the defeat of a few village Home Guard units would not have meant the conquest of the whole island. To move on, the enemy would have to take each village or community in turn. With luck, the consequent delays in the German advance, would have given time for units of the main field army to arrive. Though the Nazis would certainly have used terror tactics, it is impossible to say how long local resistance would have held out. However, what is certain, is that if the Home Guard had been called upon to fight, it would have done so bravely, with resolution and to the best of its ability. Although the Home Guard did not win any battle honours, its part in the war was an honourable one. Moreover, its value in the system of national defence was beyond question while its symbolic importance was crucial.

Despite its obvious limitations, the Home Guard was very important and worthwhile. It provided people with the opportunity to take a direct personal role in the defence of the nation by defending their own "home, hearth and family". In Norfolk, as in other parts of the country, men were inspired by Churchill's rhetoric about the great enterprise they were engaged in against the forces of darkness. The formation of the Home Guard units throughout Norfolk, was part of a great national gesture, the outward signs of the spirit of resistance – patriotic, proud and ready to repulse the enemy. They were boldly standing up to Hitler.

The Home Guard was also important for its socially leavening effects. Class distinction was certainly evident in a rural county like Norfolk, where the local squire or retired World War I officer, often assumed command of the local unit. But there was still much social mixing in the Norfolk units, which were marked by a cheerful comradeship and lack of deference. Much depended of course, on the enthusiasm and initiative of local commanders, but in general the atmosphere appears to have been positive and supportive, which ensured that the overall experience of Home

Guard life was very valuable. Involvement in the force ensured men were an integral part of the fabric of wartime morale. Even after the threat of invasion had virtually disappeared, the Home Guard still performed a variety of useful tasks, as has already been shown.

The Home Guard had begun its life during the dark days of 1940, when groups of Local Defence Volunteers, motley civilians armed with sticks, pitchforks and the odd shotgun, rallied to the call throughout Norfolk. The contrast with the well armed and equipped and professionally trained units of 1942-44 is striking. The Home Guard had come a long way in a short time, but it is perhaps the former image combining a touch of nobility and eccentricity, which survives in the public mind and guarantees its unique place in our national history. However, this account has also tried to show that the majority of the men who joined the Home Guard, took their job very seriously, and were justifiably proud of the high level of competence they had achieved as a result of commitment, considerable sacrifice and hard work.

The last word should go to a veteran of the Home Guard who served in the force from beginning to end:– "Looking back, the Home Guard was a lot of hard work and a great challenge. There was some fun and we had a real sense of achievement. We had contributed something of which we and the nation could be proud".

PART TWO
The Story of The Norfolk Resistance

CHAPTER 9

A very Secret Army

THE BACKGROUND

One of the best kept secrets of World War Two, was the existence of the British Resistance Units. These were specially trained groups of men, an elite force which would be used to counter possible Nazi invasion by acts of sabotage and destruction.

There were over 3,000 men in all, organised into units of between five and seven men stretching around the country from John o'Groat's to Lands End and Pembrokeshire. Each unit was based within 30 miles of the coast and was responsible for its own "patch" of the local countryside. These units, trained in guerrilla warfare, were "the secret army". In the event of an invasion, they would operate from cleverly camouflaged underground bunkers (Operational Bases), from which they would emerge to cause as much trouble as possible to the enemy.

While Churchill's rhetoric spoke of "fighting on the beaches", top secret plans were in place for a resistance underground, which would be ready to take on the might of the Third Reich if the Nazis ever landed on British soil.

HOW THE RESISTANCE WAS STARTED IN 1940

Various people contributed to the formation of the British Resistance. Churchill had noticed that as each country fell to the Nazi forces in the first stage of the war, very little fighting was going on **behind** the lines. He therefore ordered British officers to recruit and train suitable men to form Resistance Units. Such units it was felt, would prevent an invading force from roaming freely without hindrance as had happened in much of western Europe. Military Intelligence had long been considering the best way to cope with an invasion force on these islands.

General Thorne, Commander of XII Division, based in south east England had argued that if the main British Army was pushed back, an enemy advance could be delayed by the obstructive tactics of irregulars operating against the Nazi supply lines. He told the War Office that he needed someone to organise such units, which would be known as "stay behinds". In Kent, Sussex and Surrey, Colonel Peter Fleming, brother of Ian Fleming, creator of "James Bond", was appointed to set up the scheme in that area. Thorne's ideas were adopted by the other divisional commanders and Captain Andrew Croft was given the task of starting the Resistance in East Anglia.

However the key figure in establishing a nation-wide resistance organization was a World War 1 veteran, Colonel Colin Gubbins. He had considerable experience in observing guerrilla tactics in action in Russia, Poland and Ireland before the war. Later, in 1939-40, he helped to organise guerrilla activity in Czechoslovakia, Poland and Norway, where he formed the "Independent Companies" to fight as guerrillas against the Nazis. After the allied withdrawal from Norway in May 1940, Gubbins returned to Britain, Here he was told by MI (R) to create an "underground army". General Ironside C in C Home Forces, promised men, supplies and training and asked for weekly reports on the progress of the scheme. A copy of each report was also sent to Churchill.

RESISTANCE GROUPS TO BE KNOWN AS AUXILIARY UNITS

Gubbins believed that an invader was especially vulnerable to guerrilla activity during the first few days after landing. He therefore planned to deploy guerrilla units in a coastal strip no more than 30 miles deep, where initially, it was thought a German attack was most likely to come. This was the area stretching from Norfolk to Southampton.

To set up the scheme, he asked for 12 officers, with specialist skills, some of whom had served with him in Poland and Norway. These were known as Intelligence Officers (or IOs) and each would be responsible for a sector of the coast in the area thought to be most likely targeted by Nazi invasion plans. Gubbins chose officers of the highest quality, men with drive, initiative and understanding. Later, their numbers would be increased to 36 to cover the majority of the coastal area of the British Isles. The task

200

of these officers was to recruit patrol or unit leaders, who would in turn recruit five or six other suitable men. The units formed in this way were to be known as the *Auxiliary Units,* a suitably vague title to allay suspicion and ensure maximum flexibility of action. Soon an underground organization, military in character and secret in structure, was developing behind the main national defences which were steadily encircling the British coast during 1940. The basis for a highly secret but effectively organized Resistance movement which could continue to expand, was in place.

The start of the Norfolk Resistance Units

The founder of the Resistance Units in Norfolk was Captain Andrew Croft, who was initially responsible for the whole of East Anglia. Croft was no ordinary individual. He was a man of considerable intelligence and wide interests. After completing his education at Oxford, he went on the Trans-Greenland Expedition 1933-4 and then on an expedition to the Arctic. He had learnt to ski and fly and spoke 10 languages. In 1939 he led a military mission to Finland before returning to England, where he was asked to set up the Auxiliary Units in Norfolk, Suffolk and Essex.

Later in 1940, when more officers were appointed, Norfolk's Resistance Units became the responsibility of Captain Oxenden, MC, who was later succeeded by Captain Woodward. Because of the intense secrecy of their work, it is impossible to say how many Auxiliary Units had been formed in 1940. However, it can be concluded with reasonable certainty that the essential elements for a rapid development of the scheme in Norfolk were firmly in place.

Norfolk's Resistance Units in 1941

1941 is the first year for which there is a detailed record of the operational strength of the Auxiliary Units throughout Britain. At this point there were over 3,500 civilians recruited and organized into over 570 patrols or units. Over 500 Operational Bases (OBs or underground bunkers) had been dug and another 53 were being built. A further 85 were planned.

In Norfolk, 201 men had been recruited. They were organized into 35 units. 40 OBs had been built and another 8 were planned. It is worth noting that among all the counties in England, Scotland and Wales, only Kent, Hampshire, Somerset, East Yorkshire and

Kincardine in Scotland, had recruited more men into the Auxiliary Units than Norfolk. Within the Norfolk structure there were 11 Group Commanders who were civilian officers responsible for three of the units in their areas.

What is clear is that remarkable progress had been made in a very short time as a result of the dedication and expertise of the regular officers in charge and the character of the volunteers who were courageously prepared to put their lives on the line. An invading Nazi force would certainly have put to death any men involved in acts of violence or sabotage against them.

Although the Auxiliary Units were administered by a small staff from its HQ at Coleshill House in Oxfordshire, whose postal address was c/o GPO, Highworth, Norfolk had its local HQ for the Resistance Units nearer home. The administrative centre of the Norfolk Units was at Beeston Hall, near Neatishead, while Rackheath Hall became the control station and radio communication centre.

RECRUITMENT OF MEN TO THE NORFOLK RESISTANCE UNITS

Intelligence Officers were told to look out for men who knew the forests, woods, fields and hills of their locality. Recruitment was cautious and thorough and potential recruits had to be totally trustworthy and capable of keeping a secret. They would be approached personally and told that there was difficult, dangerous and challenging work if they were interested. The right calibre of man was usually more than ready to volunteer when approached in this way. Security vetting would be carried out by MI5 assisted by the local police who were never told of the purpose of the investigation. The men also had to sign the Official Secrets Act.

Many, though not all, were recruited from local Home Guard units. Men from a wide variety of jobs became members of the Auxiliary Units – gamekeepers (and poachers!), farmers and farm workers, blacksmiths, engineers, office workers. Temperament and character were regarded as more important than social or occupational background. They had to be the sort of men who were not only capable of living rough and blending into the countryside, but also if necessary, would go on fighting until they triumphed or were killed.

Often one recruit was asked to recommend others. This is why groups of friends or even relatives were drawn into the network.

Men who knew each other well already and worked together, for example on a farm, would be ideal recruits. Of course all the men in the Resistance Units had to continue any other voluntary work they were involved in, such as Home Guard or fire watching to allay suspicion about their activities. The wives of these men were told nothing and their families remained in complete ignorance of the fact that they were trained guerrillas. However, some wives apparently did suspect that their husbands' frequent absence at night may have involved another woman!

The fact that the secret of the Resistance Units has been so well kept, testifies to the quality of the organization and the men in it, resourceful, self-disciplined and personally courageous.

"THEY WERE ON THEIR OWN" IN 202 BATTALION

Men in the Auxiliary Units were given Home Guard uniforms if they were not already in the force. As a cover for their activities, they were officially in the Home Guard. They were later informed that they were part of a secret Battalion, No. 202, which covered northern and eastern England. No. 201 Battalion was for Scotland and No. 203 covered the south and west. However, the names of the men were never recorded on paper and the battalions do not appear on any Home Guard official records. In short, they did not exist and no one was formally enrolled in anything. The men of the Resistance Units were on their own. They could never claim the protection afforded by the Geneva Convention to uniformed official fighting men. The Home Guard uniform and the 202 flashes however, might have given them some sense of security.

THE OPERATIONAL BASES (OBs)

Guerrilla activity on the continent in the late 1930s had shown that fighting in the open against an invading or occupying force meant that the first confrontation with the enemy usually ended in disaster.

To be effective, the Auxiliary Units in Norfolk and elsewhere, needed a secret base from which they could operate. From a well camouflaged hideout, they could strike an unseen blow and then disappear to relative safety. An ancient Chinese warlord underlined the importance of a base with the maxim that, "a guerrilla without a base is no better than a desperate struggler". One of the first

An Artist's Impression of an Operational Base.
This is drawn from descriptions given by Norfolk Auxiliary Unit members and site visits. The situation of this base is under a small copse and a hollowed-out tree stump concealed the trapdoor entrance. There are two "rooms", one containing bunks and food and the other an ammunition store. Designs did vary and although most were built by the Royal Engineers, some were constructed by the groups themselves.

priorities therefore, once the units have been formed and their training begun, was to provide them with a base. The secret underground bunkers were to be known as OBs or Operational Bases.

Many of the OBs in Norfolk were built by men from the Royal Engineers, though in some units the men constructed their own base. The work was done in the utmost secrecy, usually at night or at weekends. They were stocked with food supplies to last a month, water, blankets, stoves, a radio and other essential stores. In addition, there were the military stores which confirm that the Resistance Units were better armed and equipped than any other military unit in the country. Apart from an array of weaponry from automatic guns to revolvers and daggers, plus appropriate ammunition, the men were provided with a variety of sabotage equipment, including explosives, detonators and time fuses, booby trap devices and grenades. This careful attention to detail over equipment and supplies ensured that the units would hopefully be capable of inflicting more than an isolated blow against the enemy, and also of remaining a menace to the invader for weeks.

Castle Rising Patrol.
Standing, Left to Right: Ernie Drew, Rex Robin, Stanley Warren, Jack Masters, Deryck Neville, Ted Masters,
Archie Hudson. Seated: Walter Garner
Photo with kind permission of Mr. Ray Fisher

205

The design of the OBs varied but the principles on which they were built were the same. The speedily dug underground bunkers were usually 12 feet deep and big enough to accommodate up to six men. They were made from a mixture of materials – iron, concrete and timber. The entrance was always extremely well camouflaged, as was the escape route, usually through a tunnel. Sometimes an OB made use of an existing cellar of an old house. In one case, the tunnels of a badger sett in a derelict chalk pit, were enlarged to make an effective OB. Improvisation had excelled!

The man-made structures however, were formidable bunkers. The ones dug by the Royal Engineers were lined with concrete walls two feet thick. But it was the entrance and the escape routes which displayed the greatest imagination and skill. Both were carefully concealed, and trap-door systems would be operated by cunningly hidden wires. Sometimes, above the bunkers of this type, the men would "plant" hollowed out trees which would have carried the fumes of cooking high above any enemy in the vicinity.

TRAINING TO BE GUERRILLAS

The men who were recruited into the Resistance Units were trained by professionals to the highest level of proficiency. Many of those men who experienced the training, confirm that it was very demanding, thorough and arduous. It took place on a regular weekly basis and at weekends. Much of it occurred at night. The men were kept up to the mark by the regularity of their training in Norfolk, which was complemented by specialist weekend exercises and longer summer camps. These took place at Cawston Common, Leicester Square Farm at Syderstone and at Coleshill in Oxfordshire, near the administrative HQ of the Resistance Units. The instructors were always regular army specialists.

HELP FROM HANDBOOKS

Patrol leaders and others in Norfolk who were responsible for the training were supplied with expert and up-to-date information and advice for men being prepared for guerrilla warfare. Among the publications used in Norfolk were two by Colonel Gubbins. These were, "The Art of Guerrilla Warfare" and "How to use Explosives", which became the training manuals of Resistance groups in Britain and throughout the free world.

"The 1938 Norfolk Calendar" – an Explosives Manual!

However, the key book used by operational patrol leaders and instructors in Norfolk was known as "The 1938 Norfolk Calendar", so called because of its innocent looking cover. In reality it was a saboteur's handbook which provided concise, clear, explanations and instructions on everything about explosives and how to use them. The "Calendar" covered a wide range of sabotage techniques, including fuses, detonators, delay mechanisms, grenades, incendiaries, booby trap mechanisms, booby traps and improvised mines. Another section of the book showed how to blow up tanks, railway lines, aeroplanes, armoured vehicles, etc., and also how to destroy petrol, ammunition and food dumps. There was further very practical advice about storing explosives, methods of lighting and throwing instructions.

Resistance Units became much more than Explosives Experts

The training undergone by the men covered a wide variety of skills. Among those which they acquired were, map reading, stalking (often taught by Lovat Scouts), reconnoitering buildings or other targets, camouflage, unarmed combat (known as "Thuggery"), security and management of the OB and of course weapon training in many different weapons.

Weapons– "These men must have Revolvers"

The Resistance Units were among the best, if not the best, armed and equipped units in Britain in the early 1940s. They were fully trained in a wide range of weaponry which included automatic Thompson machine guns, Tommy guns and Stens, .303 Rifles and in some cases .22 Rifles with telescopic lens and silencer. All of them were also provided with revolvers, at Churchill's behest, plus daggers and truncheons. The units also had plentiful supplies of ammunition.

The men were also equipped with a range of explosives and bombs, such as sticky bombs, anti-tank grenades, land mines and booby trap devices. They were the first to be issued with plastic explosives rather than the traditional gelignite which was inclined to "sweat" if not properly stored and become dangerous.

Once they had been fully trained, the units assumed responsibility for their own local arms and equipment, which were regularly replenished and updated where appropriate. It seems that everything was done to provide the men with the best of what was available. Their weapons and ammunition stores were subject to inspections by army officers at regular intervals, ensuring the highest standards were maintained.

NORFOLK RESISTANCE UNITS ON EXERCISE

Routine exercises included night patrol, stalking an "enemy" and reconnoitering the estates of big country houses in the area. The latter was to obtain information which could be used later in the event of an invasion and the enemy takeover of a local manor house as a local HQ and base. Another very useful exercise was the employment of the units to test the security and defence of local airfields and camps of regular army units. Such exercises tested one of the most important skills of the guerrilla, namely the ability to move silently, unobtrusively and stealthily. Men were frequently reminded of one of the maxims of an officer in charge of training at the Coleshill HQ of the Auxiliary Units, which was, "Don't hurry and be killed".

A CHALLENGE FOR RESISTANCE UNITS – EXERCISE "FLORENCE"

By 1942, with the German army concentrating on the invasion of Russia, the possibility of a military attack on Britain seemed unlikely. However, there was no respite for the Auxiliary Units in Norfolk. In June many of them were informed of an exercise in which they would be involved. The scenario was that the German offensive on Russia had failed and Nazi troops had adopted defensive positions on the eastern front. At the same time, they had begun to transfer large numbers of troops back to the west. By 2 June the Resistance Units were told to prepare for an early invasion of Britain, with "stand-by" procedure. On 4 June they had to be in a state of complete readiness for the attack and two days later, "Action Stations" was under way. The objective of a number of Resistance Units, was to recapture Coltishall aerodrome after a paratroop attack and to disrupt enemy bridgeheads at Wells, Binham and Weybourne, which had been subject to enemy bombing.

With exercises like this, the Auxiliary Units were kept very realistically trained and in a constant state of readiness. Sometimes training sessions were lengthy and a letter from a group commander in east Norfolk to patrol leaders apologized for the duration of a recent class. He then suggested that the next time, patrol leaders bring a primus stove and each man bring "a pinch of tea a piece, so a brew can be made"!

An Auxiliary Unit can always Improve its Skills

Although there were frequent courses, usually at Cawston and Syderstone, where the instruction was by experts in different fields, occasionally a cancellation occurred. Group commanders were reminded by GHQ Highworth, that Auxiliary Units could always get on with something useful. This emphasises the idea that they were self-sufficient, self-operating units, constantly improving by continual training. They could plan scouting operations, improve the OB door camouflage or lay multiple charges to keep their explosives skills up to the mark.

Camps and Competitions

An annual camp and competition was held at Leicester Square farm, Syderstone. Apart from being updated on existing guerrilla techniques, units would be given other useful advice. On one camp in 1942, detailed information on German military routines and procedures was provided. Men were told how the Nazis defend their tanks, their sentry patterns and what they did to secure a captured airfield. Detailed extracts from German military manuals on tactics, etc. were also available.

Another annual event was the Coleshill Shield Competition. The men were tested on observation and given a night patrol exercise. In this they were given two and a half hours to penetrate the "enemy" defences, which had two sentries posted at least 20 yards from the target. They had to place a magnet on the target, avoid the trip wires and return to their base some 1,000 yards away. After this the men would be given efficiency tests on explosives, map reading, weaponry, booby traps and setting time fuses.

At a weekend course at Leicester Square farm, held in 1943, the men were kept particularly busy. The programme lasted from 4pm on Saturday until 4.15pm Sunday. It included sessions on the

Letter of thanks from GHQ Coleshill to a Group Commander.
With kind permission of Mr. R. Bartram

Dear Bartram,

A line to thank you for the trouble you took over my visit, and also for the exceptionally hard work which I know you must have put in over this show.

I cannot over emphasise the importance of keeping going at full blast through these rather difficult times, and I know that since you took over your group you have improved it out of all knowledge.

Hoping to see you soon.

Yours ....
Lt. Col.

following: shooting, reconnoitering a night scheme, a day scheme, a night scheme, respirator drill, arms inspection, explosives, booby traps, telephones, grenades, camouflage, sabotage and unarmed combat. The men had to be mentally as well as physically tough to cope with such demanding training. On Monday morning after such a course, they would have to be back to work!

During a patrol explosives competition at Syderstone, men were told to solve five problems from a list of ten. These included, destroying a dump of aeroplane bombs, an aeroplane, a petrol dump, an armoured vehicle and a heavy gun. Felling a tree in a certain direction and setting a booby trap to fire a shrapnel mine could also be tackled. Dummy detonators were used and safety pins left in all mechanisms. The marking of these tests was rigorous. Different points were awarded for such things as, drawing of stores, making up charges, placing of charges, camouflage and amount of explosives used. The professional manner of guerrilla training ensured that the Auxiliary Units were well prepared for the worst if it came.

THE SITUATION BY THE END OF 1942

After a hasty and very improvised beginning in 1940, the organization of the Auxiliary Units in Norfolk had made great progress. The units were a sophisticated and powerful instrument for resistance activity. Churchill had always admired the scheme and believed that the Auxiliary Units were a very useful addition to the regular forces. Judging by the evidence of the Norfolk units, the men in them had been turned into highly trained, well equipped and confident resistance fighters, who were very clear about their role in the overall system of strategic and tactical defence.

A VERY SECRET "ORGANIZATION"

It would be wrong to regard the Auxiliary Units as part of a centrally controlled and tight-knit system. This would have made it easier to destroy. Colonel Gubbins and his successors were never' the "head of the British Underground".

Because of the intense secrecy, which was preserved throughout the war, (and long after it), the members of the Resistance would usually only know the men who were in their unit. Also they remained ignorant of any OB other than their own. One Norfolk sergeant explosives instructor was blindfolded before being taken to an other OB to ensure its location remained secret. Even when two or three units attended a course, the anonymity and confidentiality of each, was preserved. This was one of the great strengths of the system in resistance terms, for in the event of one unit being captured, its members would have no information about the other units. Each unit was trained and equipped to work independently on the initiative of its patrol leader. The vast majority of the men in the Norfolk Resistance remain ignorant to this day of colleagues in other parts of the county who also served. It could be said, that never had so much, been kept secret by so few, for so long. This achievement was a great tribute to the character of the men who were recruited throughout Norfolk for such potentially dangerous work.

THE CHAIN OF COMMAND

However, for the units to function effectively, there was a means of communication for the purposes of security, training and continual updating of skills. From the HQ at Coleshill, c/o Highworth Post Office, the Norfolk Intelligence Officers (regular army captains) would receive instructions and information. They in turn relayed this to the Group Commanders (civilians, often Home Guard officers), who were responsible for three Auxiliary Units in their area. The group commanders would deal directly with the patrol leader of each Auxiliary Unit under their command. And of course he would ensure that men in his unit were fully briefed accordingly. This "system" was flexible enough to incorporate the military expertise of various regular army units which were based in Norfolk, to assist with training. Also, the intelligence officers, (Captains Oxenden and Woodward) would visit each Auxiliary Unit from time to time to check on things and to boost morale. In this way the Norfolk Resistance grew from strength to strength, retaining the vital ingredient of secrecy at all times.

DISCIPLINE AND SECURITY IN THE
NORFOLK OPERATIONAL BASES (OBs)

The intelligence officers who managed the Resistance Units in Norfolk ensured that good advice and practical help was given to the men in the units. Captain Woodward's memo on OB discipline and security, pays great attention to detail. Among the instructions sent to group commanders, who relayed these to the units were the following:–

> *"One man will be responsible for seeing that no light is left on in the OB, no gas is left on, camouflage is replaced and that hatches are fastened.*
> *No man will enter the OB without permission of the Patrol Leader.*
> *The OB will not be approached by the same route on all occasions.*
> *The position of the Rendezvous will be varied for all occasions except "Action Stations".*
> *In the OB hang up that which will hang up.*
> *See that tidiness is everyone's business.*
> *Lights – Candles give least strain to the eyes, but must be used in sconces or candlesticks".*

ADVICE ABOUT SURVIVING UNDERGROUND

Every conceivable problem about living in an OB was considered by those in charge of the Auxiliary Unit scheme. Everything from ventilation and camouflage to sleep patterns and smoking, was included in a "Lecture" or printed handout of practical advice on "OB Discipline". A list of the subjects so comprehensively covered in this document, follows:– food and water, rum, smoking, sleep, light, cooking, washing, waste disposal, care of arms and stores, mental dullness, physical fitness and recreation. A few extracts from this lecture are quoted to illustrate its flavour and attention to detail.

> *"No frying is to be permitted on any account.*
> *Patrols must eat to live, and not the reverse, and should therefore take a pride in their economy of food rather than in extravagant meals.*
> *Seal up the Rum jar after each time it is breached. Be scrupulously fair in its distribution and not over lavish. Best issue on return from Patrol.*
> *Smoking must be controlled (10–15 minutes in each hour must be sufficient). It is not only a question of fresh air, but the give-away of smoke fumes from the ventilator.*

Light. The outlet must be continually checked for "Black Out".

Dirt and damp are the chief enemies of the Arms and Stores.

Constant care and cleaning necessary and should be routine.

Cleanliness of OB is essential, for care of arms, etc. but also psychologically.

Mental dullness is inevitable and must be relieved by mental gymnastics, and by a few minutes rest in the open air on emerging from the OB.

Extinguish all lights for 10 minutes before emerging so that men are not bewildered by contrast.

Give each man a specific task in OB maintenance so that he has something definite to do.

Beware of pessimism and despondency, which are the natural outcome of failure and casualties. Any ill feeling which arises from some mistake or patrol, should be checked.

Our work requires the highest state of fitness. Patrol Leaders must not allow unfit men to proceed on duty. Have a supply of health salts or pills. First aid sets must be kept clean and a personal check of Morphine tablets made by the Patrol Leader.

General Amenities – Playing cards, dart board, radio. slippers or canvas shoes, lavatory paper, matches, pencils, needles and thread, soap, vacuum flask, etc".

24 Hours of an Auxiliary's Life (Winter)

From time to time, a unit would have to spend 24 hours at its OB as part of the training. This is how the time would be organised.

1430	*Reveille.*
1515	*Meal – hot tea – cold food.*
1600-1700	*Clean OB, wash up, make beds, inspect weapons, stores & equipment.*
1700-1800	*Stand easy – smoking allowed for 15 mins.*
1800-2030	*Prepare for Night Patrol.*
2030-2045	*Emerge and rest in open air.*
2045-0545	*Patrol – during absence, hot meal is cooked by next-day's Observer.*

| 0600 | Hot meal – after which Observer moves to his task. |
| 0700-1400 | Lights Out. |

The Observer's OB and Telephone – Improving Security

This was a one man OB or "hide" which would enable a member of a patrol to go to ground if the enemy was nearby, avoiding the need to open up the patrol's OB, disturbing its camouflage and thus jeopardizing the lives of the whole patrol. A telephone link would enable the observer to maintain contact with his patrol. The one man OB formed a rendezvous for the neighbouring patrol's message carriers to meet, but the location of the patrol OB was kept secret from personnel in other patrols. *(See page 236)*

Observer's OBs had to be well camouflaged, weatherproof, easy of access and in view of the patrol OB, to enable the observer to warn the patrol of enemy presence. The issue of telephones, wire and periscopes would make the system workable. In case of enemy discovery of the telephone, a password preceded all conversations.

"Don't Tamper with the Rum"

In 1943, all Norfolk Resistance Units leaders received the following memo from their group commanders:– "There appears to have been tampering with RUM in parts of the country. Vigorous disciplinary action will be taken in future as well as payment for any consumed". There is no evidence to suggest that Norfolk units were guilty of such offences. The story is included to illustrate the high standards which were expected and maintained by members of the resistance who would have undoubtedly enjoyed and deserved a drink of rum after a long night patrol.

The Beginning of the end of the Auxiliary Units

By 1944, the prospect of an invasion was very unlikely, but the units continued to function and attend training activities. However, early in the year the Norfolk units were amalgamated with those throughout East Anglia under the command of one intelligence officer.

By now some units had lost members who had been called up to serve in the regular forces. Among these was John Fielding of

Norwich, who trained as a paratrooper and joined the very dangerous mission, "Operation Bullbasket". This was part of an SOE (Special Operations Executive) plan to sabotage and disrupt German communications in France (May 1944), to distract attention from the Normandy coast, the focus of the D Day invasion plans.

John Fielding's training as a Norfolk resistance fighter had been excellent preparation for the guerrilla activity in which he now became involved in France.

At the time of D Day (June 1944) some members of the Norfolk Resistance were transferred to the south coast and the Isle of Wight to help with security patrols.

STAND DOWN OF THE AUXILIARY UNITS

In November 1944, the C in C, Home Forces wrote to the GHQ of the Auxiliary Units at Coleshill, to say that because of the improved war situation, the units which had been of such value to the country, could now be "Stood Down". He sent his congratulations to all men who had served and added that although their work could not receive any publicity, their secrecy should be regarded by them as a matter of special pride.

A THANK YOU LETTER AND A BADGE

In due course, everyone who had served in an Auxiliary Unit received a letter from GHQ Coleshill, signed by Colonel Douglas. It included the following words of tribute:–

"You were invited to do a job which would require more skill and coolness, more hard work and greater danger than was demanded of any other voluntary organization. In the event of "Action Stations" being ordered you knew well the kind of life you were in for. But you were picked men and (we) knew that you would continue to fight whatever the conditions, with, or if necessary, without orders.

In view of the fact that your lives depended on secrecy, no public recognition will be possible. But those in the most responsible positions at General HQ, Home Forces, knew what was done and what would have been done, if you had been called upon. They know it well. It will not be forgotten".

By 1942, many members of the Auxiliary Units wore 202 Battalion flashes on their Home Guard uniform. They did not refer to a Home Guard battalion and there is no official record of such a battalion. However, after the war, the men received a badge with 202 inscribed on it. It is worn with justifiable pride and has been described as "the Badge of Courage" which singled out the wearer as a resistance fighter.

THE PRESS IS TOLD

In April 1945, the War Office told the press that a resistance organization had existed in Britain since 1940. The Times published a leading article. Colonel Gubbins wanted the men to have the Defence Medal, but this did not happen, perhaps because of the secrecy and also because there was no official record of the men's service. So in the VE Parades, while representatives of the Armed Forces and the voluntary organizations marched proudly together, the Auxiliary Units remained apart, their secret role receiving no public recognition at the time. It is fitting that in 1996, the Ministry of Defence finally authorised the award of the Defence Medal to the men who had served in the Resistance Units for at least three years.

CLEARING UP AFTER THE WAR

Many of the OBs in Norfolk, as in other parts of the country, had huge stores of ammunition, explosives, fuse wire, detonator cord, booby traps, time switches, grenades, etc. These had to be made safe and teams of military experts came round to collect weapons and stores and blow up items which could not be moved. Some men doubtless retained some items as souvenirs of their time in the Resistance. Sometimes, a patrol leader whose OB was not found, had to destroy his own stores.

THE IMPORTANCE OF THE NORFOLK AUXILIARY UNITS

Although they may have not made the supreme sacrifice, the resistance fighters *were* prepared to do so. *They were part of an elite secret group, over 270 in number out of a total of 3,000 for the whole of the British Isles.* They should be remembered for what they did and also for what they might have done if a Nazi force had ever invaded these islands. They too stood up to Hitler.

However, they were not just a guerrilla force to combat German occupation, defend their immediate locality and test the security of our regular forces in the area. The formation of the Auxiliary Units in 1940, gave Colonel Gubbins a chance to test his theories about guerrilla warfare. The experience gained was later used by him and others in the founding of the SOE (Special Operations Executive). The work of the Auxiliary Units had a direct influence on resistance activity behind the German lines in occupied Europe. John Fielding's work in France in 1944, prior to the D Day landings, has already been mentioned. When some of the younger members of the units were called up for regular army service, their training was ideal for a commando role abroad.

While serving in the Auxiliary Units the men tested and proved the value of a wide range of guerrilla weapons such as plastic explosives and timing devices. The officers who organised things in Norfolk and elsewhere, learned valuable lessons which they were able to use, when they were later employed to lead resistance groups in occupied Europe. Andrew Croft, who set up the organization in Norfolk, later served in commando operations and the SOE.

HOW SUCCESSFUL WOULD THE RESISTANCE HAVE BEEN IF THE GERMANS HAD INVADED?

It is impossible to say with any certainty, though there is encouraging evidence, that they would have achieved some damaging blows against an invading force. We should remember the quality of the training, their arms and equipment and above all the confidence of many of the men who served, that they would have caused some serious problems for the enemy. Certainly the Nazis had not encountered an effective Resistance on the continent in the opening campaigns of the war. To quote John Fielding, who went on to successful guerrilla activity against the Nazis in France, "We were confident that we could cause a considerable amount of mayhem". Some have argued that some of the units might have survived a few weeks at most: others are more pessimistic. It is true that though their fighting spirit may have been fierce, the prospects of six men living indefinitely in relative isolation in an underground bunker, would not have been great. Furthermore, seasonal changes in the weather, such as falling leaves and the coming of snow, would have reduced their natural cover.

The Resistance Units must have realised the certain prospect of retribution if they were caught. Reprisals against themselves, their families and the local community would have followed. However, this knowledge perhaps would have inspired them to strike some telling blows first. Invasion is never easy and the Nazis would initially try to establish a bridgehead against a fierce counter attack. The diversionary and disruptive tactics of the resistance could have made a valuable contribution in the struggle, out of all proportion to its numbers. Churchill and senior military commanders recognised that above all, the enemy should not be allowed to maraud freely through the countryside, if it succeeded in establishing a bridgehead. It was in such a situation that the Resistance Units might have played a crucial role.

Speculation on likely scenarios following an invasion is a fascinating exercise. However, it is more important to recognize the significance of the Resistance Units. The story of the "Secret Army" is an illustration of heroism and the willingness of volunteers to display the highest standards of courage, self-discipline and self-sacrifice in the defence of their country against a tyrannical foe. For that they should always be remembered with pride.

EXTRACTS FROM THE 1942 DIARY OF A MEMBER OF THE NORFOLK RESISTANCE

Jan	8	*Parade at Earlham OB*
	13	*See Turner about duty*
	20	*At Earlham OB*
Feb	8	*Collect rifles and revolvers from Veterans Club*
	15	*Tunnel caved in, but mended very satisfactorily*
	22	*Meet Turner to go to OB and collect corrugated iron*
Mar	1	*Rifle shooting at Whitlingham sandpits*
	5	*Take car to Beeston with others to see Capt. Woodward (the Intelligence Officer)*
	6	*Woodward gives general lecture at Veterans Club*
	15	*Pick up others to go to Whitlingham for Tommy gun firing*
	18	*Night patrol at Cringleford OB*

	23	NCOs meeting at Veterans Club
	29	Earlham OB inspection by Capt. Woodward
	30	Marston Lane night patrol
Apr	1	Patrol at Sprowston OB
	5	Cringleford OB inspected by Capt. Woodward
	11	Night operations at Earlham Park OB
	12	Parade Veterans Club re court enquiry re Xs revolver
		Parade Hellesdon OB to fetch equipment
	16	Got call-up papers
	18	Patrol at Hellesdon OB
	27	Blitz starts – big damage in Norwich eg, City Station, Mile Cross and Vauxhall Street
	29	More Blitz – helped to fight fire in Newmarket Road
May	3	Full kit inspection by Capt. Woodward – didn't come
	6	Woodward inspects kit
	11	Visit to Veterans Club by Capt. Oxenden and questions
	14	Parade at Grammar School in the Close for observation training for competition
	17	Parade Earlham OB for camouflaging
	20	Went to OB to measure for bunks in evening, but found courting couple 15 yards from OB
	21	Measured for bunks in OB
	24	Haines picked me up in car to go to Marston Lane to collect timber
	25	Finish getting timber ready for collection
	26	Haines collected timber in car for use at OB
	27	Made start in erecting structure
	28	Haines took me to OB to do reconnaissance for a patrol competition
	30	11pm competition night patrol. Sleep in OB
	31	Continued competition at Whitlingham sandpits 8am
Jun	2	Picked up by Haines to go to X's OB to collect wire netting. Collected rubber truncheons to take to our OB and clean up after Saturday night
	9	OB Inspection by Colonel X. In OB all night
	16	In OB all night
28–7 Jul		Parades and/or activities on every day
Jul	11	Combined operations scheme. Attacked St Faiths aerodrome. At OB all night and Sunday morning
	19	At Whitlingham sandpits
	24	Travel to Coleshill

25–26	Weekend training at Coleshill
Aug 1–2	All night working on tunnel
3	To Feltwell aerodrome for recce for Saturday night
8	Combined attack on St Faiths. Changed to Feltwell. Quite successful as 12 aircraft destroyed, battle HQ and electricity power sabotaged
17	Concreted floor of OB
23	Parade at Whitlingham sandpits
31	Opened rum at Earlham OB
Sep 5	Competition night patrol 9pm and sleep in OB
6	Sprowston OB won all Norfolk patrol competition
20	Climbing up sides of sandpits with gas masks and firing Tommy guns
27	Met Haines to take wood for trap-door to OB Climbing sides of Whitlingham sandpits again
Oct 4	Go to Wroxham for lecture on explosives
10	Arrive at OB at 5pm to remain there for 36 hours
12	7pm at OB. King visited Norwich
18	To Wroxham for competition final
24–25	At OB for 36 hours
Nov 1	Practice for competition at Whitlingham Pits
7	Night patrol
13–15	At Coleshill for competition
Dec 3	Night patrol
10	Night patrol
12	Attack on Wroxham. Arrive back at OB 4am
22	Post mortem on attack on Wroxham

The diary reveals in considerable detail how wide and varied the training of an Auxiliary was. The OB was of course, the focal point of activities, but lectures, inspections, exercises, patrols, competitions and visits to the HQ of the Auxiliary Units at Coleshill underline the thorough and professional approach. It is clear that the Norwich OBs were built by the men themselves, as was the case in a number of others in different parts of the county. Finally, the diary illustrates how men in the Resistance Units were kept purposefully employed and intensively trained for their role.

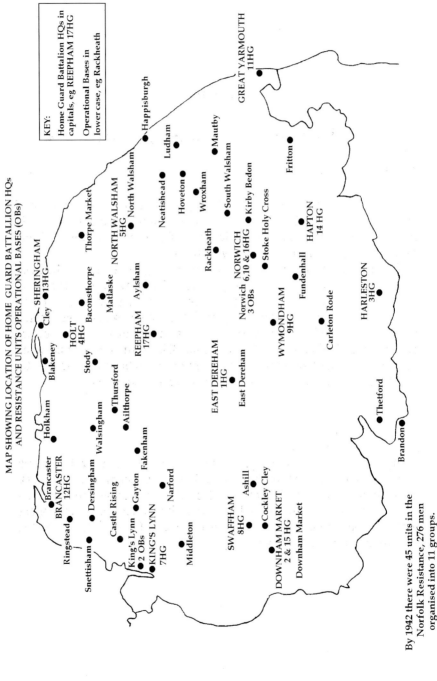

MAP SHOWING LOCATION OF HOME GUARD BATTALION HQs AND RESISTANCE UNITS OPERATIONAL BASES (OBs)

KEY:

Home Guard Battalion HQs in capitals, eg REEPHAM 17HG

Operational Bases in lower case, eg Rackheath

GREAT YARMOUTH 11HG

Happisburgh

Ludham

Mautby

SHERINGHAM

Cley ●13HG

Thorpe Market

North Walsham

NORTH WALSHAM 5HG

Neatishead

Hoveton

Wroxham

South Walsham

Fritton

Baconsthorpe

Matlaske

Aylsham

Rackheath

Kirby Bedon

Stoke Holy Cross

HOLT 4HG

Blakeney

Stody

REEPHAM 17HG

NORWICH 6,10 & 16HG

Norwich 3 OBs

HAPTON 14 HG

Fundenhall

Holkham

Thursford

Ailthorpe

EAST DEREHAM 1HG

East Dereham

WYMONDHAM 9HG

Carleton Rode

HARLESTON 3HG

Brancaster

BRANCASTER 12HG

Dersingham

Walsingham

Fakenham

Narford

Ringstead

Castle Rising

King's Lynn

Gayton

2 OBs

KING'S LYNN 7HG

Middleton

SWAFFHAM 8HG

Ashill

Cockley Cley

Thetford

Snettisham

DOWNHAM MARKET 2 & 15 HG

Downham Market

Brandon

By 1942 there were 45 units in the Norfolk Resistance, 276 men organised into 11 groups.

222

CHAPTER 10

Personal Memories of the Norfolk Resistance

Mr. D.L. Daglish,
Dereham.

I was living at Baconsthorpe during the war and I was recruited into a unit of No. 202 Battalion there. There were four of us in the unit plus a sergeant, John Seaman. The other three were Tony Smith, Hedley Smith and Harry Adlard.

Our underground OB (Operational Base) was in the right hand corner of Baconsthorpe Castle grounds. There were two rooms in the OB, one being where we had meetings with our CO, Capt. Duncan from North Walsham, and the other where we stored ammunition and explosives, such as detonators, gun cotton, bullets, plastic fuses, i.e. Orange line, Bickford, cortex and hand grenades. We had an underground tunnel too, where we could enter at one end and escape through the other if necessary.

Mr. Peter Harcourt,
son of H.T. Harcourt.

My father was the sergeant in the Blakeney patrol and he recruited me into the patrol when I was 16 years old. The OB, now filled in, was at Wiveton. After the war, some time pencils were found on my father's farm and the police came to collect them. Other members of the patrol were G. Cubitt, J. Betts, E. Parsons and A. Holman.

I remember one Sunday morning when our CO came to check our supplies. He was very concerned because all our boxes of gelignite had begun to "sweat". This was very dangerous and could have caused a massive explosion, so the Army came and took that lot away.

We had plenty of training and much of it was very tough. I remember we went with several other Norfolk units on a course at Coleshill, near Swindon. On another occasion, we had a two week course at Leicester Square Farm, Syderstone. Of course, we had plenty of weapon training too. We had revolvers and our CO, Capt. Duncan was a wizard on how to use these revolvers. One Sunday, as a demonstration, he put six walnut shells on a wall and stood some 12 yards back, then split every shell. He had been abroad and seen action, being sent home as a result of a bad wound, but he certainly knew how to teach us revolver skills. We were also issued with very strong magnets, so that we could use them to clamp a stick of dynamite to an enemy tank.

We also spent several Sunday mornings at Lodge Hill, Sheringham, learning how to crawl under real fire from the Army. They threw thunder flashes at us which made a terrific bang, to teach us to keep our heads down under fire. Another part of our training, was to run a certain distance with a gas mask on, then through a tear gas chamber to check our equipment and also to see how fit we were.

The most interesting course lasted 3 weeks on the Isle of Wight, based at Sandown. There we were asked to take over guard duties on the airfields, to let the regulars take some leave. We were well armed with .303 Lee Enfield rifles, a striker board sewn to one trouser leg and a dagger down the other leg. We also carried a Smith & Wesson .38 revolver. Incidentally, on our way to the Isle of Wight, via London, we had to take cover from a "Doodlebug" which hit a cinema and killed several people.

With all the training, we got very tired, as we still had our jobs on the farm. When we weren't on duty, we spent several nights fire watching on Kelling Heath and Holt Lows. Sometimes, we found incendiary bombs which had dropped in soft ground and not exploded. We took them home and set them off at the first opportunity, to watch the phosphorous sparks. Looking back, this was very unwise!

When the war was over, like other Auxiliary Units throughout the country, we had no official recognition. However, we were given a small badge, which I still wear with pride in my buttonhole, as in our own way, we did what we could to help the war effort. During the day we were ordinary men working on the farms, but at night and other times, we were doing our bit to defeat Nazi tyranny. My memories of the comradeship in the Auxiliary Unit are still very vivid. Baconsthorpe Castle was very overgrown and neglected at the time of the war, but now it has been transformed into a beautiful place and our underground base is now a lovely goldfish pond.

Mr. Max Cremer,
Calthorpe, Nr. Erpingham.

When the Government appealed for volunteers to join the Home Guard, I enrolled at Erpingham Village Hall. I was issued with an old .300 American rifle which I trained with. Later, I was asked by a Capt. Bray, if I would volunteer to join an underground movement (202 Battalion), which would be trained in the use of explosives. In my unit there was Sergeant Scott, a local farmer, John Everett, son of another farmer, Raymond Buller, known as "Timmy" and myself, just the four of us. Our underground base was in a wood between the Cromer and North Walsham roads, known as Thorpe Market.

We were issued with Smith and Wesson revolvers. Timmy and myself had an American Lewis machine gun between us. We were trained in the use of explosives by various specialists in the Army, and I remember that we trained two or three times a week. I think that Major Kett-Cremer was in charge of our operation. At the time it was believed that the Germans might land on the North Norfolk coast. Our job was to be behind the German lines after they had landed and moved inland. We would then operate from our underground base and blow up bridges, railway lines and carry out other acts of sabotage against the enemy.

Mr. A.N. Other,
Aylsham.

I was in charge of an Auxiliary Unit of six men, mainly gamekeepers, poachers and farm workers. They were all good men with a superb knowledge of the local countryside, and of course they were all good shots.

At the start of the war I had been a special constable, but I joined the Home Guard as soon as it was formed. Then one day, a regular army captain approached me to offer more interesting work before I was called up for the regular forces myself. I did some basic training in Yorkshire, then returned to Norfolk and was actively involved in 202 Battalion for about two years.

The training was frequent, professional and invariably at night. We always wore Home Guard uniform and as far as the rest of the Home Guard were concerned and the community generally, we were part of the Home Guard. In fact, I was in a highly secret unit. I was very proud of my men, whose skill and bravery were exceptional. Our underground base was in the woods 2-3 miles north of Aylsham. One of the skills we were taught was how to move silently. One night, I remember I was in the woods when suddenly someone touched my shoulder. I was amazed because I had not heard or seen anyone approaching. On another occasion, during a night training exercise, I came across my men standing about 20 yards from our underground base. When I asked them why they had not gone in, I was told that they couldn't because a courting couple were making love on the "roof", oblivious of course of what was actually below them!

During another training day in the midlands, two of us were in a dugout with a live grenade each. I threw mine but my colleague dropped his with the lever "on" i.e. live! Well, the lever fell out and, cool as a cucumber, I picked it up and threw it out of the dugout, saving both of us from disaster.

We were trained to act as guerrillas in the event of a German invasion. However, we were not frightened for ourselves, because morale was excellent and we were extremely well armed. Our main concern was for our women, because once it was realized we were operating behind German lines following an invasion, they would be prime targets.

At the end of the war, we had loads of ammunition and explosives to dispose of. We were told to remove detonators, put it underground and burn it. All rifles and Stens etc. were handed in.

In conclusion, 202 Battalion did not wear black (SAS style) uniform as suggested in a TV documentary. We always wore Home Guard uniform, and to all intents and purposes, that's what we were.

Mr. Jack Gamble,
Wattlefield.

As the manager of Wattlefield estate, I was in a "reserved" occupation, so could not join the regular forces. However, I did join the Home Guard when it was started in 1940. We had two meetings a week in the Drill Hall in Pople Street, Wymondham. We had parades, drill, etc. and weapon training at weekends. Night watch from the Abbey Tower was cold and unpleasant.

Then one day, out of the blue, a friend asked me if I would like to be transferred to another branch of the Home Guard. He couldn't tell me what it was about, but said it was very interesting. As I was not particularly enthusiastic about the local Home Guard unit, I said, "Yes". In due course I joined 202 Battalion, where I became a member of one of a number of small units which were being trained for guerrilla warfare. The training included the use of high explosives, blocking roads by felling trees and stretching thin, high tension wire across the road to stop enemy motor cyclists.

Our role was to be left behind if local inhabitants were evacuated in the event of an invasion. Our HQ was an underground base. We would live off the land and many houses in the area would be booby-trapped to create as much nuisance and diversion as possible to the enemy.

The training was intensive and on many weekends, from Friday to Sunday, we trained at Leicester Square Farm. Specialist army units taught us all the latest ideas and methods. Every time that new devices were discovered in North Africa, left by the German army, they were used by our instructors. We had to crawl under live machine gun fire at night, which was very unpleasant and particularly hard on the knees. I borrowed a pair of leather knee pads from a local thatcher, which were a great help when we did this sort of training. On Sunday nights we would come home totally exhausted after a weekend in which regular army sergeants had worked us extremely hard. But of course we were expected to carry on our usual job the next day. Looking back, I don't know how we did it. Sometimes after one of those training weekends I could hardly walk.

During the week in the evening, our duties were to test security at searchlight units and other military establishments, as there were a number of army units based in the area. These exercises lasted for most of the night and we would arrive home between

West Norfolk Group of Patrols

Back row: Aubrey Brown, ?, Jack Masters, ?, Dick Libbey, Edwin Seaman, Ray Mallett, Ron Bennett, Rex Robin, ?, Deryck Neville, ?.   Middle row: Stanley Warren, Walter Garner, Harold Spreckley, Robinson, Capt. J. Hardy, Maurice Newnes, H. Haggas, Attwood, Cheddar Walker, D. Sneezum.   Front row: Archie Hudson, ?, Ernie Drew, ?, Bill Ely, ?, ?, Ted Masters.

Photo with kind permission of Mr. Ray Fisher

4 and 5 o'clock in the morning, thus getting a couple of hours sleep before going off to work. One of our raids was on a military arsenal outside Norwich. We tried to gain information by listening to conversation in pubs, without success. The raid was a failure and we were all captured. All the trees and bushes round the camp were bugged so that if you stood on a twig, the noise would echo around from loud speakers. We always felt that someone had told them that we were going to test them that night.

However, we were often very successful in these exercises and on one occasion, after listening in pubs, some members of my unit were invited back to the camp and shown around. Little did they know that we were planning to raid them later that week! On another occasion we were told to test a searchlight unit. Again we went to the local pub, got friendly and then were invited up to the site to see everything. Later in the week we put the searchlight out of action.

Although our uniform was the same as the Home Guard, we always carried a revolver. We were not allowed to carry any formal identification except a military pass. If we were stopped by the police, etc. they had to contact our HQ in Wiltshire.

As D-Day approached we were put on special alert. We were asked to volunteer to go to the south coast to provide back-up in the event of any German counter-attack, or problems arising from the invasion of France. We were very disappointed when our names were not among those chosen for this assignment.

We had been trained to a high level of skill by various experts so that we could lay booby traps, carry out many acts of sabotage against an enemy, move silently and of course use various weapons efficiently. In short, we were trained to create as much havoc as possible for any enemy who landed.

Mrs. R.M. Wroth,
North Elmham.

My late husband was a member of the secret underground movement. During the war we were farming at Holkham, but it was not until after the war that he told me about their meeting place. One day long after the war was over he took me to his unit's hideaway which was in Holkham Park, about three miles from the sea. However, I refused to go into it via a hollowed out tree which was the tunnel entrance to the secret bunker.

When he went out on training, of course I never knew where he was and he was often out all night. I do remember that he had a number of gas masks, telephones and revolvers, which he kept out of sight in a bedroom. In 1944, my husband was sent to the Southampton area and he said that he had never seen so many ships in his life - "enough to walk across the Channel".

Mr. G. Warman,
Ashwellthorpe.

I was 17 in 1940 and I joined the Home Guard soon after it was started. In due course, I was recruited into the 202 Battalion by my boss Mr. Bothway. Our underground base was built by the men in our unit, mainly on Sunday mornings, at Fundenhall. The names of the other men were, P. Myhill, J. Moore, L. Lawn, T. Drew, P. Howes and J. Gamble.

There was a hollow tree stump to cover the door into our bunker. To open the hatch there was a drainpipe with a wire through it. If you pulled the wire it released the catch which opened the hatch. We stored ammunition, bombs and various items of equipment there, but we never slept in it. At the end of the war, the ammunition was removed, but we blew up all the phosphorous bombs.

Our unit had its own car, which was a Wolseley. Two of us had to sit on a plank of wood at the back. Apart from the usual weapons, we had revolvers and daggers. We did a lot of training and many exercises. On one occasion, we had to attack some tanks on Mousehold Heath but because it was a very moonlight night, we did not get very far. In 1942, we were sent to the Suffolk coast at Dunwich, where we lived with the army and went on coastal patrols because it was thought at the time that an invasion might come.

The office in charge of our unit was Capt. Mitchell and our Sergeant was Mr. R. Bothway.

Mr. B. Bowman,
Coltishall.

In 1940, as a young apprentice, I joined the Home Guard. Then one day I was called into the CO's office at the Drill Hall, Chapelfield Gardens, where a panel of officers asked me lots of questions starting with my age. I said 16, "no I mean 18". "I thought that's what you said", commented one of the officers. Then they asked me if I wanted to join a special organization. As I had to sign the Official Secrets Act, it sounded more exciting than the Home Guard. It seems that I had already been security vetted by the police and MI5 and my family background had been investigated. After I had been accepted into 202 Battalion, I faced a lot of intensive training by experts in their fields on explosives and time fuses. I was often sent to Syderstone and South Creake where regular soldiers from different regiments taught us unarmed combat, fieldcraft and camouflage and weaponry. We had to train while under machine gun fire and having tear gas blown at us and at the same time shoot back. It was certainly tough training. However, we were expected to be quiet, disciplined people who kept all our activities secret.

My unit was one of three in the Norwich area and our underground base was in Rackheath Woods near the airfield. It was built by regular army engineers. There were bunks, food to last a month and plenty of ammunition and supplies. The entrance was a concealed, counter-weighted trap-door. Sometimes we would have training weekends at our underground bunkers.

We were specially trained in sabotage skills and one of our exercises involved getting through airfield security at Rackheath and then "blowing up" the planes. Another part of our training was in unarmed combat which we practised in a field behind Norwich School. This class was taken by a very strong man, Jack Ridgeway, who had taken a "Mr. Atlas" course. No one could outfight him but he taught us a few tricks!

Of course, my parents knew nothing of all this. They thought I was in the Home Guard as I always wore Home Guard uniform and flashes which was the cover for all our secret activities. My identity card enabled me to travel wherever I was needed. I think that the local HQ of the Resistance Units was at Beeston Hall. Once a week we would meet at the Veterans Club in Princes Street to discuss future plans. Everything was very secret and I only knew the names of the men in my unit. Each unit trained separately.

Morale was excellent and we were not frightened of an invasion. If the Germans did come, we wanted to be able to do something and put our training to good use. We were very well armed and our OB was stacked with ammunition. I had a Tommy gun, a Winchester rifle with telescopic sight, a revolver and a dagger. Some of these I kept in my wardrobe. I had been taught a great deal in a short time and before I joined the Home Guard I had never done any shooting.

In the weeks before D-Day in 1944, we were sent to the Isle of Wight to assist in its defence and as reinforcements.

Towards the end of the war I realised how secret and anonymous my career in the Auxiliary Units had been. While in the unit I had passed my driving test and various other exams. However, when I was called up for regular service, the army authorities had no record of this and I had to take the driving test and other tests all over again.

Mr. C.G. Haines,
Norwich.

In 1940, I was an engineer at Laurence Scott and so in a "reserved" occupation. I was originally in the Army Cadets and very happy to serve in 202 Battalion from October 1940 until its disbandment in 1944. I was 26 years old in 1940 when I was approached by someone who was already a member of an Auxiliary Unit. I had been security vetted and my family background checked. My father had been a company sergeant Major, I was in the local Army Cadet Force and I had done quite a lot of boxing. When I was recruited I had to tell my family that I was in a local anti-tank unit.

I was in one of the three Auxiliary Units in Norwich. My underground base was in the grounds of the University of East Anglia. I remember that Churchill did not like the word "hideout" which is sometimes used to describe the OBs. Ours was 12 by 8 feet and there was an entrance passage, an explosives store and an area for our bunks. Once we spent 48 hours in the OB to see how we would cope. There were six men in my unit and I only knew my own group so that I could never give the game away as to the whereabouts of others.

We were provided with a variety of weapons. I had a .38 revolver, a knife, knuckle duster, Tommy gun and Sten and a .22 rifle with a telescopic lens. Our training was by regulars and was very thorough and severe. It included weaponry, night work, map reading, explosives and unarmed combat. Each member of my unit tried to become an expert in two of these areas; mine were unarmed combat and map reading. Sometimes we went to Aldershot and Highworth where different units of regulars gave us further specialist training - it was very thorough. In one training exercise we were taken on a Friday night and dropped at a spot on the map, somewhere in Wiltshire. We had to find our way to a certain place on a heath, which we did, but we could not get in. On our return journey we had to cross a six foot dyke and one of our unit, "Daredevil" Fielding tried to jump it and fell in. On another occasion we went to Cawston Heath where we were trained in the skills of unarmed combat by a 6 foot 4 inch Scottish sergeant major. He showed us every hold you could use to disarm someone. We came back from that session black and blue!

We had training every weekend and regular meetings at the Veterans Club in Norwich, where talks on various subjects were given; one of these was by a Scottish ghillie on how to tickle a trout. At Highworth, I remember being shown a tree stump with a well weathered flap. You pressed a concealed button, a trap door opened and we all went down into a bunker. The whole thing was perfectly camouflaged, something which was always stressed in our training. We had to have good stamina and be very fit. One exercise we had to do involved each man in the unit putting 3 rounds in the magazine, then running 25 yards wearing a respirator, then 3 targets came up at which you fired. Then you removed the respirator and ran back to hand the Tommy gun to the next man. The regulars said it couldn't be done under 3 minutes, but I was pleased to do it twice in 2 minutes 56 seconds. I was always first in the assault course, too.

My unit included my brother, Sid Littlewood and John Fielding. Later in the war, the younger members were called up into the regular forces and the standard dropped somewhat, because there were less men to choose from. My unit had a sergeant, a corporal, lance corporal and three privates. Disbanded in 1944, we handed in weapons, ammunition and gelignite because it "sweated". Later, I got a letter of thanks and a badge. If an invasion had come, we would have reported to our OB and then been on our own, to cause as much trouble as we could.

Mr. John Fielding,
Norwich.

I joined the Home Guard at the end of 1940. At the time I was articled to an accountant. While at school at Felstead I had been in the ATC and enjoyed the activities. When I was recruited into the Auxiliary Units, I was excited by the prospects of special training and fresh challenges. Our group commander was Capt.

Eades and another officer was Lt. Buxton. The regular officers in charge of us were Capt. Oxenden and Capt. Woodward. At first we had regular meetings at the Veterans Club in Norwich, at the junction of Princes Street and Redwell Street.

Our OB, or underground base, was on the golf course at Earlham, now part of the University of East Anglia grounds, between Bluebell Road and the University grounds. I helped to build this bunker and I knew about two more in the Norwich area, which were in Plumstead Road and Marston Lane. They are all now filled in. The one I helped to dig, was 12 feet down, completely flat on top and overgrown so that it was totally concealed. We used to work on it at weekends.

The training we received was very good. I went to Coleshill a number of times and received special instruction in sabotage techniques. These skills gave me a lot of confidence. We believed that we could create a considerable amount of mayhem for an enemy. We were certainly not frightened of the Germans and I looked forward to getting stuck in if they did invade us. We had been well trained and were confident that we could do a lot of damage to an enemy by destroying vehicles, petrol dumps, etc.

In 1943, I was called up and went to Scotland where I was taught to parachute. In 1944, I was among a group of irregulars (some of whom were ex-202 Battalion) who were dropped into France to disrupt German communications and generally sabotage the enemy's positions. So some of the skills I had first learnt as a member of the Auxiliary Units were now used in German occupied France during Operation "Bullbasket".

The former Veteran's Club in Princes Street, Norwich, where members of "202" would attend meetings.

234

Mr. R. Clutterham,
Ashill.

In 1940, I was a farm worker which was a "reserved" occupation. When they appealed for Local Defence Volunteers I joined up. I was 27 at the time and I was not in the LDV/Home Guard very long before my career in the Auxiliary Units began. One day a man came to interview me at my boss, Mr. Broadhead's house at Burys Hall. I was asked if I would like to do something more interesting than the Home Guard. Apparently, I had been watched for a month to see the sort of people I mixed with and what we talked about. If I wanted to join this special organization I was told that I would have to sign the Official Secrets Act.

Our OB (underground base) was built by the Royal Engineers under the boarded floor of a shed, with a trap door entry. There was an escape hatch in the cart shed next door. I remember a day when someone parked a tractor with its front wheels over the hatch! We had to stay down in the bunker for 36 hours without coming out to see if we could cope. There were bunks each side, with explosives underneath and on shelves. There was a toilet, a light and an army phone. The air outlet from the bunker was a drainpipe on the side of the farm shed. We took it in turns being in charge of the unit which consisted of seven men. One of our look-outs was in a hollow oak tree opposite Burys Hall. We used to get in through a trap-door in the bottom and go up inside the tree, where sometimes we would sleep. As the tree was on a hill we had a good view of all around.

My wife knew nothing about my activities in the Auxiliary Units, although she did sometimes notice men going towards the tree and wondered what was going on. I told my family I was in the Home Guard and wore that uniform. When I went on weekend courses, I did not get back until 4am on Monday morning sometimes. Then I had to go to work! One night when there were German planes about, my wife did not go to bed but slept in the chair in the living room. I arrived home from a patrol with my face all blackened and when I opened the door my wife woke up and I frightened her to death.

Our training was by experts and all seven of us had revolvers. I had a Thompson sub-machine gun and another member had a Sten. I had 1300 rounds of ammunition under the bed and my machine gun was kept up the chimney. We all went through an explosives course and we were very well supplied with explosives

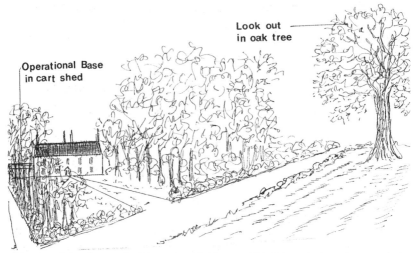

Operational Base
in cart shed

Look out
in oak tree

The site of the observer's OB was in a field some 300-400 yards from the cart shed.

"One of our lookouts was in a hollow oak tree. We used to get in with a trapdoor at the bottom and go up inside the tree and sometimes sleep there. It was on top of a hill and so we could see a lot". Mr. Clutterham.

"I used to see people crossing the road to the tree and wondered what they were doing". Mrs. Clutterham.

The site of Ashill operational base was under this cart shed at Burys Hall on the right hand side.

in our bunker. I remember that there was a huge explosion reported in London. What had happened was that a German bomb had hit an Auxiliary Unit bunker, full of explosives. Because of the force of the explosion people thought it must have been a new type of bomb.

We were not frightened about the Germans coming and felt confident as a result of our training. It was important that we did not get captured if there was an invasion. We were given three tablets (morphine), one to ease the pain if injured, two to knock us out and three to kill ourselves if taken prisoner.

One day, on an exercise, we were told we were going to Leicester Square. However, we discovered we were at a farm in North Creake! We had to crawl along under fire and they threw thunder flashes at us. I was hit in the leg but not badly. It was the same weekend we were told that some Germans had tried to land and were stopped by setting the sea on fire. That was probably a small commando expedition which failed. On another occasion, we were taken blindfolded to another OB on the Broads, near Wroxham I believe. We went through a trap door, along a tunnel, around a corner and into a very large room.

Sometimes we had to test security on airfields. One night we went to try and get on to Marham aerodrome. We all got under the perimeter wire and made crosses on the Mosquitos parked on the runway, to prove that we had got in. We never saw anyone and later heard that another unit had got in on the same night. A week later we went again, the searchlights were on, we were half way through the defences with Sanderson getting under the wire, when a guard came along. Eventually we were challenged and when we got back I found that I had been the last to be captured.

One night there was a plan to drop us behind enemy lines in France. We were to be taken by lorry to Bodney aerodrome and then flown by Ventura aircraft. But at the last minute a phone message told us we would not be going. Later, I heard that 40 planes went out but only 10 or 12 returned. This happened some time after D-Day.

Although I shouldn't have done, I once used some explosives from the OB to uproot an old tree stump. I put it in a tin dolly tub and set it off. A little later my neighbour came to the door asking if I had done anything with a bit of tin as it had come over his fence and knocked all his tomatoes down! My unit was disbanded in 1944 and I became an explosives instructor in the

Home Guard. The other members of my unit were, K. Broadhead (Ashill) Sergeant, W. Burroughs (Carbrooke), G. Dewing (Bradenham). W. Sanderson (Bodney). S. Mortimer (Saham Toney) and D. Fake (Ashill). My identity card was marked 202 GHQ Reserve, Home Guard.

Mr. D. Fake,
Ashill.

I was the youngest member of the unit at 16 years. I had to sign the Official Secrets Act and was in the Auxiliary Unit from 1940-1944.

On one exercise at an airfield, someone challenged us and said, "What are you doing here? This is a free French aerodrome. They shoot first and ask questions later". It was the only Free French airfield in Norfolk and apparently we should not have been on it. On another occasion, we were so well camouflaged that another man stood on my hand without realising it. I knew that there were OBs at Cockley Cley and Wroxham.

Army Form B.2606.

**MILITARY
IDENTITY CARD No. M 632585**

Surname Bartram
Surname at Birth Bartram
Other Names William, David, George.
(and rank or designation) Lieut.

Sex Male

Unit or occupation

Address 33. Newmarket,
Beccles, Suffolk.

Nationality British

Nationality at Birth British

Second Nationality, if any Tivetshall St. Mary,
Place of Birth Nr. Norwich.

Year of Birth 1900

Issued by

t.d.t 202 (G H Q. Reserve
Date 4th. January 1944.

35

Photograph of Bearer
partly overstamped
with official stamp

Signature of Bearer

Visible distinguishing marks
Scar on chin.

The identity card of a 202 member.

238

A very rare photograph taken in 1944 of members of 202 Battalion on the Norfolk/Suffolk border. Members identified are:– Back row: 1st left Kenny Pink, 3rd left Lennie Hall, 7th left Reggie Goffin. Centre row: Middle E.D.G. Bartram (Group Commander), 7th left Cecil Poll, 8th left "Wag" West. Front row: Centre Billy Hazell, far right Gordon Driver.

Photograph with kind permission of Mr. R. Bartram

Mr. J. Seaman,
Baconsthorpe.

I was formerly in the Territorial Army and classed as a "reserve" for an indefinite period. I had to come back to Baconsthorpe to farm. One day an army officer came to see me to ask me to join a special Home Guard unit, the 202 Battalion which was a separate organization whose members wore Home Guard tabs. I was responsible for training six Auxiliary Units in the area. An officer approved the members of the units. They were recruited from the farming community who knew the countryside well, for example, gamekeepers.

My unit was based at Baconsthorpe Castle which was very overgrown at the time because the Ministry of Works had not yet taken it over. The OB was an Anderson shelter set in one of the dungeons of the old castle. It was made of wood and corrugated iron and you can still see the whitewash where it was. Inside the OB was stored 1500 cwt of ammunition and explosives. Each man in the unit had a Sten gun, .38 revolver, knife and rubber truncheon. There were hand grenades galore. First aid kit contained shell and standard dressings and morphia. I never trained men near their OBs to ensure maximum secrecy was maintained.

When I was taken to the North Walsham bunker, I was blindfolded to ensure I would not know where it was. Its situation was particularly well chosen.

My special duties were instructing the men in the use of explosives. I had special authorization from the GHQ Home Forces Highworth, to obtain supplementary petrol for use on my visits to train Auxiliary Units in the area. The document said that any enquiry about my work or the journey should me made to GHQ Highworth, (the HQ of the Auxiliary Units).

If invasion did occur, the role of the Auxiliary Units was to go to ground, wait for the enemy to move inland, and then emerge to sabotage shell and petrol dumps and to attack tanks, and generally disrupt German communications. We used to go to Coleshill in Wiltshire for training, where Lovat scouts taught the skills of stalking. Norfolk was an area vulnerable to attack, but the Auxiliary Units were part of the regional defence scheme which included regulars and Home Guard units. Our doctor was part of another level in the organization and had a secret wireless behind the chimney in the roof.

Some of the documents I was issued with were, a "1938 Calendar" with a training manual about explosives inside, a special constable's warrant and two ID cards, one of which was a 202 ID. Another item of cover was a document saying I was a member of Erpingham District Committee of the Norfolk Agricultural Executive!

Men in the units realised the job was dangerous and knew that if they got caught by the enemy, they would be tortured or killed. That was why they had morphine tablets as standard equipment. The units were kept strictly apart and rarely visited another bunker, so they could not give further information to the enemy.

Our job was *not* to engage the enemy but to *engage in sabotage.* As part of our training at Coleshill we were given a dummy charge and taken out in a truck for two or three miles at night. We had a map with a dump in a wood marked on it. The dump was guarded by Lovat scouts dressed in German uniform. We had to get in, set the explosives and then get away.

In 1944, I was sent to Sandown, Isle of Wight to help guard the PLUTO pipeline and petrol dump and 700 tons of fuel a day passed through it to France after D-Day. To guard the compound we were issued with a pick axe handle and an Alsatian dog!

When I came out of the Auxiliary Units I had to sign the Official Secrets Act. After the war I received a special 202 badge instead of a medal.

Mr. R. Bartram,
Beccles.

My father was the Area Group Commander of the North Suffolk 202 Battalion, based in Beccles, which included the border area with Norfolk and Gillingham. Fifty years ago I remember taking coded messages from a "Captain Blackbird" relating to my father's unit without any knowledge of what it was all about.

Mr. Roger Parker,
son of Mr. Harold William Parker, Norwich.

My father was in a "reserved" occupation and served in the Home Guard. I had a hunch he was in the "secret army" too but could never be certain until it was confirmed to the author by another member of his patrol, Bert Bowman. The OB was near the Salhouse Road, opposite the Heartsease estate.

Mr. G.R.E. Stanton,
son of Mr. R.S.S. Stanton, Dersingham.

My father was a Group commander of patrols in the Dersingham/Kings Lynn area. I knew there was an OB in Sandringham Woods *somewhere*. I remember that one rhododendron always flowered later than the rest because it had been dug up and replanted after the OB had been constructed.

Mr. H. Dawson,
Dareham.

About 25 years ago I was talking to a man in his office when I noticed a peculiar paperweight. He invited me to pick it up and examine it. It was irregular cube-shaped, with jagged grooves with a screw plug in one side. I thought it was a piece of shrapnel but in fact it was a lump of coal, used by the Resistance during the war as cover for an explosive device which they would place in locomotive tenders. He told me he did not know how he came by the object. However, soon after this he died and I found out later that he had been a member of the "underground army" section of the Home Guard.

Mr. Ray Allen,
Cley.

My brother Dick was in 202 Battalion and was proud of the guerrilla skills he learnt in his unit, which he believed would enable him to blow up important places if the Germans had landed.

The underground bunker of his unit was in an old lime kiln which appeared as just a slight hump on the ground's surface. Down below however, it was like a brick tower with tunnels coming off either side of it. You could hardly see it then although there is now much more earth on it. Down in the bunker he told me that they had everything they needed in the event of an invasion, like food, ammunition, explosives, stores, etc.

Mr. Dennis G. Seaman,
Walsingham.

I was an Army cadet, aged 14, and attached to a special unit as a scout. Its OB was in the woods on the Walsingham estate: there was an escape tunnel, a steel ladder, bunks and ammunition. A hollow tree some 15 metres from the OB was used as a lookout; entrance to it was via a foxhole. If the Germans landed, I had to burn my uniform and provide the secret unit with useful information. The C.O. was a Lt. D.C. Carey, a local farmer, and most of the men in his patrol worked on his farm. Two members of the patrol were Sid Beckham and George Abel.

Mr. Jim Baldwin,
Fakenham.

An incident I shall never forget was in the mid 1950s and concerns a school teacher, L.S. Harris, a clever man who came from the Wroxham area. One morning at school he asked us if we had heard the radio news that day, which some of us had. An announcement was made confirming that a secret underground army had been formed in Britain during the invasion scare of 1940. Mr. Harris said that he was at last free to tell us that he was a member of that organization. He then told us boys some details about the "secret army". I was spellbound by the story and will never forget the occasion.

Author's note: Mr. Harris served in the Auxiliary Units, Norfolk's "secret army" from 1940-43.

Mr. A.J. Harrison,
Rollesby, Great Yarmouth.

I became a member of a group in 202 Battalion in 1942 based at Halesworth. There were six of us and I served until I was called up in 1944. I still have my copy of the "1938 Calendar", which was our instruction manual on the use of various booby traps, time delay pencils, explosive charges and their fuses, anti personnel devices, etc. Our concrete underground bunker was near the windmill at Holton. We had a variety of weapons including, Sten guns, .38 revolvers, Thompson machine guns and rifles. I remember doing exercises, and on one occasion we were taken to somewhere near Woodbridge, where we had to practise blowing up trees in the grounds of a country house. We had gelignite but also were given some of the new plastic explosive. We were trained in a variety of skills such as shooting, sabotage, unarmed combat, etc. I had signed the Official Secrets Act and my family knew nothing of my activities.

Chris and Gerald Allen,
sons of Mr. Victor Allen, Hoveton.

Our father, Victor Allen, was in the Hoveton unit and we are proud to have his 202 badge. Before he died he told us that the OB was near Hoveton Hall. When we eventually found it, the roof was still intact and inside we discovered the frames of the bunks, together with pipe work which was part of the ventilation system. However, part of the escape tunnel had collapsed. While searching the area, we also found the entrance to an observer's OB, still accessible after all these years.

Mr. Anthony Bailey,
Thursford.

Our first OB was built in Thursford wood by the Army though they didn't know what it was for. Because it was near a spring it got flooded, so we dug our own OB near Thursford Hall, camouflaging it with trees over the top. The entrance was beneath an outside lavatory seat with a trap door contraption. In the OB was a gas stove, telephone and escape tunnel. We trained around Thursford and South Creake, and we also went to Coleshill. The men in my patrol were T. Brock, E. Davies, Alfred Smith, Anthony Bailey, Bernard Flint, A. Smith and A. Scargill.

Mrs. Mary Davies,
widow of Edward Davies, Thursford.

My husband was in the Auxiliaries as well as the Home Guard. I have his 202 badge. Edward was a carpenter and he and his mates built their own OB at Thursford, dug into the chalk and sandpits on the Thursford/Cley road. There was enough ammunition in our bedroom to blow up the whole village! I was not to touch it! Of course I didn't know what was going on except that my bag was already packed and in the event of an invasion, I had to leave. Edward was a quiet man and didn't say much. At the end of the war all their ammunition and explosives were handed in.

Mr. Ray Fisher,
Castle Rising.

My uncle, Archie Hudson, was in the Auxiliaries. I have a photo of his patrol wearing pistols and also a letter of thanks from Col. Douglas. I believe their OB was in Castle Rising and a Mr. Garner was the sergeant and Capt. Hardy was in charge of a group of patrols in that area. At the end of the war, the North Walsham unit was told to dig a hole and blow up all their grenades, etc. one at a time. But they got fed up because it was taking so long so they put them all in the hole and detonated the lot simultaneously.

Mr. Ronald Hill,
Cley.

My patrol was at Cley and its members were Sgt. Harcourt, Sgt. Nicky Newstead, Harry Hart, Jack Barnard, Brian Ramm and Ronald Hill. We trained at Walsingham and Leicester Square farm, which included live firing 18″ above our heads. I was in 202 for 18 months, had a pistol and 300 rounds of ammunition as did the rest. Our OB was at "the Hangs" a hilly area on the Cley/Kelling road. There was another OB at Blakeney.

Mr. Alec Newstead,
Ailthorpe.

I am the only surviving member of my patrol and I have never spoken about the subject before. I was 18 when I joined the Auxiliary Units after being approached by farmer Cedric Thistleton-Smith, who was the commander of the local patrol. Our OB in Ailthorpe Wood, close to Little Snoring airfield, was built by the Royal Engineers. It had four bunks, a 200 gallon water tank, calor gas for light and heat, together with about 40 lbs of explosives, time pencils, etc. The main roof of the OB has collapsed and part of the tunnel probably, though the main structure, including a booby trap, still exists. Our training, mostly by regular soldiers, took place at Leicester Square farm where there was an army base. We were sent out on 5 mile patrols and had to blow up aircraft and ammunition dumps. We also did pistol training at Walsingham. If an invasion occurred in 1940, we would go underground and remain there for 48 hours, before beginning a campaign of sabotage against the enemy. Other memebers of the patrol included Sgt. Guy Savory, Charles Cornwall and John Burgess. We were very separate from the Home Guard who sometimes trained above our OB which they knew nothing about.

Mr. R. Mallett,
Narford.

I was in the Narford patrol which consisted of seven men, four farmers, a tractor driver, a gamekeeper who was the salt of the earth, and myself. Other men in the group were D. Sneezum, R.R. Bennett, Capt. J.L. Hardy, D.S.O., M.C., W. Welham and

.

G.F. Attwood. As I was the youngest I am probably the only surviving member. Our OB was in the grounds of Narford Hall near Narborough – the roof has now fallen in. There were other OBs in the area but because of the secret nature of our organization, I did not know their location. During training we were visited by Capt. Woodward, but the key figure was the charismatic Major J.L. Hardy. He was a veteran of World War One. He had lost a leg, but wrote books including "I Escape". At Sandhurst, he had won the pistol shooting competition.

At Rougham where I lived for a time, there was a communications centre unit, with wiring under the bark of the tree going to the top, brilliantly disguised. The transmitting unit was concealed inside an oil drum. If the Germans had landed we would have done something to upset them but I don't think we could have lasted long. At the end of the war we had to dispose of one and half cwt of explosives and ammunition.

SELECT BIBLIOGRAPHY

B. Collier, *The Defence of the UK*, HMSO (1957)
W. Churchill, *Their Finest Hour*, Vol. 2 of *History of World War Two*, Cassells (1948-54)
P. Fleming, *Invasion 1940*, Rupert Hart Davis (1957)
C. Graves, *The Home Guard of Great Britain*, Hutchinson (1943)
A.G. Street, *From Dusk till Dawn*, Blandford Press (1945)
N. Longmate, *The Real Dad's Army*, Arrow Books (1974)
    If Britain had Fallen, BBC & Hutchinson of London (1972)
D. Johnson, *East Anglia at War*, Jarrolds (1992)
R. Douglas Brown, *Anglia at War* (6 vols.), Terence Dalton (1980-1994)
S.P. Mackenzie, *The Home Guard*, Oxford University Press (1993)
P.K. Kemp, *History of the Norfolk Regiment* (1919-1951)
D. Lampe, *The Last Ditch*, London (1968)
J. Brophy, *Home Guard Proficiency*, London (1942)
    Advanced Training for the Home Guard, London (1941)
J. Langdon-Davies, *The Home Guard Training Manual*, John Murray & the Pilot Press (1940)
    The Home Guard Fieldcraft Manual, John Murray & the Pilot Press (1942)
    Qualifications for & governing the condition of Home Guard Proficiency Badges and Certificates
    Home Guard Instructions – Battlecraft & Battle Drill for the Home Guard
    Home Guard Instructions – Patrolling & Summer Training (1944)
Britannia Magazine, *Journal of the Norfolk Regiment*, No. 27 (1946)